CLEP

College Level Examination Program

**Business
Series**

Copyright © 2016

All rights reserved. No part of the material protected by this copyright notice may be reproduced or utilized in any form or by any means, electronic or mechanical, including photocopying or recording or by any information storage and retrievable system, without written permission from the copyright holder.

To obtain permission(s) to use the material from this work for any purpose including workshops or seminars, please submit a written request to:

XAMonline, Inc.
21 Orient Avenue
Melrose, MA 02176
Toll Free: 1-800-301-4647
Email: info@xamonline.com
Web: www.xamonline.com
Fax: 1-617-583-5552

Library of Congress Cataloging-in-Publication Data
Wynne, Sharon

CLEP Business Series/ Sharon Wynne
    ISBN: 978-1-60787-582-6

1. CLEP   2. Study Guides   3. Business

Disclaimer:

The opinions expressed in this publication are the sole works of XAMonline and were created independently from the College Board, or other testing affiliates. Between the time of publication and printing, specific test standards as well as testing formats and website information may change that are not included in part or in whole within this product. XAMonline develops sample test questions, and they reflect similar content as on real tests; however, they are not former tests. XAMonline assembles content that aligns with test standards but makes no claims nor guarantees candidates a passing score.

Cover photo provided by © Can Stock Photo Inc./robwilson39/10942021; © Can Stock Photo Inc./labamba/11404236; © Can Stock Photo Inc./radiantskies/11700565; © Can Stock Photo Inc./Bialasiewicz /17186541; © Can Stock Photo Inc. /karenr /7601053

Printed in the United States of America
CLEP Business Series
ISBN: 978-1-60787-582-6

TABLE OF CONTENTS

Financial Accounting 1

    Sample Test 3

    Answer Key 27

    Rationales 28

Information Systems 78

    Sample Test 80

    Answer Key 104

    Rationales 105

Business Law 156

    Sample Test 158

    Answer Key 180

    Rationales 181

Principles of Management 233

    Sample Test 235

    Answer Key 263

    Rationales 264

Principles of Marketing 318

    Sample Test 319

    Answer Key 341

    Rationales 342

FINANCIAL ACCOUNTING

Description of the Examination
The Financial Accounting examination covers skills and concepts that are generally taught in a first-semester undergraduate financial accounting course. Colleges may award credit for a one-semester course in financial accounting.

The exam contains approximately 75 questions to be answered in 90 minutes. Some of these are pretest questions that will not be scored. Any time candidates spend on tutorials or providing personal information is in addition to the actual testing time.

Knowledge and Skills Required
Questions on the Financial Accounting examination require candidates to demonstrate one or more of the following abilities.

- Familiarity with accounting concepts and terminology
- Preparation, use and analysis of accounting data and financial reports issued for both internal and external purposes
- Application of accounting techniques to simple problem situations involving computations
- Understanding the rationale for Generally Accepted Accounting Practices and Procedures

The subject matter of the Financial Accounting examination is drawn from the following topics. The percentages next to the main topics indicate the approximate percentage of exam questions on that topic.

20-30% General Topics
- Generally Accepted Accounting Principles
- Rules of Double-Entry Accounting/Transaction Analysis/Accounting Equation
- The Accounting Cycle
- Business Ethics
- Purpose of, Presentation of, and Relationships Between Financial Statements
- Forms of Business

20-30% The Income Statement
- Presentation Format Issues
- Recognition of Revenues and Expenses
- Cost of Goods Sold
- Elasticity
- Irregular Items
- Profitability Analysis

30-40% The Balance Sheet
- Cash and Internal Controls
- Valuation of Accounts and Notes Receivable (including bad debts)
- Valuation of Inventories
- Acquisition and Disposal of Long-Term Assets
- Depreciation/Amortization/ Depletion
- Intangible Assets
- Accounts and Notes Payable
- Long-Term Liabilities
- Owner's Equity
- Preferred and Common Stock
- Retained Earnings
- Liquidity, Solvency, Activity Analysis

FINANCIAL ACCOUNTING

5-10%   **The Statement of Cash Flows**
- Indirect Method
- Cash Flow Analysis
- Operating, Financing and Investing Activities

1-5%   **Miscellaneous**
- Investments
- Contingent Liabilities

SAMPLE TEST

DIRECTIONS: Read each item and select the best response.

1. **Sale – March**
   Delivery - April
   Payment – May
   Warranty – 1 Year
   Warranty expense reported in:

   A. March

   B. April

   C. March of the following year

   D. April of the following year

   E. When the warranty ends

2. **Amortization of prepaid insurance appears on:**

   A. Balance sheet only

   B. Balance sheet and cash flows statement

   C. Balance sheet and income statement

   D. Income statement and cash flows statement

   E. Cash flows statement and balance sheet

3. **Starting inventory - $1,000**
   Purchases - $15,000
   Ending inventory - $2,000
   COGS - $____:

   A. 12,000

   B. 16,000

   C. 14,000

   D. 17,000

   E. 15,000

4. **Which of the following appears separately, net of income tax, on an income statement:**

   A. Gross Profit

   B. Loss on Discontinued Operations

   C. Gain on Sale of a Truck

   D. Interest Expense

   E. Tax expense

FINANCIAL ACCOUNTING

5. **Business loan worth $1 million
   Interest rate is 0%
   Repayment period is 10 years
   Payments are made annually
   This is recorded as:**

   A. A current liability of $1 million

   B. A long-term liability of $1 million

   C. Current liability of $100,000 and a long-term liability of $900,000

   D. Note payable of $100,000 and bond payable of $900,000

   E. Long-term liability of $100,000 and current liability of $900,000

6. **Which of the following appears as a cash flow from investing activities:**

   A. Revenues from the sale of goods

   B. Paying interest to bondholders

   C. Paying a dividend to preferred shareholders

   D. Sale of machinery for scrap

   E. COGS

7. **The government agency which regulates financial reporting of publicly-traded companies is:**

   A. IRS

   B. FASB

   C. AICPA

   D. SEC

   E. DoD

8. **The professional organization which issues accounting credentials is:**

   A. FASB

   B. AICPA

   C. IRS

   D. SEC

   E. DoD

9. **The organization is charge of establishing GAAP is:**

   A. IRS

   B. FASB

   C. AICPA

   D. SEC

   E. FBI

10. The accounting equation states:

    A. Assets = Liabilities + Equity

    B. Equity = Liabilities - Assets

    C. Equity = Liabilities + Assets

    D. Assets = Equity – Liabilities

    E. Assets = Equity/Liabilities

11. Which of the following is not a basic accounting principle:

    A. Matching

    B. Audit

    C. Objectivity

    D. Realization

    E. Economic entity assumption

12. ____ does not appear on the income statement:

    A. EBIT

    B. Interest expense

    C. Accumulated depreciation

    D. Depreciation Expense

    E. Operating income

13. Company A had one owner whose personal assets were protected, then someone bought a 50% stake in the business using a similar structure. Company A is now:

    A. LLC

    B. Corporation

    C. Partnership

    D. LLP

    E. Partnership

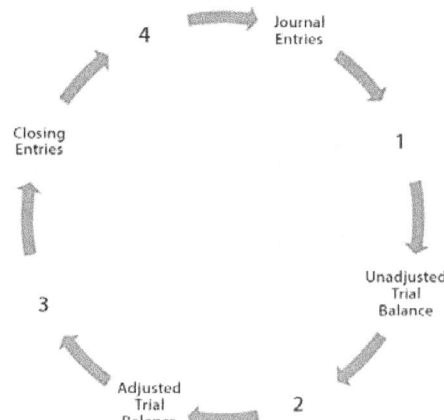

14. Financial Statements belong at point ____:

    A. 1

    B. 3

    C. 4

    D. 2

    E. None of these

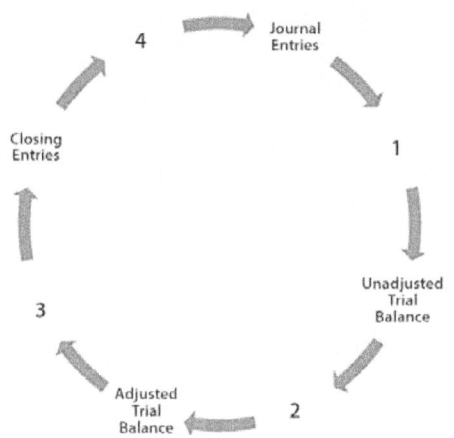

15. Ledger belongs at point _____:

    A. 1

    B. 3

    C. 2

    D. 4

    E. None of these

16. The cost of equity using the dividend capitalization model is:

    A. (Dividends per share/Market Value)+Dividend growth

    B. Pr^t

    C. $B_s(r_m-r_f)$

    D. $((E/V)*C_e)+((D/V)*C_D)$

    E. Assets = Liabilities + Equity

17. The cost of equity using CAPM model is:

    A. (Dividends per share/Market Value)+Dividend growth

    B. $B_s(r_m-r_f)$

    C. Pr^t

    D. $((E/V)*C_e)+((D/V)*C_D)$

    E. Assets = Liabilities + Equity

18. The after-tax cost of debt is:

    A. $(Pr^t)-T$

    B. Pr^t

    C. $((E/V)*C_e)+((D/V)*C_D)$

    D. $B_s(r_m-r_f)$

    E. Assets = Liabilities + Equity

19. Unrealized holding gain or loss would be a typical entry for:

    A. Operations derivatives

    B. Option derivatives

    C. Forward derivatives

    D. Cash flow hedges

    E. COGS

20. A short-term investment in a partner company would be listed in the balance sheet as _____:

    A. Trading security

    B. Held-to-maturity investment

    C. Available for sale

    D. Long-term asset

    E. Short-term liability

21. Which of the following is not a contingent asset or contingent liability:

    A. Issued corporate bonds

    B. Unexercised options

    C. Pending lawsuit

    D. Insurance coverage

    E. Unexercised futures contract

22. A contingent liability which will be recorded in the accounts of the balance sheet and income statement, rather than as a note is:

    A. Future losses on a futures contract

    B. Future losses on an options contract

    C. Insurance coverage

    D. Losses resulting from a petty lawsuit

    E. COGS

23. The left is _____, the right is _____:

    A. Credit, Credit

    B. Debit, Debit

    C. Credit, Debit

    D. Debit, Credit

    E. None of these

24. In a t-account, debits _____ expenses, and _____ revenues:

    A. Increase, decrease

    B. Decrease, increase

    C. Increase, increase

    D. Decrease, decrease

    E. None of these

25. Company A pays $10,000 on a $1 million loan they borrowed 5 years ago at a rate of 5%. The t-account transaction will include:

    A. A $10,000 credit to assets, and a $10,000 debit to liabilities

    B. $10,000 debit to assets, a $10,000 credit to short-term liabilities, and a $10,000 credit to long-term liabilities

    C. A $10,000 debit to assets, and a $10,000 credit to liabilities

    D. A $10,000 credit to assets, a $10,000 debit to liabilities, and a $40,000 credit to liabilities

    E. A $50,000 credit to assets

26. Where would you look to assess whether Company A's financial statements are fair and accurate:

    A. Auditor's report

    B. Financial statement notes

    C. Management discussion

    D. Footnotes to the balance sheet

    E. Business news website

27. The purchase of a large machine by issuing corporate bonds is reported as:

    A. Cash inflow of the financing section

    B. Noncash financing and investing activity

    C. Cash outflow of the financing section

    D. Cash outflow of the investing section

    E. Cash outflow of the operating section

28. Beginning capital: $1.2 million
    Ending capital: $800,000
    Withdrawals: $1 million
    Net Income/Loss:

    A. $2,200,000

    B. $200,000

    C. $1,400,000

    D. $600,000

    E. $750,000

29. **The listing of all account balances to demonstrate an equivalent total value of debits and credits is:**

    A. Ledger

    B. Trial balance

    C. Journal

    D. Balance sheet

    E. Income statement

30. **In 1 year, a furniture store sells a $3,000 living room set on 6-month 0% store credit for $5,000. On the balance sheet this would be:**

    A. Increase notes receivable by $5,000, and decrease inventories for $5,000

    B. Increase accounts receivable by $5,000, decrease inventories for $3,000, and increase owner's equity for $2,000.

    C. Increase owner's equity for $5,000, and decrease inventories for $5,000

    D. Increase accounts receivable by $3,000, decrease inventories by $3,000, and increase owner's equity by $5,000.

    E. Increase long-term liabilities by $5,000 and increase inventories by $3,000

31. **Deferred income tax liability results from:**

    A. Depreciation on assets

    B. Contingent liability

    C. Short-term differences in GAAP and tax accounting law

    D. Unrealized gains

    E. COGS

32. **The difference between EPS and diluted EPS is:**

    A. Diluted EPS assumes the distribution of dividends on preferred shares

    B. Diluted EPS assumes the exercising of all convertible shares

    C. Diluted EPS assumes the distribution of dividends on common shares

    D. Diluted EPS assumes the exercising of all convertible bonds

    E. Diluted EPS assumes a net loss

33. Company A $1.4 million in net income for the year, 235,000 common shares outstanding, and 5,000 convertible shares. It's EPS is:

    A. $5.96

    B. $5.83

    C. $1.165 million

    D. $6.09

    E. $5.90

34. The listing of the names and numbers of all accounts is:

    A. Chart of accounts

    B. Index of accounts

    C. Book of accounts

    D. Reference of accounts

    E. List of accounts

	2013	2014	2015
Revenue			
Distribution Solutions	2,025.00	2,314.00	
Technology Solutions	2,984.00		3,124.00
Total Revenue		5,378.00	5,676.00
Cost of Revenues			
Cost of Sales		0.00	
Total Cost of Revenues		0.00	
Gross Income	5,009.00		
Gross Margin (%)			100.0%
SG&A Expense	3,065.00	3,192.00	3,164.00
Research & Development Expenses	347.00	364.00	376.00
Restructuring & Other cash charges (Gains)	0.00	0.00	0.00
Other Operating Expenses (Gains)	(5.00)	493.00	(20.00)
(EBITDA)		1,329.00	
(EBITDA Margin)	32.0%		
Depreciation & Amortization	124.00		148.00
Total Operating Expense	3,531.00	4,182.00	3,668.00
Operating Income (EBIT)			2,008.00
Operating Income Margin (EBIT Margin)	29.5%	22.2%	
Interest Expense (Income)		144.00	187.00
Interest & Other Income (Expense)	121.00	12.00	43.00
Interest & Investment Expense (Income)	21.00	132.00	
Net Income Before Taxes (EBT)	1,457.00		1,864.00
Provision for Income Taxes (Benefit)		241.00	
Effective Tax Rate	32.1%		32.2%
Net Income from Continuing Operations			
Income from Discontinued Operations, After-Tax Non-Recurring (Items), Accounting	1.00		0.00
(Preferred Dividends)	0.00		0.00
Net Income (E)		823.00	

35. What trend is found through a horizontal analysis of gross income for the period 2013-2015:

    A. A 12% growth rate

    B. A 12% reduction in 2014 followed by 13.3% growth in 2015

    C. A 88.2% growth rate

    D. A 13.3% growth rate

    E. A 13.3% reduction in 2014 followed by a 12% growth in 2015

	2013	2014	2015
Revenue			
Distribution Solutions	2,025.00	2,314.00	
Technology Solutions	2,984.00		3,124.00
Total Revenue		5,378.00	5,676.00
Cost of Revenues			
Cost of Sales		0.00	
Total Cost of Revenues		0.00	
Gross Income	5,009.00		
Gross Margin (%)			100.0%
SG&A Expense	3,065.00	3,192.00	3,164.00
Research & Development Expenses	347.00	364.00	376.00
Restructuring & Other cash charges (Gains)	0.00	0.00	0.00
Other Operating Expenses (Gains)	(5.00)	493.00	(20.00)
(EBITDA)		1,329.00	
(EBITDA Margin)	32.0%		
Depreciation & Amortization	124.00		148.00
Total Operating Expense	3,531.00	4,182.00	3,668.00
Operating Income (EBIT)			2,008.00
Operating Income Margin (EBIT Margin)	29.5%	22.2%	
Interest Expense (Income)		144.00	187.00
Interest & Other Income (Expense)	121.00	12.00	43.00
Interest & Investment Expense (Income)	21.00	132.00	
Net Income Before Taxes (EBT)	1,457.00		1,864.00
Provision for Income Taxes (Benefit)		241.00	
Effective Tax Rate	32.1%		32.2%
Net Income from Continuing Operations			
Income from Discontinued Operations, After-Tax Non-Recurring (Items), Accounting (Preferred Dividends)	1.00		0.00
	0.00		0.00
Net Income (E)		823.00	

36. **Calculate the EBIT margin for 2015:**

    A. 32.3%

    B. 21.4%

    C. 35.4%

    D. 35.3%

    E. 35.1%

37. **Use comparative vertical analysis to explain the change in net income from 2013-2014:**

    A. A 24.7% decrease in net income is primarily explained by an unusually low 16.7% EBITDA margin

    B. A 16.7% increase in net income is primarily explained by an unusually high 24.7% EBITDA margin

    C. A 16.7% decrease in net income is primarily explained by an unusually low 24.7% EBITDA margin

    D. A 24.7% increase in net income is primarily explained by an unusually high 16.7% EBITDA margin

    E. A 16.7% decrease in net income is primarily explained by an unusually high 24.7% EBITDA margin

FINANCIAL ACCOUNTING

38. Net profit margin is calculated as:

    A. (Net income*100)/Net sales

    B. (Net sales/100)*Net income

    C. (Net income*100)/operating margin

    D. (Gross income*100)/net sales

    E. (Net sales*100)/operating margin

39. Total assets = $25,000
    Shareholder's equity = $5,000
    Revenue = $10,000
    Net income = $2,000
    Structure a DuPont equation model:

    A. (5)(2.5)(0.2)

    B. (0.2)(0.4)(5)

    C. (2.5)(0.4)(5)

    D. (0.2)(0.08)(2)

    E. (5)(0.2)(0.08)

40. Total assets = $25,000
    Shareholder's equity = $5,000
    Revenue = $10,000
    Net income = $2,000
    The simplified DuPont calculation is the same as___, with a value of ____:

    A. Return on assets, 0.08

    B. Return on equity, 0.4

    C. Profit margin, 0.2

    D. Equity multiplier, 5.0

    E. Return on equity, 0.8

41. The sole proprietor's drawing account is closed to the:

    A. Shareholder's equity account

    B. General ledger

    C. Income summary account

    D. Owner's capital account

    E. Cash flows statement

42. ____ appears on the balance sheet:

    A. Accumulated depreciation

    B. Depreciation expense

    C. Accumulated amortization

    D. Amortization expense

    E. Accumulated interest expense

FINANCIAL ACCOUNTING

43. Recording revenues when they are earned is seen in ____ accounting, and when the money is received in ___ accounting:

    A. Accrual, Tax

    B. Forensic, Accrual

    C. Accrual, Cash

    D. Cash, Accrual

    E. Tax, Forensic

44. ____ will not cause a change to shareholder equity under accrual accounting:

    A. Purchase of treasury shares

    B. Issuing a dividend

    C. Sale of inventory at a profit

    D. Purchase of equipment

    E. Loss from discontinued operations

45. The purpose of cross-indexing is to:

    A. Function as a reference between fiscal years

    B. Function as a reference between financial statements

    C. Function as a reference between the general ledger and subsidiary ledger

    D. Function as a reference between the journal and the ledger

    E. Function as a reference between the journal and the income statement

46. Company A buys a machine for $1 million, which is expected to last 10 years with a salvage value of $5,000. Using straight-line method, the entry after 1 year is:

    A. Depreciation expense: $99,500
       Acc. Depreciation: $99,500

    B. Depreciation expense: $100,000
       Acc. Depreciation: $100,000

    C. Acc. Depreciation: $99,500
       Owner's Equity: $99,500

    D. Depreciation expense: $100,000
       Owner's Equity: $100,000

    E. Acc. Depreciation: $100,000
       Depreciation expense: $100,000

47. Company A pays $10,000 for 4 years of prepaid insurance. After 1 year, the adjusting entry is:

   A. $2,500 credit of prepaid insurance
      $10,000 debit of insurance expense

   B. $2,500 credit of prepaid insurance
      $2,500 debit of insurance expense

   C. $2,500 debit of prepaid insurance
      $2,500 credit of insurance expense

   D. $2,500 debit of prepaid insurance
      $10,000 credit of insurance expense

   E. $10,000 credit of prepaid insurance
      $2,500 debit of accrued insurance

48. LIFO liquidation occurs when:

   A. A company using LIFO sells older inventory, causing a distortion of profit margin

   B. A company using LIFO sells older inventory, causing a distortion of sales

   C. A company using FIFO switches to LIFO, causing a distortion in inventory value

   D. A company using LIFO switches to FIFO, causing a distortion in inventory value

   E. A company using FIFO switches to LIFO, causing a distortion of profit margin

49. Company A accepts prepayment of $10,000 for 100 units, and in the first year they ship 50%, but in that time the market price dropped to $750 per unit. After that transaction:

   A. $5,000 unearned revenue
      $5,000 revenue

   B. ($5,000) unearned revenue
      ($5,000) revenue

   C. $10,000 unearned revenue
      $5,000 revenue

   D. ($10,000) unearned revenue
      ($5,000) revenue

   E. $5,000 unearned revenue
      $5,000 assets

50. Sales = $750,000
    Gross Margin = 35%
    COGS = _____:

   A. $487,500

   B. $262,500

   C. $225,000

   D. $478,500

   E. ($478,500)

51. Starting Inventory = $50,000
    Ending Inventory = $40,000
    Purchases = $120,000
    COGS = ____:

    A. $130,000

    B. $110,000

    C. $90,000

    D. $30,000

    E. $60,000

Accounts Receivables	$30,000
Average Accounts Receivables	$30,000
Average Inventory	$80,000
Average Total Assets	$200,000
Cash Equivalents	$10,000
COGS	$250,000
Current Liabilities	$60,000
Ending Inventory	$80,000
Marketable Securities	$2,000
Net credit sales	$30,000
Net Income	$75,000
Net Sales	$500,000
Operating Cash Flows	$150,000
Operating Income	$150,000
Total Assets	$200,000
Total Equity	$196,000
Working Capital	$150,000

52. Calculate days sales in receivables:

    A. 12.1

    B. 25.7

    C. 18.5

    D. 21.9

    E. 20.9

Accounts Receivables	$30,000
Average Accounts Receivables	$30,000
Average Inventory	$80,000
Average Total Assets	$200,000
Cash Equivalents	$10,000
COGS	$250,000
Current Liabilities	$60,000
Ending Inventory	$80,000
Marketable Securities	$2,000
Net credit sales	$30,000
Net Income	$75,000
Net Sales	$500,000
Operating Cash Flows	$150,000
Operating Income	$150,000
Total Assets	$200,000
Total Equity	$196,000
Working Capital	$150,000

53. Calculate accounts receivables turnover in days:

    A. 365

    B. 82.2

    C. 251.9

    D. 45.3

    E. 180

Accounts Receivables	$30,000
Average Accounts Receivables	$30,000
Average Inventory	$80,000
Average Total Assets	$200,000
Cash Equivalents	$10,000
COGS	$250,000
Current Liabilities	$60,000
Ending Inventory	$80,000
Marketable Securities	$2,000
Net credit sales	$30,000
Net Income	$75,000
Net Sales	$500,000
Operating Cash Flows	$150,000
Operating Income	$150,000
Total Assets	$200,000
Total Equity	$196,000
Working Capital	$150,000

54. Calculate the quick ratio:

    A. 0.6

    B. 0.3

    C. 0.7

    D. 0.5

    E. 0.4

Accounts Receivables	$30,000
Average Accounts Receivables	$30,000
Average Inventory	$80,000
Average Total Assets	$200,000
Cash Equivalents	$10,000
COGS	$250,000
Current Liabilities	$60,000
Ending Inventory	$80,000
Marketable Securities	$2,000
Net credit sales	$30,000
Net Income	$75,000
Net Sales	$500,000
Operating Cash Flows	$150,000
Operating Income	$150,000
Total Assets	$200,000
Total Equity	$196,000
Working Capital	$150,000

55. Calculate the net profit margin:

A. 13%

B. 14%

C. 15%

D. 16%

E. 17%

Accounts Receivables	$30,000
Average Accounts Receivables	$30,000
Average Inventory	$80,000
Average Total Assets	$200,000
Cash Equivalents	$10,000
COGS	$250,000
Current Liabilities	$60,000
Ending Inventory	$80,000
Marketable Securities	$2,000
Net credit sales	$30,000
Net Income	$75,000
Net Sales	$500,000
Operating Cash Flows	$150,000
Operating Income	$150,000
Total Assets	$200,000
Total Equity	$196,000
Working Capital	$150,000

56. Calculate ROA:

A. 0.375

B. 0.35

C. 0.3

D. 0.5

E. 0.4

Accounts Receivables	$30,000
Average Accounts Receivables	$30,000
Average Inventory	$80,000
Average Total Assets	$200,000
Cash Equivalents	$10,000
COGS	$250,000
Current Liabilities	$60,000
Ending Inventory	$80,000
Marketable Securities	$2,000
Net credit sales	$30,000
Net Income	$75,000
Net Sales	$500,000
Operating Cash Flows	$150,000
Operating Income	$150,000
Total Assets	$200,000
Total Equity	$196,000
Working Capital	$150,000

57. Calculate ROE:

A. 0.25

B. 0.28

C. 0.3

D. 0.38

E. 0.4

Accounts Receivables	$30,000
Average Accounts Receivables	$30,000
Average Inventory	$80,000
Average Total Assets	$200,000
Cash Equivalents	$10,000
COGS	$250,000
Current Liabilities	$60,000
Ending Inventory	$80,000
Marketable Securities	$2,000
Net credit sales	$30,000
Net Income	$75,000
Net Sales	$500,000
Operating Cash Flows	$150,000
Operating Income	$150,000
Total Assets	$200,000
Total Equity	$196,000
Working Capital	$150,000

58. Given an interest expense of $50,000 calculate times earned interest:

A. 12.4

B. 5.8

C. 3

D. 1.5

E. 3.5

Accounts Receivables	$30,000
Average Accounts Receivables	$30,000
Average Inventory	$80,000
Average Total Assets	$200,000
Cash Equivalents	$10,000
COGS	$250,000
Current Liabilities	$60,000
Ending Inventory	$80,000
Marketable Securities	$2,000
Net credit sales	$30,000
Net Income	$75,000
Net Sales	$500,000
Operating Cash Flows	$150,000
Operating Income	$150,000
Total Assets	$200,000
Total Equity	$196,000
Working Capital	$150,000

59. **Given long-term liabilities of $100,000, calculate D/E and debt ratio:**

    A. 0.8

    B. 0.82

    C. 0.95

    D. 1.2

    E. 0.9

Accounts Receivables	$30,000
Average Accounts Receivables	$30,000
Average Inventory	$80,000
Average Total Assets	$200,000
Cash Equivalents	$10,000
COGS	$250,000
Current Liabilities	$60,000
Ending Inventory	$80,000
Marketable Securities	$2,000
Net credit sales	$30,000
Net Income	$75,000
Net Sales	$500,000
Operating Cash Flows	$150,000
Operating Income	$150,000
Total Assets	$200,000
Total Equity	$196,000
Working Capital	$150,000

60. **Given long-term liabilities of $200,000, calculate operating cash flows to total debt:**

    A. 0.89

    B. 0.65

    C. 0.58

    D. 0.42

    E. 0.6

Accounts Receivables	$30,000
Average Accounts Receivables	$30,000
Average Inventory	$80,000
Average Total Assets	$200,000
Cash Equivalents	$10,000
COGS	$250,000
Current Liabilities	$60,000
Ending Inventory	$80,000
Marketable Securities	$2,000
Net credit sales	$30,000
Net Income	$75,000
Net Sales	$500,000
Operating Cash Flows	$150,000
Operating Income	$150,000
Total Assets	$200,000
Total Equity	$196,000
Working Capital	$150,000

61. **Calculate the equity multiplier:**

    A. 2.5

    B. 2

    C. 0.5

    D. 1

    E. 1.5

62. Company A purchases a machine for $100,000 with a 5 year life and $10,000 scrap value Using double-declining method, the end-of-year value at year 2 is:

    A. $60,000

    B. $21,000

    C. $36,000

    D. $24,000

    E. $48,000

63. Company A purchases a machine for $100,000 with a 5 year life and $10,000 scrap value Using the sum of years' digits method, the annual depreciation in year 4 is:

    A. $18,000

    B. $12,000

    C. $46,000

    D. $28,000

    E. $15,000

64. Upon total liquidation, who is the last to receive financial consideration:

    A. Employees

    B. Bondholders

    C. Preferred shareholders

    D. Common shareholders

    E. IRS

65. Upon total liquidation, who is 2nd to receive financial consideration:

    A. Employees

    B. Bondholders

    C. Preferred shareholders

    D. Common shareholders

    E. ATF

66. Which of the following is not an intangible asset:

    A. Goodwill

    B. Brand licensing

    C. Current patents

    D. Distribution contracts

    E. Copyrights

67. FV = $10,000
    r = 7%
    t = 2 years
    PV = _____:

    A. $21,400

    B. $4,673

    C. $8,734

    D. $11,400

    E. $7,345

68. **A 2/1 stock split will affect the total equity value held by each shareholder by:**

    A. It will reduce their share value by 50%

    B. It will increase their share value by 100%

    C. It will increase their share value by 50%

    D. No change

    E. It will reduce their share value by 100%

69. **$75,000 corporate bond, 4% coupon
    $2,500 par value
    7 years until maturity
    The semi-annual journal entry is:**

    A. $1,500

    B. $3,000

    C. $2,900

    D. $0

    E. $4,500

70. **Company A has operating income of $1 million, interest expense of $100,000, and a tax rate of 35%. With 100,000 common shares, the EPS is:**

    A. $5.85

    B. $5.5

    C. $2.8

    D. $1.8

    E. $6

71. **P/E is:**

    A. The minimum estimate of value per share based on asset book value

    B. The market estimate of the NPV of future earnings per share

    C. The minimum estimate of value per share based on the asset market value

    D. The market estimate of the value of future dividends

    E. The market estimate of enterprise value

FINANCIAL ACCOUNTING

72. **Items on the balance sheet are listed in order of:**

    A. Most liquid to least liquid across categories

    B. Least liquid to most liquid in each category

    C. Most liquid to least liquid in each category

    D. Least liquid to most liquid across categories

    E. Highest to lowest value

73. **The ideal debt-to-equity ratio is:**

    A. 1

    B. 1/2

    C. 2/1

    D. Cost of Debt = Cost of Equity

    E. 1.5

74. **In corporate valuation, what would cause the enterprise and equity value models to be much higher than the NPV model:**

    A. Poor capital management resulting in high WACC and low DCF

    B. Market expectation of increasing rates on variable bonds

    C. Investors pushing the market price up in anticipation of earnings and dividends well beyond practical NPV calculations.

    D. Nothing

    E. NPV is always the lowest value

75. **EV is calculated as:**

    A. Equity market value – debt market value + cash and investments

    B. Equity market value + Debt market value – cash and investments

    C. Equity market value – debt market value – cash and investments

    D. –Equity market value + debt market value – cash and investments

    E. –Equity market value – debt market value – cash and investments

FINANCIAL ACCOUNTING

76. Start of year -
    Price = $50/unit, profit margin 10%
    Inventory = 500 units, $45/unit cost

    End of year -
    No units sold due to market drop
    New market price = $30/unit
    Inventory replacement = $25/unit

    Calculate the value of inventory at lower of cost or market:

    A. $25,000

    B. $22,500

    C. $15,000

    D. $12,500

    E. $12,000

77. Cost of PPE less accumulated depreciation is:

    A. Salvage value

    B. Market value

    C. Book value

    D. Present value

    E. Future value

78. Inflows: $500/year at 10%
    Outflows: $475/year at 4%
    The NPV of year 5 cash flows is:

    A. ($79.95)

    B. $79.95

    C. ($79.96)

    D. $79.96

    E. $79.9

79. Order received on Jan 1
    Order fulfilled on Feb 1
    Payment received on Mar 1
    The sale is recorded on ____ using accrual method, and on ____ using cash method:

    A. Jan 1, Feb 1

    B. Jan 1, Mar 1

    C. Feb 1, Mar 1

    D. Feb 1, Jan 1

    E. Mar 1, Feb 1

80. Which of the following is included in the footnotes of a cash flows statement:

    A. Sale of a machine at scrap value

    B. Payment of a dividend

    C. Incurring debt

    D. Repayment of debt using equity shares

    E. COGS

FINANCIAL ACCOUNTING

81. **GAAP stands for:**

    A. Generally accepted accounting principles

    B. Generally accepted accounting practices

    C. General accepted accounting procedures

    D. General accounting and audit practices

    E. General accounting and audit principles

82. **The post-closing trial balance:**

    A. Recording activity in the period between closing and the next fiscal year

    B. Verify that debits and credits are equal after closing all temporary accounts

    C. Tests the balance sheet accounts before formally reporting financial statements for the year

    D. An audit performed after operations close for the day

    E. Verify that debits and credits are equal before closing temporary accounts

83. **The dividend puzzle refer to:**

    A. The ambiguity of when you need to own a stock in order to earn upcoming dividends

    B. The tendency for quickly growing companies to issue dividends despite potential for financing using retained earnings

    C. The tendency for dividend stocks to have higher market value despite no differences in financial value

    D. The tendency for non-dividend stocks to have higher market value despite no differences in financial value

    E. The uncertainty of how frequently dividends will be issues relative to dividend value

84. **Which of the following is not a type of equity financing:**

    A. Venture capital

    B. Personal loan

    C. Stock IPO

    D. Online crowdsourcing

    E. Personal funding

FINANCIAL ACCOUNTING

85. When unusually-high returns are offered by an investment manager, and are paid using the funds of new investors, it's called:

    A. Ponzi scheme

    B. Pump and dump

    C. Insider trading

    D. Bid rigging

    E. Shenanigans

86. The use cash inflows from a short-term repurchase agreement, recorded as a sale, to temporarily pay-down debt and falsify balance sheet accounts was committed by:

    A. Enron

    B. Healthsouth

    C. Lehman Brothers

    D. Bernie Madoff

    E. Worldcom

87. Nonoperating revenues and expenses is included in the _____ presentation of the income statement:

    A. Multi-step

    B. Single-step

    C. Expanded

    D. Simplified

    E. Overflow

88. The marginal revenue product is:

    A. The amount of additional revenue generated by selling one additional product

    B. The comparative margins of profit between different products

    C. The comparative margins of revenue between different products

    D. The amount of additional revenue generated with one additional unit of any specific input factor

    E. The comparative margins of operating income between products

89. A worker makes $500/week salary. They quit in the middle of the day on Monday to pursue a job paying $600/week. What is the associated wages payable:

    A. $50

    B. $100

    C. $500

    D. $0

    E. $150

90. **A cash flow statement which uses cash flows to adjust the net income is using the _____ method:**

    A. Net income method

    B. Direct method

    C. Indirect method

    D. Adjusting method

    E. Correcting method

Cash Flow From Operations		
Net Earnings		
Additions to Cash		
Depreciation		
Decrease in Accounts Receivable		
Increase in Accounts Payable		
Increase in Taxes Payable		
Subtractions From Cash		
Increase in Inventory		
Net Cash from Operations		
Cash Flow From Investing		
Equipment		
Cash Flow From Financing		
Notes Payable		
Cash Flow for FY Ended		

91. **This is an example of:**

    A. Indirect method cash flow statement

    B. Direct method cash flow statement

    C. Adjusting method cash flow statement

    D. Net income method cash flow statement

    E. Correcting method of cash flow statement

92. **Participating preferred shares:**

    A. Come with voting rights

    B. Also receive common dividends

    C. Can be converted into common shares

    D. Can be repurchased by the issuer at par value at any time

    E. Can be converted into bonds

93. **Convertible shares can _____ and convertible bonds can _____:**

    A. Convert into common shares, convert into preferred shares

    B. Convert into bonds, convert into preferred shares

    C. Convert into bonds, convert into common shares

    D. Convert into common shares, convert into common shares

    E. Convert into preferred shares, convert into preferred shares

94. **Deferred shares:**

    A. Are shares, the issuing of which are deferred

    B. Raise equity financing, the accrual of which is deferred until the following year

    C. Have their dividends deferred until all other dividends are paid

    D. Do not exist

    E. Have their dividends deferred until their sale

95. **___ is not in the cash flow statement:**

    A. Financing activities

    B. Funding activities

    C. Investing activities

    D. Operating activities

    E. Operating or financing activities

96. **To convert LIFO into FIFO:**

    A. COGS(LIFO)-1/2(Average beginning inventory*inflation rate)

    B. COGS(FIFO) - ΔFIFO reserve

    C. COGS(LIFO) - ΔLIFO reserve

    D. COGS(average)-1/2(LIFO beginning inventory*inflation rate)

    E. COGS(average)+1/2(Average beginning inventory*inflation rate)

97. **To convert FIFO into LIFO:**

    A. COGS(LIFO) - ΔLIFO reserve

    B. COGS(average)-1/2(Average beginning inventory*inflation rate)

    C. COGS(FIFO) - ΔFIFO reserve

    D. COGS(LIFO)-1/2(FIFO beginning inventory*inflation rate)

    E. COGS(average)+1/2(Average beginning inventory*inflation rate)

FINANCIAL ACCOUNTING

98. **What can cause a difference in the tax expense and taxes payable:**

    A. Change in inventory valuation methods

    B. Uncollectible account receivable under the cash method

    C. Differences in the depreciation method used for reporting and tax purposes

    D. Tax fraud

    E. Net losses

99. **(EBIT+FC)/EBIT is:**

    A. Financial leverage

    B. Operating leverage

    C. Combined leverage

    D. Statistical leverage

    E. Mechanical leverage

100. **EBIT/(EBIT-Interest Expense) is:**

    A. Combined leverage

    B. Financial leverage

    C. Statistical leverage

    D. Financial leverage

    E. Mechanical leverage

FINANCIAL ACCOUNTING

Answer Key

Question Number	Correct Answer	Your Answer	Question Number	Correct Answer	Your Answer	Question Number	Correct Answer	Your Answer
1	B		35	D		69	A	
2	C		36	C		70	A	
3	C		37	C		71	B	
4	B		38	A		72	C	
5	C		39	B		73	D	
6	C		40	B		74	C	
7	D		41	D		75	B	
8	B		42	A		76	D	
9	B		43	C		77	C	
10	A		44	D		78	C	
11	B		45	D		79	B	
12	C		46	A		80	D	
13	D		47	B		81	A	
14	B		48	A		82	B	
15	A		49	A		83	C	
16	A		50	A		84	B	
17	B		51	A		85	A	
18	A		52	D		86	C	
19	B		53	A		87	A	
20	A		54	C		88	D	
21	A		55	C		89	A	
22	D		56	A		90	C	
23	D		57	D		91	A	
24	A		58	C		92	B	
25	A		59	B		93	D	
26	A		60	C		94	C	
27	B		61	D		95	B	
28	B		62	C		96	C	
29	B		63	B		97	B	
30	B		64	D		98	C	
31	C		65	B		99	B	
32	B		66	D		100	D	
33	A		67	C				
34	A		68	D				

FINANCIAL ACCOUNTING

RATIONALES

1. **Sale – March**
   Delivery - April
   Payment – May
   Warranty – 1 Year
   Warranty expense reported in:

   A. March

   B. April

   C. March of the following year

   D. April of the following year

   E. When the warranty ends

The answer is B
Warranties are reported at the time they begin.

2. **Amortization of prepaid insurance appears on:**

   A. Balance sheet only

   B. Balance sheet and cash flows statement

   C. Balance sheet and income statement

   D. Income statement and cash flows statement

   E. Cash flows statement and balance sheet

The answer is C
The change in value appears on the income statement, while the new value is found on the balance sheet.

FINANCIAL ACCOUNTING

3. **Starting inventory - $1,000**
   Purchases - $15,000
   Ending inventory - $2,000
   COGS - $_____:

   A. 12,000

   B. 16,000

   C. 14,000

   D. 17,000

   E. 15,000

The answer is C
Starting inventory plus purchases contribute to the COGS for the period, but the ending inventory will contribute to the next period.

4. **Which of the following appears separately, net of income tax, on an income statement:**

   A. Gross Profit

   B. Loss on Discontinued Operations

   C. Gain on Sale of a Truck

   D. Interest Expense

   E. Tax expense

The answer is B
As a significant one-time contributor to finances, discontinued operations are listed separately so as not to mislead investors.

FINANCIAL ACCOUNTING

5. **Business loan worth $1 million**
   Interest rate is 0%
   Repayment period is 10 years
   Payments are made annually
   This is recorded as:

   A. A current liability of $1 million

   B. A long-term liability of $1 million

   C. Current liability of $100,000 and a long-term liability of $900,000

   D. Note payable of $100,000 and bond payable of $900,000

   E. Long-term liability of $100,000 and current liability of $900,000

The answer is C
Current liabilities include anything that will be due in less than 12 months. Notes and bonds payable refer specifically to promissory notes and bonds, leaving everything due after 12 months as generic long-term liabilities.

6. **Which of the following appears as a cash flow from investing activities:**

   A. Revenues from the sale of goods

   B. Paying interest to bondholders

   C. Paying a dividend to preferred shareholders

   D. Sale of machinery for scrap

   E. COGS

The answer is C
Dividend activities are considered investing activities.

FINANCIAL ACCOUNTING

7. The government agency which regulates financial reporting of publicly-traded companies is:

    A. IRS

    B. FASB

    C. AICPA

    D. SEC

    E. DoD

The answer is D
The Securities and Exchange Commission is tasked with regulating public company financial management and reporting.

8. The professional organization which issues accounting credentials is:

    A. FASB

    B. AICPA

    C. IRS

    D. SEC

    E. DoD

The answer is B
The American Institute of CPAs is the professional organization which is responsible, among other things, for establishing the qualifications of being a CPA.

FINANCIAL ACCOUNTING

9. **The organization is charge of establishing GAAP is:**

    A. IRS

    B. FASB

    C. AICPA

    D. SEC

    E. FBI

The answer is B
The Financial Accounting Standards Board establishes reporting policy.

10. **The accounting equation states:**

    A. Assets = Liabilities + Equity

    B. Equities = Liabilities - Assets

    C. Equity = Liabilities + Assets

    D. Assets = Equity – Liabilities

    E. Assets = Equity/Liabilities

The answer is A
Conversely, equity can be calculated as Equity = Assets - Liabilities

11. **Which of the following is not a basic accounting principle:**

    A. Matching

    B. Audit

    C. Objectivity

    D. Realization

    E. Economic entity assumption

The answer is B
Auditing is the activity of verifying accounts, not a principle.

FINANCIAL ACCOUNTING

12. ____ does not appear on the income statement:

   A. EBIT

   B. Interest expense

   C. Accumulated depreciation

   D. Depreciation expense

   E. Operating income

The answer is C
Accumulated depreciation appears on the balance sheet

13. Company A had one owner whose personal assets were protected, then someone bought a 50% stake in the business using a similar structure. Company A is now:

   A. LLC

   B. Corporation

   C. Partnership

   D. LLP

   E. Partnership

The answer is D
LLP is a limited liability partnership

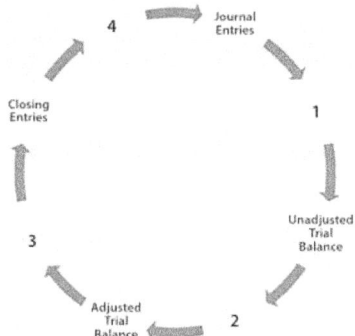

14. Financial Statements belong at point ____:

A. 1

B. 3

C. 4

D. 2

E. None of these

The answer is B
After the adjusted trial balance, financial statements are created.

FINANCIAL ACCOUNTING

15. **Ledger belongs at point _____:**

    A. 1

    B. 3

    C. 2

    D. 4

    E. None of these

The answer is A
Journal entries are moved to the general ledger.

16. **The cost of equity using the dividend capitalization model is:**

    A. (Dividends per share/Market Value)+Dividend growth

    B. Pr^t

    C. $B_s(r_m - r_f)$

    D. $((E/V)*C_e)+((D/V)*C_D)$

    E. Assets = Liabilities + Equity

The answer is A
The dividend capitalization model is used primarily by those concerned with income-generating equity investments.

FINANCIAL ACCOUNTING

17. **The cost of equity using CAPM model is:**

    A. (Dividends per share/Market Value)+Dividend growth

    B. $B_s(r_m-r_f)$

    C. Pr^t

    D. $((E/V)*C_e)+((D/V)*C_D)$

    E. Assets = Liabilities + Equity

The answer is B
The CAPM model defines the cost of equity as the amount of incurred financial risk.

18. **The after-tax cost of debt is:**

    A. $(Pr^t)-T$

    B. Pr^t

    C. $((E/V)*C_e)+((D/V)*C_D)$

    D. $B_s(r_m-r_f)$

    E. Assets = Liabilities + Equity

The answer is A
The cost of debt is equal to the rate of interest paid

19. **Unrealized holding gain or loss would be a typical entry for:**

    A. Operations derivatives

    B. Option derivatives

    C. Forward derivatives

    D. Cash flow hedges

    E. COGS

The answer is B
One may choose whether to exercise an options contract

FINANCIAL ACCOUNTING

20. **A short-term investment in a partner company would be listed in the balance sheet as _____:**

    A. Trading security

    B. Held-to-maturity investment

    C. Available for sale

    D. Long-term asset

    E. Short-term liability

The answer is A
Trading securities are not expected to be held until maturity.

21. **Which of the following is not a contingent asset or contingent liability:**

    A. Issued corporate bonds

    B. Unexercised options

    C. Pending lawsuit

    D. Insurance coverage

    E. Unexercised futures contract

The answer is A
Bonds that have already have no contingent outcomes except in special cases.

22. **A contingent liability which will be recorded in the accounts of the balance sheet and income statement, rather than as a note is:**

    A. Future losses on a futures contract

    B. Future losses on an options contract

    C. Insurance coverage

    D. Losses resulting from a petty lawsuit

    E. COGS

The answer is D
Once a lawsuit is settled, it is no longer contingent.

```
        Account Name
  _____
           |
           |
           |
           |
```

23. The left is ____, the right is ____:

    A. Credit, Credit

    B. Debit, Debit

    C. Credit, Debit

    D. Debit, Credit

    E. None of these

The answer is D
In this context, the terms debit and credit mean nothing more than left and right.

24. In a t-account, debits ____ expenses, and ____ revenues:

    A. Increase, decrease

    B. Decrease, increase

    C. Increase, increase

    D. Decrease, decrease

    E. None of these

The answer is A
Debits have an inverse effect on opposites, such as expenses and revenues.

FINANCIAL ACCOUNTING

25. **Company A pays $10,000 on a $1 million loan they borrowed 5 years ago at a rate of 5%. The t-account transaction will include:**

    A. A $10,000 credit to assets, and a $10,000 debit to liabilities

    B. $10,000 debit to assets, a $10,000 credit to short-term liabilities, and a $10,000 credit to long-term liabilities

    C. A $10,000 debit to assets, and a $10,000 credit to liabilities

    D. A $10,000 credit to assets, a $10,000 debit to liabilities, and a $40,000 credit to liabilities

    E. A $50,000 credit to assets

The answer is A
Each individual transaction includes only two account entries.

26. **Where would you look to assess whether Company A's financial statements are fair and accurate:**

    A. Auditor's report

    B. Financial statement notes

    C. Management discussion

    D. Footnotes to the balance sheet

    E. Business news website

The answer is A
The auditor's report states that the finances have been reviewed, though scandals in recent years have shown that even large auditors are subject to pressure from their major clients.

FINANCIAL ACCOUNTING

27. The purchase of a large machine by issuing corporate bonds is reported as:

    A. Cash inflow of the financing section

    B. Noncash financing and investing activity

    C. Cash outflow of the financing section

    D. Cash outflow of the investing section

    E. Cash outflow of the operating section

The answer is B
No cash is being used in this transaction, meaning no cash flows.

28. **Beginning capital: $1.2 million**
    Ending capital: $800,000
    Withdrawals: $1 million
    Net Income/Loss:

    A. $2,200,000

    B. $200,000

    C. $1,400,000

    D. $600,000

    E. $750,000

The answer is B
Beginning capital+withdrawals-ending capital

FINANCIAL ACCOUNTING

29. **The listing of all account balances to demonstrate an equivalent total value of debits and credits is:**

    A. Ledger

    B. Trial balance

    C. Journal

    D. Balance sheet

    E. Income Statement

The answer is B
The trial balance is used to test whether the account balances are accurate.

30. **In 1 year, a furniture store sells a $3,000 living room set on 6-month 0% store credit for $5,000. On the balance sheet this would be:**

    A. Increase notes receivable by $5,000, and decrease inventories for $5,000

    B. Increase accounts receivable by $5,000, decrease inventories for $3,000, and increase owner's equity for $2,000.

    C. Increase owner's equity for $5,000, and decrease inventories for $5,000

    D. Increase accounts receivable by $3,000, decrease inventories by $3,000, and increase owner's equity by $5,000.

    E. Increase long-term liabilities by $5,000 and increase inventories by $3,000

The answer is B
When a company earns more value than it lost, it increases the value of the company.

FINANCIAL ACCOUNTING

31. **Deferred income tax liability results from:**

    A. Depreciation on assets

    B. Contingent liability

    C. Short-term differences in GAAP and tax accounting law

    D. Unrealized gains

    E. COGS

The answer is C
Differences in timing in the recognition of transactions can create this problem.

32. **The difference between EPS and diluted EPS is:**

    A. Diluted EPS assumes the distribution of dividends on preferred shares

    B. Diluted EPS assumes the exercising of all convertible shares

    C. Diluted EPS assumes the distribution of dividends on common shares

    D. Diluted EPS assumes the exercising of all convertible bonds

    E. Diluted EPS assumes a net loss

The answer is B
Convertible shares would increase the volume of shares outstanding

33. **Company A $1.4 million in net income for the year, 235,000 common shares outstanding, and 5,000 convertible shares. It's EPS is:**

    A. $5.96

    B. $5.83

    C. $1.165 million

    D. $6.09

    E. $5.90

The answer is A
Convertible shares aren't included in standard EPS calculations.

FINANCIAL ACCOUNTING

34. The listing of the names and numbers of all accounts is:

A. Chart of accounts

B. Index of accounts

C. Book of accounts

D. Reference of accounts

E. List of accounts

The answer is A
The chart of accounts acts as a reference guide.

	2013	2014	2015
Revenue			
Distribution Solutions	2,025.00	2,314.00	
Technology Solutions	2,984.00		3,124.00
Total Revenue		5,378.00	5,676.00
Cost of Revenues			
Cost of Sales		0.00	
Total Cost of Revenues		0.00	
Gross Income	5,009.00		
Gross Margin (%)			100.0%
SG&A Expense	3,065.00	3,192.00	3,164.00
Research & Development Expenses	347.00	364.00	376.00
Restructuring & Other cash charges (Gains)	0.00	0.00	0.00
Other Operating Expenses (Gains)	(5.00)	493.00	(20.00)
(EBITDA)		1,329.00	
(EBITDA Margin)	32.0%		
Depreciation & Amortization	124.00		148.00
Total Operating Expense	3,531.00	4,182.00	3,668.00
Operating Income (EBIT)			2,008.00
Operating Income Margin (EBIT Margin)	29.5%	22.2%	
Interest Expense (Income)		144.00	187.00
Interest & Other Income (Expense)	121.00	12.00	43.00
Interest & Investment Expense (Income)	21.00	132.00	
Net Income Before Taxes (EBT)	1,457.00		1,864.00
Provision for Income Taxes (Benefit)		241.00	
Effective Tax Rate	32.1%		32.2%
Net Income from Continuing Operations			
Income from Discontinued Operations, After-Tax Non-Recurring (Items), Accounting	1.00		0.00
(Preferred Dividends)	0.00		0.00
Net Income (E)		823.00	

FINANCIAL ACCOUNTING

35. What trend is found through a horizontal analysis of gross income for the period 2013-2015:

A. A 12% growth rate

B. A 12% reduction in 2014 followed by 13.3% growth in 2015

C. A 88.2% growth rate

D. A 13.3% growth rate

E. A 13.3% reduction in 2014 followed by a 12% growth in 2015

The answer is D
Horizontal analysis means to compare trends in a single indicator over time.

	2013	2014	2015
Revenue			
Distribution Solutions	2,025.00	2,314.00	
Technology Solutions	2,984.00		3,124.00
Total Revenue		5,378.00	5,676.00
Cost of Revenues			
Cost of Sales		0.00	
Total Cost of Revenues		0.00	
Gross Income	5,009.00		
Gross Margin (%)			100.0%
SG&A Expense	3,065.00	3,192.00	3,164.00
Research & Development Expenses	347.00	364.00	376.00
Restructuring & Other cash charges (Gains)	0.00	0.00	0.00
Other Operating Expenses (Gains)	(5.00)	493.00	(20.00)
(EBITDA)		1,329.00	
(EBITDA Margin)	32.0%		
Depreciation & Amortization	124.00		148.00
Total Operating Expense	3,531.00	4,182.00	3,668.00
Operating Income (EBIT)			2,008.00
Operating Income Margin (EBIT Margin)	29.5%	22.2%	
Interest Expense (Income)		144.00	187.00
Interest & Other Income (Expense)	121.00	12.00	43.00
Interest & Investment Expense (Income)	21.00	132.00	
Net Income Before Taxes (EBT)	1,457.00		1,864.00
Provision for Income Taxes (Benefit)		241.00	
Effective Tax Rate	32.1%		32.2%
Net Income from Continuing Operations			
Income from Discontinued Operations, After-Tax Non-Recurring (Items), Accounting	1.00		0.00
(Preferred Dividends)	0.00		0.00
Net Income (E)		823.00	

FINANCIAL ACCOUNTING

36. **Calculate the EBIT margin for 2015:**

    A. 32.3%

    B. 21.4%

    C. 35.4%

    D. 35.3%

    E. 35.1%

The answer is C
EBIT is also called operating income

	2013	2014	2015
Revenue			
Distribution Solutions	2,025.00	2,314.00	
Technology Solutions	2,984.00		3,124.00
Total Revenue		5,378.00	5,676.00
Cost of Revenues			
Cost of Sales		0.00	
Total Cost of Revenues		0.00	
Gross Income	5,009.00		
Gross Margin (%)			100.0%
SG&A Expense	3,065.00	3,192.00	3,164.00
Research & Development Expenses	347.00	364.00	376.00
Restructuring & Other cash charges (Gains)	0.00	0.00	0.00
Other Operating Expenses (Gains)	(5.00)	493.00	(20.00)
(EBITDA)		1,329.00	
(EBITDA Margin)	32.0%		
Depreciation & Amortization	124.00		148.00
Total Operating Expense	3,531.00	4,182.00	3,668.00
Operating Income (EBIT)			2,008.00
Operating Income Margin (EBIT Margin)	29.5%	22.2%	
Interest Expense (Income)		144.00	187.00
Interest & Other Income (Expense)	121.00	12.00	43.00
Interest & Investment Expense (Income)	21.00	132.00	
Net Income Before Taxes (EBT)	1,457.00		1,864.00
Provision for Income Taxes (Benefit)		241.00	
Effective Tax Rate	32.1%		32.2%
Net Income from Continuing Operations			
Income from Discontinued Operations, After-Tax Non-Recurring (Items), Accounting	1.00		0.00
(Preferred Dividends)	0.00		0.00
Net Income (E)		823.00	

FINANCIAL ACCOUNTING

37. **Use comparative vertical analysis to explain the change in net income from 2013-2014:**

    A. A 24.7% decrease in net income is primarily explained by an unusually low 16.7% EBITDA margin

    B. A 16.7% increase in net income is primarily explained by an unusually high 24.7% EBITDA margin

    C. A 16.7% decrease in net income is primarily explained by an unusually low 24.7% EBITDA margin

    D. A 24.7% increase in net income is primarily explained by an unusually high 16.7% EBITDA margin

    E. A 16.7% decrease in net income is primarily explained by an unusually high 24.7% EBITDA margin

The answer is C
In 2014 the company experienced significant one-time operating expenses.

38. **Net profit margin is calculated as:**

    A. (Net income*100)/Net sales

    B. (Net sales/100)*Net income

    C. (Net income*100)/operating margin

    D. (Gross income*100)/net sales

    E. (Net sales*100)/operating margin

The answer is A
Net profit margin is a measure of profitability.

FINANCIAL ACCOUNTING

39. Total assets = $25,000
    Shareholder's equity = $5,000
    Revenue = $10,000
    Net income = $2,000
    Structure a DuPont equation model:

    A. (5)(2.5)(0.2)

    B. (0.2)(0.4)(5)

    C. (2.5)(0.4)(5)

    D. (0.2)(0.08)(2)

    E. (5)(0.2)(0.08)

The answer is B
The DuPont equation details those things which contribute to ROE.

40. Total assets = $25,000
    Shareholder's equity = $5,000
    Revenue = $10,000
    Net income = $2,000
    The simplified DuPont calculation is the same as___, with a value of ____:

    A. Return on assets, 0.08

    B. Return on equity, 0.4

    C. Profit margin, 0.2

    D. Equity multiplier, 5.0

    E. Return on equity, 0.8

The answer is B
Through cross-multiplication, DuPont = ROE

FINANCIAL ACCOUNTING

41. The sole proprietor's drawing account is closed to the:

A. Shareholder's equity account

B. General ledger

C. Income summary account

D. Owner's capital account

E. Cash flows statement

The answer is D
In a sole proprietorship, the owner's assets are intrinsically linked to the company assets, and subject to the owner's use without restriction.

42. ____ appears on the balance sheet:

A. Accumulated depreciation

B. Depreciation expense

C. Accumulated amortization

D. Amortization expense

E. Accumulated interest expense

The answer is A
Accumulated depreciation is the total amount of depreciation expense.

FINANCIAL ACCOUNTING

43. Recording revenues when they are earned is seen in ____ accounting, and when the money is received in ___ accounting:

   A. Accrual, Tax

   B. Forensic, Accrual

   C. Accrual, Cash

   D. Cash, Accrual

   E. Tax, Forensic

The answer is C
Accrual accounting is concerned with when the money is obligated to them, while cash accounting awaits the actual cash transaction.

44. ____ will not cause a change to shareholder equity under accrual accounting:

   A. Purchase of treasury shares

   B. Issuing a dividend

   C. Sale of inventory at a profit

   D. Purchase of equipment

   E. Loss from discontinued operations

The answer is D
A decrease in cash is associated with an equivalent increase in capital.

45. The purpose of cross-indexing is to:

   A. Function as a reference between fiscal years

   B. Function as a reference between financial statements

   C. Function as a reference between the general ledger and subsidiary ledger

   D. Function as a reference between the journal and the ledger

   E. Function as a reference between the journal and the income statement

The answer is D
Cross-indexing helps to more easily track account entries.

FINANCIAL ACCOUNTING

46. Company A buys a machine for $1 million, which is expected to last 10 years with a salvage value of $5,000. Using straight-line method, the entry after 1 year is:

   A. Depreciation expense: $99,500
      Acc. Depreciation: $99,500

   B. Depreciation expense: $100,000
      Acc. Depreciation: $100,000

   C. Acc. Depreciation: $99,500
      Owner's Equity: $99,500

   D. Depreciation expense: $100,000
      Owner's Equity: $100,000

   E. Acc. Depreciation: $100,000
      Depreciation expense: $100,000

The answer is A
Salvage value is considered when calculating the value of useful life

47. Company A pays $10,000 for 4 years of prepaid insurance. After 1 year, the adjusting entry is:

   A. $2,500 credit of prepaid insurance
      $10,000 debit of insurance expense

   B. $2,500 credit of prepaid insurance
      $2,500 debit of insurance expense

   C. $2,500 debit of prepaid insurance
      $2,500 credit of insurance expense

   D. $2,500 debit of prepaid insurance
      $10,000 credit of insurance expense

   E. $10,000 credit of prepaid insurance
      $2,500 debit of accrued insurance

The answer is B
Prepaid account deplete at a constant rate given time or utilization.

FINANCIAL ACCOUNTING

48. LIFO liquidation occurs when:

A. A company using LIFO sells older inventory, causing a distortion of profit margin

B. A company using LIFO sells older inventory, causing a distortion of sales

C. A company using FIFO switches to LIFO, causing a distortion in inventory value

D. A company using LIFO switches to FIFO, causing a distortion in inventory value

E. A company using FIFO switches to LIFO, causing a distortion of profit margin

The answer is A
During a time of inflation (most of the time), LIFO liquidation will result in inflated profitability records.

49. Company A accepts prepayment of $10,000 for 100 units, and in the first year they ship 50%, but in that time the market price dropped to $750 per unit. After that transaction:

A. $5,000 unearned revenue
   $5,000 revenue

B. ($5,000) unearned revenue
   ($5,000) revenue

C. $10,000 unearned revenue
   $5,000 revenue

D. ($10,000) unearned revenue
   ($5,000) revenue

E. $5,000 unearned revenue
   $5,000 assets

The answer is A
Since unearned revenue is considered a liability, a positive value will increase total liability value.

FINANCIAL ACCOUNTING

50. Sales = $750,000
    Gross Margin = 35%
    COGS = _____ :

    A. $487,500

    B. $262,500

    C. $225,000

    D. $478,500

    E. ($478,500)

The answer is A
Sales(1-r)

51. Starting Inventory = $50,000
    Ending Inventory = $40,000
    Purchases = $120,000
    COGS = ___ :

    A. $130,000

    B. $110,000

    C. $90,000

    D. $30,000

    E. $60,000

The answer is A
All the inventory either bought in a period, or brought from a prior period is considered, except that which is moving into the next period.

Accounts Receivables	$30,000
Average Accounts Receivables	$30,000
Average Inventory	$80,000
Average Total Assets	$200,000
Cash Equivalents	$10,000
COGS	$250,000
Current Liabilities	$60,000
Ending Inventory	$80,000
Marketable Securities	$2,000
Net credit sales	$30,000
Net Income	$75,000
Net Sales	$500,000
Operating Cash Flows	$150,000
Operating Income	$150,000
Total Assets	$200,000
Total Equity	$196,000
Working Capital	$150,000

52. **Calculate days sales in receivables:**

    A. 12.1

    B. 25.7

    C. 18.5

    D. 21.9

    E. 20.9

The answer is D
Accounts Receivables/(Net sales/365)

53. **Calculate accounts receivables turnover in days:**

    A. 365

    B. 82.2

    C. 251.9

    D. 45.3

    E. 180

The answer is A
Average Accounts Receivables/(Net credit sale/365)

Accounts Receivables	$30,000
Average Accounts Receivables	$30,000
Average Inventory	$80,000
Average Total Assets	$200,000
Cash Equivalents	$10,000
COGS	$250,000
Current Liabilities	$60,000
Ending Inventory	$80,000
Marketable Securities	$2,000
Net credit sales	$30,000
Net Income	$75,000
Net Sales	$500,000
Operating Cash Flows	$150,000
Operating Income	$150,000
Total Assets	$200,000
Total Equity	$196,000
Working Capital	$150,000

54. Calculate the quick ratio:

    A. 0.6

    B. 0.3

    C. 0.7

    D. 0.5

    E. 0.4

The answer is C
(Cash+Securities+AR)/Current liabilities

55. Calculate the net profit margin:

    A. 13%

    B. 14%

    C. 15%

    D. 16%

    E. 17%

The answer is C
(Net income*100)/Net Sales

Accounts Receivables	$30,000
Average Accounts Receivables	$30,000
Average Inventory	$80,000
Average Total Assets	$200,000
Cash Equivalents	$10,000
COGS	$250,000
Current Liabilities	$60,000
Ending Inventory	$80,000
Marketable Securities	$2,000
Net credit sales	$30,000
Net Income	$75,000
Net Sales	$500,000
Operating Cash Flows	$150,000
Operating Income	$150,000
Total Assets	$200,000
Total Equity	$196,000
Working Capital	$150,000

56. **Calculate ROA:**

    A. 0.375

    B. 0.35

    C. 0.3

    D. 0.5

    E. 0.4

The answer is A
Net income/Average total assets

57. **Calculate ROE:**

    A. 0.25

    B. 0.28

    C. 0.3

    D. 0.38

    E. 0.4

The answer is D
Net Income/Equity

Accounts Receivables	$30,000
Average Accounts Receivables	$30,000
Average Inventory	$80,000
Average Total Assets	$200,000
Cash Equivalents	$10,000
COGS	$250,000
Current Liabilities	$60,000
Ending Inventory	$80,000
Marketable Securities	$2,000
Net credit sales	$30,000
Net Income	$75,000
Net Sales	$500,000
Operating Cash Flows	$150,000
Operating Income	$150,000
Total Assets	$200,000
Total Equity	$196,000
Working Capital	$150,000

58. Given an interest expense of $50,000 calculate times earned interest:

A. 12.4

B. 5.8

C. 3

D. 1.5

E. 3.5

The answer is C
EBIT/Interest expense

Accounts Receivables	$30,000
Average Accounts Receivables	$30,000
Average Inventory	$80,000
Average Total Assets	$200,000
Cash Equivalents	$10,000
COGS	$250,000
Current Liabilities	$60,000
Ending Inventory	$80,000
Marketable Securities	$2,000
Net credit sales	$30,000
Net Income	$75,000
Net Sales	$500,000
Operating Cash Flows	$150,000
Operating Income	$150,000
Total Assets	$200,000
Total Equity	$196,000
Working Capital	$150,000

59. Given long-term liabilities of $100,000, calculate D/E and debt ratio:

   A. 0.8

   B. 0.82

   C. 0.95

   D. 1.2

   E. 0.9

The answer is B
Total Debt/Total Equity

Accounts Receivables	$30,000
Average Accounts Receivables	$30,000
Average Inventory	$80,000
Average Total Assets	$200,000
Cash Equivalents	$10,000
COGS	$250,000
Current Liabilities	$60,000
Ending Inventory	$80,000
Marketable Securities	$2,000
Net credit sales	$30,000
Net Income	$75,000
Net Sales	$500,000
Operating Cash Flows	$150,000
Operating Income	$150,000
Total Assets	$200,000
Total Equity	$196,000
Working Capital	$150,000

60. Given long-term liabilities of $200,000, calculate operating cash flows to total debt:

A. 0.89

B. 0.65

C. 0.58

D. 0.42

E. 0.6

The answer is C
EBIT/Total debt

Accounts Receivables	$30,000
Average Accounts Receivables	$30,000
Average Inventory	$80,000
Average Total Assets	$200,000
Cash Equivalents	$10,000
COGS	$250,000
Current Liabilities	$60,000
Ending Inventory	$80,000
Marketable Securities	$2,000
Net credit sales	$30,000
Net Income	$75,000
Net Sales	$500,000
Operating Cash Flows	$150,000
Operating Income	$150,000
Total Assets	$200,000
Total Equity	$196,000
Working Capital	$150,000

61. **Calculate the equity multiplier:**

    A. 2.5

    B. 2

    C. 0.5

    D. 1

    E. 1.5

The answer is D
Total assets/Total equity

62. **Company A purchases a machine for $100,000 with a 5 year life and $10,000 scrap value. Using double-declining method, the end-of-year value at year 2 is:**

    A. $60,000

    B. $21,000

    C. $36,000

    D. $24,000

    E. $48,000

The answer is C
Double-declining depreciation accelerates the rate of depreciation

FINANCIAL ACCOUNTING

63. Company A purchases a machine for $100,000 with a 5 year life and $10,000 scrap value. Using the sum of years' digits method, the annual depreciation in year 4 is:

    A. $18,000

    B. $12,000

    C. $46,000

    D. $28,000

    E. $15,000

The answer is B
The sum of years' digits uses the actual numbers in the years of useful life.

64. Upon total liquidation, who is the last to receive financial consideration:

    A. Employees

    B. Bondholders

    C. Preferred shareholders

    D. Common shareholders

    E. IRS

The answer is D
Since common shareholders are the owners, they are the ones subject to the most loss potential.

FINANCIAL ACCOUNTING

65. Upon total liquidation, who is 2nd to receive financial consideration:

A. Employees

B. Bondholders

C. Preferred shareholders

D. Common shareholders

E. AFT

The answer is B
Debtors always get their share before owners.

66. Which of the following is not an intangible asset:

A. Goodwill

B. Brand licensing

C. Current patents

D. Distribution contracts

E. Copyrights

The answer is D
Intangible assets aren't physical objects but still have intrinsic value.

67. FV = $10,000
r = 7%
t = 2 years
PV = _____:

A. $21,400

B. $4,673

C. $8,734

D. $11,400

E. $7,345

The answer is C
FV/(1+r)^t

68. A 2/1 stock split will affect the total equity value held by each shareholder by:

A. It will reduce their share value by 50%

B. It will increase their share value by 100%

C. It will increase their share value by 50%

D. No change

E. It will reduce their share value by 100%

The answer is D
Although each share is worth half of its previous price, each shareholder will have twice as many shares.

69. $75,000 corporate bond, 4% coupon
    $2,500 par value
    7 years until maturity
    The semi-annual journal entry is:

    A. $1,500

    B. $3,000

    C. $2,900

    D. $0

    E. $4,500

The answer is A
4% of $75,000 is $3,000, semi-annual (6 months) is $1,500

70. Company A has operating income of $1 million, interest expense of $100,000, and a tax rate of 35%. With 100,000 common shares, the EPS is:

    A. $5.85

    B. $5.5

    C. $2.8

    D. $1.8

    E. $6

The answer is A
Subtract interest expense before calculating taxes.

FINANCIAL ACCOUNTING

71. P/E is:

    A. The minimum estimate of value per share based on asset book value

    B. The market estimate of the NPV of future earnings per share

    C. The minimum estimate of value per share based on the asset market value

    D. The market estimate of the value of future dividends

    E. The market estimate of enterprise value

The answer is B
P/E is an extremely common measure of market value.

72. Items on the balance sheet are listed in order of:

    A. Most liquid to least liquid across categories

    B. Least liquid to most liquid in each category

    C. Most liquid to least liquid in each category

    D. Least liquid to most liquid across categories

    E. Highest to lowest value

The answer is C
Liquidity in assets refers to how easily they can be turned into cash, while in liabilities it is those which are due the soonest.

73. The ideal debt-to-equity ratio is:

    A. 1

    B. 1/2

    C. 2/1

    D. Cost of Debt = Cost of Equity

    E. 1.5

The answer is D
A company will pursue the cheapest capital financing until they have equal price.

FINANCIAL ACCOUNTING

74. **In corporate valuation, what would cause the enterprise and equity value models to be much higher than the NPV model:**

    A. Poor capital management resulting in high WACC and low DCF

    B. Market expectation of increasing rates on variable bonds

    C. Investors pushing the market price up in anticipation of earnings and dividends well beyond practical NPV calculations.

    D. Nothing

    E. NPV is always the lowest value

The answer is C
Enterprise and equity value models both include market share price, which is frequently less conservative in its estimates.

75. **EV is calculated as:**

    A. Equity market value – debt market value + cash and investments

    B. Equity market value + Debt market value – cash and investments

    C. Equity market value – debt market value – cash and investments

    D. –Equity market value + debt market value – cash and investments

    E. –Equity market value – debt market value – cash and investments

The answer is B
Enterprise value refers to the market value of their capital

FINANCIAL ACCOUNTING

76. Start of year -
    Price = $50/unit, profit margin 10%
    Inventory = 500 units, $45/unit cost

    End of year -
    No units sold due to market drop
    New market price = $30/unit
    Inventory replacement = $25/unit

    Calculate the value of inventory at lower of cost or market:

    A. $25,000

    B. $22,500

    C. $15,000

    D. $12,500

    E. $12,000

The answer is D
The current cost of replacement is the current cost value, which is lower than the market value since price is higher than cost per unit.

77. Cost of PPE less accumulated depreciation is:

    A. Salvage value

    B. Market value

    C. Book value

    D. Present value

    E. Future value

The answer is C
The book value is the value of the remaining life of capital as stated in the financial records.

78. Inflows: $500/year at 10%
    Outflows: $475/year at 4%
    The NPV of year 5 cash flows is:

    A. ($79.95)

    B. $79.95

    C. ($79.96)

    D. $79.96

    E. $79.9

The answer is C
It's possible to have negative NPV despite having positive FV.

79. Order received on Jan 1
    Order fulfilled on Feb 1
    Payment received on Mar 1
    The sale is recorded on ____ using accrual method, and on ____ using cash method:

    A. Jan 1, Feb 1

    B. Jan 1, Mar 1

    C. Feb 1, Mar 1

    D. Feb 1, Jan 1

    E. Mar 1, Feb 1

The answer is B
Accrual method concerns itself with obligation while cash method is only concerned with completion.

FINANCIAL ACCOUNTING

80. Which of the following is included in the footnotes of a cash flows statement:

A. Sale of a machine at scrap value

B. Payment of a dividend

C. Incurring debt

D. Repayment of debt using equity shares

E. COGS

The answer is D
As a non-cash transaction, this is included as a footnote.

81. GAAP stands for:

A. Generally accepted accounting principles

B. Generally accepted accounting practices

C. General accepted accounting procedures

D. General accounting and audit practices

E. General accounting and audit principles

The answer is A
Yes, it's pronounced "gap", like the Grand Canyon is a gap.

82. The post-closing trial balance:

A. Recording activity in the period between closing and the next fiscal year

B. Verify that debits and credits are equal after closing all temporary accounts

C. Tests the balance sheet accounts before formally reporting financial statements for the year

D. An audit performed after operations close for the day

E. Verify that debits and credits are equal before closing temporary accounts

The answer is B
At the end of the year when all the temporary accounts are closed, it's important to ensure that everything is still balanced given so much recent activity.

FINANCIAL ACCOUNTING

83. **The dividend puzzle refer to:**

    A. The ambiguity of when you need to own a stock in order to earn upcoming dividends

    B. The tendency for quickly growing companies to issue dividends despite potential for financing using retained earnings

    C. The tendency for dividend stocks to have higher market value despite no differences in financial value

    D. The tendency for non-dividend stocks to have higher market value despite no differences in financial value

    E. The uncertainty of how frequently dividends will be issues relative to dividend value

The answer is C
No one is really sure why dividend stocks have higher market price despite the fact that non-dividend stocks maintain that value through retained earnings.

84. **Which of the following is not a type of equity financing:**

    A. Venture capital

    B. Personal loan

    C. Stock IPO

    D. Online crowdsourcing

    E. Personal funding

The answer is B
A loan is a type of debt.

85. **When unusually-high returns are offered by an investment manager, and are paid using the funds of new investors, it's called:**

    A. Ponzi scheme

    B. Pump and dump

    C. Insider trading

    D. Bid rigging

    E. Shenanigans

The answer is A
Colloquially, "Robbing Peter to pay Paul."

86. **The use cash inflows from a short-term repurchase agreement, recorded as a sale, to temporarily pay-down debt and falsify balance sheet accounts was committed by:**

    A. Enron

    B. Healthsouth

    C. Lehman Brothers

    D. Bernie Madoff

    E. Worldcom

The answer is C
Lehman used an account called Repo 105 to classify a short-sale as a long-sale, hiding the assets offshore.

87. Nonoperating revenues and expenses is included in the ____ presentation of the income statement:

   A. Multi-step

   B. Single-step

   C. Expanded

   D. Simplified

   E. Overflow

The answer is A
Multi-step income statements provide much more detailed information, though small businesses typically only really need a single-step income statement.

88. **The marginal revenue product is:**

   A. The amount of additional revenue generated by selling one additional product

   B. The comparative margins of profit between different products

   C. The comparative margins of revenue between different products

   D. The amount of additional revenue generated with one additional unit of any specific input factor

   E. The comparative margins of operating income between products

The answer is D
For each increase in labor, production will increase, but at a decreasing rate for each additional person.

FINANCIAL ACCOUNTING

89. A worker makes $500/week salary.
    They quit in the middle of the day on Monday to pursue a job paying $600/week. What is the associated wages payable:

    A. $50

    B. $100

    C. $500

    D. $0

    E. $150

The answer is A
You still need to pay your employees for the time they worked, no matter how the relationship ended.

90. A cash flow statement which uses cash flows to adjust the net income is using the _____ method:

    A. Net income method

    B. Direct method

    C. Indirect method

    D. Adjusting method

    E. Correcting method

The answer is C
The indirect method is generally considered to be less detailed, but reconciles accounts.

Cash Flow From Operations		
Net Earnings		
Additions to Cash		
Depreciation		
Decrease in Accounts Receivable		
Increase in Accounts Payable		
Increase in Taxes Payable		
Subtractions From Cash		
Increase in Inventory		
Net Cash from Operations		
Cash Flow From Investing		
Equipment		
Cash Flow From Financing		
Notes Payable		
Cash Flow for FY Ended		

91. **This is an example of:**

    A. Indirect method cash flow statement

    B. Direct method cash flow statement

    C. Adjusting method cash flow statement

    D. Net income method cash flow statement

    E. Correcting method of cash flow statement

The answer is A
The entire difference between direct and indirect methods are found in Cash Flow from Operations, while the rest is the same in both.

92. **Participating preferred shares:**

    A. Come with voting rights

    B. Also receive common dividends

    C. Can be converted into common shares

    D. Can be repurchased by the issuer at par value at any time

    E. Can be converted into bonds

The answer is B
Participating shares get preferred and common dividends.

93. **Convertible shares can _____ and convertible bonds can _____:**

    A. Convert into common shares, convert into preferred shares

    B. Convert into bonds, convert into preferred shares

    C. Convert into bonds, convert into common shares

    D. Convert into common shares, convert into common shares

    E. Convert into preferred shares, convert into preferred shares

The answer is D
Everything convertible converts to common shares at a rate which is either specified (convertible shares) or at the equivalent market price (bonds).

94. **Deferred shares:**

    A. Are shares, the issuing of which are deferred

    B. Raise equity financing, the accrual of which is deferred until the following year

    C. Have their dividends deferred until all other dividends are paid

    D. Do not exist

    E. Have their dividends deferred until their sale

The answer is C
Deferred shares are typically held by executives, if issued at all

95. **___ is not in the cash flow statement:**

    A. Financing activities

    B. Funding activities

    C. Investing activities

    D. Operating activities

    E. Operating or financing activities

The answer is B
Funding activities is not a part of the cash flow statement

FINANCIAL ACCOUNTING

96. To convert LIFO into FIFO:

　A. COGS(LIFO)-1/2(Average beginning inventory*inflation rate)

　B. COGS(FIFO) - ΔFIFO reserve

　C. COGS(LIFO) - ΔLIFO reserve

　D. COGS(average)-1/2(LIFO beginning inventory*inflation rate)

　E. COGS(average)+1/2(Average beginning inventory*inflation rate)

The answer is C
The LIFO reserve is used to more accurately report financial state for those companies using LIFO inventory valuations.

97. To convert FIFO into LIFO:

　A. COGS(LIFO) - ΔLIFO reserve

　B. COGS(average)-1/2(Average beginning inventory*inflation rate)

　C. COGS(FIFO) - ΔFIFO reserve

　D. COGS(LIFO)-1/2(FIFO beginning inventory*inflation rate)

　E. COGS(average)+1/2(Average beginning inventory*inflation rate)

The answer is B
The conversion from FIFO to LIFO is extremely rare, since it would both require an analysis of long-periods of inventory management simply to create value distortions.

98. What can cause a difference in the tax expense and taxes payable:

　A. Change in inventory valuation methods

　B. Uncollectible account receivable under the cash method

　C. Differences in the depreciation method used for reporting and tax purposes

　D. Tax fraud

　E. Net losses

The answer is C
Differences in timing between GAAP and tax laws are reconciled in the long-run.

FINANCIAL ACCOUNTING

99. ΔEBIT/ΔSales is:

   A. Financial leverage

   B. Operating leverage

   C. Combined leverage

   D. Statistical leverage

   E. Mechanical leverage

The answer is B
Operating leverage looks at how revenue translates into income

100. EBIT/(EBIT-Interest Expense) is:

   A. Combined leverage

   B. Financial leverage

   C. Statistical leverage

   D. Financial leverage

   E. Mechanical leverage

The answer is D
Financial leverage looks at the cost of debt.

INFORMATION SYSTEMS

Description of the Examination

The Information Systems examination covers material that is usually taught in an introductory college-level business information systems course. Questions test knowledge, terminology, and basic concepts about information systems as well as the application of that knowledge. The examination does not emphasize the details of hardware design and language-specific programming techniques. References to applications such as word processing or spreadsheets do not require knowledge of a specific product. The focus is on concepts and techniques applicable to a variety of products and environments. Knowledge of arithmetic and mathematics equivalent to that of a student who has successfully completed a traditional first-year high school algebra course is assumed.

The examination contains approximately 100 questions to be answered in 90 minutes. Some of these are pretest questions and will not be scored. The time candidates spend on tutorials and providing personal information is in addition to the actual testing time.

Note: Prior to October 2015, this examination was called Information Systems and Computer Applications.

Knowledge and Skills Required

Questions on the Information Systems examination require candidates to demonstrate knowledge of the following content. The percentages next to each main topic indicate the approximate percentage of exam questions on that topic.

10% **Office Applications**
- Productivity software(word processing, spreadsheet, presentation package, end-user database package)
- Operating systems (memory management, file management, interfaces, types of OS)
- Office systems (e-mail, conferencing, collaborative work, document imaging, system resources)

15% **Internet and World Wide Web**
- Internet and other online services and methods (World Wide Web, protocol, Web search engines, Web bots, intranet, cloud computing, communications, push/pull technology, W3C)
- Web browsers (URLs, protocols, standards, history, cookies, resource allocation)
- Web technologies (HTML, XML, JavaScript)
- Website development (analysis, design, functionality, accessibility)

15% **Technology Applications**
- Specialized systems (knowledge management, expert systems, TPS/OLTP, DSS, GIS, BI, workflow management, project management)
- E-commerce/E-business (EDI, standards, tools, characteristics, types of transactions, business models)
- Enterprise-wide systems (ERP, CRM, SCM)
- Data management (data warehousing, data mining, networking, security, validation, migration, storage, obsolescence)

INFORMATION SYSTEMS

- Business strategies (competition, process reengineering, process modeling, TQM, Web 2.0)
- Information processing methods (batch, real-time, transaction)

15% Hardware and Systems Technology
- Devices (processing, storage, input and output, telecommunications, networking)
- Functions (computer, telecommunications, network hardware)
- Network architectures (local area, wide area, VPN, enterprise)
- Computer architectures (mainframe, client/server, operating systems)
- Wireless technologies (Wi-Fi, cellular, satellite, mobile, GPS, RFID)

10% Software Development
- Methodologies (prototyping, SDLC, RAD, CASE, JAD, Agile)
- Processes (feasibility, systems analysis, systems design, end-user development, project management)
- Implementation (testing, training, data conversion, system conversion, system maintenance, post-implementation activities, post-implementation review, documentation)
- Standards (proprietary, open source)
- User interface design
- Development and purpose of standards

10% Programming Concepts and Data Management
- Programming logic (Boolean, arithmetic, SQL)
- Methodologies (object-oriented, structured)
- Data (concepts, types, structures, digital representation of data)
- File (types, structures)
- Database management systems (relational, hierarchical, network, management strategies)

25% Social and Ethical Implications and Issues
- Economic effects (secure transactions, viruses, malware, cost of security)
- Privacy concerns (individual, business, identity theft)
- Property rights (intellectual, legal, ownership of materials, open-source software)
- Effects of information technology on jobs (ergonomics, virtual teams, telecommuting, job design)
- Technology's influence on workforce strategies (globalization, virtual teams, telecommuting, outsourcing, insourcing)
- Careers in IS (responsibilities, occupations, career path, certification)
- Computer security and controls (system application, personal computer, disaster recovery)
- Social networking (benefits, risks, ethics, technology, Web 2.0)

INFORMATION SYSTEMS

SAMPLE TEST

DIRECTIONS: Read each item and select the best response.

1. **What does a .gif picture file stand for?**
   (Office Applications)

   A. Graphical Interface Format

   B. Graphics Interior Format

   C. Graphical Interchanging Format

   D. Graphics Interchange Format

   E. Giant Interface Format

2. **It allows you to personalize your document, protect your document, and identify the ownership of the document.**
   (Social and Ethical Implications and Issues)

   A. Picture background

   B. Confidential

   C. Watermark

   D. Washout

   E. Identity Pin

3. **The acronym USB stands for?**
   (Hardware and Systems Technology)

   A. Universal Series Bus

   B. Universal Serial Bus

   C. Union Series Bus

   D. Unified Serial Bus

   E. Universal Station Bus

4. **There is a huge system of interconnected networks on the Internet. What are *networks*?**
   (Hardware and Systems Technology)

   A. Two or more computers connected together

   B. Programs that go on searches

   C. Groups of programmers

   D. Television stations

   E. A group of software

5. **Which of the following is *not* a unique feature of e-commerce technology?**
   (Technology Applications)

   A. interactivity

   B. social technology

   C. global broadcasting

   D. richness

   E. Universal standards

INFORMATION SYSTEMS

6. Inadequate database capacity is an example of the _____ dimension of business problems.
   (Programming Concepts and Data Management)

   A. technology

   B. organizational

   C. people

   D. management

   E. serial

7. When is the best time to secure dedicated backup servers, networks and either hot sites or redundant and independent sites?
   (Social and Ethical Implications and Issues)

   A. As soon as possible after a disaster declared

   B. Prior to any disaster

   C. Prior to establishing the disaster recovery planning team

   D. Once "business as usual" is established after a disaster is declared.

   E. Once other financial concerns have been taken care of.

8. What do *directories* do?
   (Internet and World Wide Web)

   A. List the information you search for

   B. List addresses and phone numbers

   C. List information by categories

   D. List information for librarians

   E. Confuse those searching for information.

9. Interactivity in the context of e-commerce can be described as the
   (Technology Applications)

   A. ability to physically touch and manipulate a product.

   B. complexity and content of a message.

   C. ability of consumers to create and distribute content.

   D. establishing of a portal to buy products.

   E. enabling of two-way communication between consumer and merchant.

INFORMATION SYSTEMS

10. Who often performs system testing and acceptance testing respectively?
    (Software Development)

    A. Senior programmers and professional testers.

    B. Technical system testers and potential customers.

    C. Independent test team and users of the system.

    D. Development team and customers of the system.

    E. Customers of the system and the technical team.

11. Which of the problems below best characterizes a result of software failure?
    (Software Development)

    A. Damaged reputation

    B. Lack of methodology

    C. Inadequate training

    D. Regulatory compliance

    E. Poor management

12. _____ computing refers to applications and services that run on a distributed network using virtualized resources.
    (Internet and World Wide Web)

    A. Distributed

    B. Cloud

    C. Soft

    D. Parallel

    E. Hard

13. Which test support tool can be used to enforce coding standards?
    (Software Development)

    A. Static analysis tool

    B. Performance testing tool

    C. Test comparator

    D. Test management tool

    E. Enforcement tool

14. What are the three main search expressions, or operators, recognized by Boolean logic?
    (Programming Concepts and Data Management)

    A. FROM, TO, WHOM

    B. AND, OR, NOT

    C. SEARCH, KEYWORD, TEXT

    D. AND, OR, BUT

    E. AND, TO, BUT

INFORMATION SYSTEMS

15. Which of the following statements about meta-search engines is NOT true?
    (Internet and World Wide Web)

    A. Meta-search engines scan multiple search engines simultaneously.

    B. Meta-search engines are a waste of time because they provide very few results.

    C. Meta-search engines provide results based on the keyword(s) submitted.

    D. Meta-search engines can save time, but you shouldn't rely on them exclusively.

    E. Meta-search engines take input from a user and simultaneously send out queries to a third party search engine for results.

16. This is programming that protects the resources of a private network from users from other networks.
    (Social and Ethical Implications and Issues)

    A. Cybernetics

    B. Firewall

    C. Server-side include

    D. Intranet

    E. Server protection

17. What test can be conducted for off-the-shelf software to get market feedback?
    (Software Development)

    A. Beta testing

    B. Usability testing

    C. Alpha testing

    D. COTS testing

    E. Trial and error testing

18. When the computer is started, a bootstrap or Initial Program Load (IPL) begins testing the system. Where is this bootstrap program stored?
    (Hardware and Systems Technology)

    A. RAM

    B. ROM

    C. hard drive

    D. virtual memory

    E. DNS

19. A software robot that systematically searches the Web is a:
    (Internet and World Wide Web)

    A. search engine

    B. web rabbit

    C. weblog

    D. spider

    E. net catch

20. **What principle is best described when test designs are written by a third-party?**
    (Software Development)

    A. Exploratory testing

    B. Independent testing

    C. Integration testing

    D. Interoperability testing

    E. Designer testing

21. **What should a software developer use to document each variable in a software solution?**
    (Software Development)

    A. Data dictionary

    B. Data file

    C. Data flow diagram

    D. Structured data types

    D. Data notebook

22. **While compiling a program the following error message occurred:**

    unexpected '=' in code line 57

    What is the most likely cause of this message?
    (Programming Concepts and Data Management)

    A. Line 57 causes an incorrect output.

    B. A global variable has not been initialized.

    C. Line 57 was missing.

    D. The syntax rules of the programming language have not been followed.

    E. The incorrect logical or arithmetic operator has been used in a calculation.

23. **Antivirus software**
    (Social and Ethical Implications and Issues)

    A. needs to be installed only when your computer is networked.

    B. needs to be installed once you have detected a virus on your computer.

    C. needs to be updated regularly in order to ensure protection from newly created viruses.

    D. works quickest when you install multiple antivirus programs from different companies.

    E. Needs to be reinstalled daily.

INFORMATION SYSTEMS

24. The maximum amount of data that can be transmitted electronically during a given period of time is known as
    (Programming Concepts and Data Management)

    A. frequency.

    B. broadband.

    C. fiber-optic.

    D. broadwidth

    E. bandwidth.

25. One of the purposes of software requirements specifications (SRS) is to provide
    (Software Development)

    A. the breakdown of a problem into its component parts.

    B. instructions of users, describing how to use the new solution.

    C. instructions to programmers on how the new program works.

    D. evaluation criteria to ensure solution requirements have been met.

    E. brainstorming of a program's most desired features.

26. Which one of the following techniques would capture data to measure the *effectiveness* of a software solution?
    (Programming Concepts and Data Management)

    A. Surveying users

    B. Measuring average login time

    C. Running the network under load

    D. Timing the execution of a process

    E. Measuring average wait time

27. The most appropriate data structure to store information about customer orders on a computer's hard drive is a
    (Programming Concepts and Data Management)

    A. file.

    B. character.

    C. one-dimensional array.

    D. two-dimensional array.

    E. document

28. A validation check used to ensure that entered data is a number is called
    (Programming Concepts and Data Management)

    A. a type check.

    B. a range check.

    C. a character check.

    D. an existence check.

    E. a calculation check.

29. Network technicians can use error logs to measure the
    (Hardware and Systems Technology)

    A. speed of a network.

    B. usability of a network.

    C. reliability of a network.

    D. maintainability of a network.

    E. redundancy of a network.

30. Who founded Google?
    (Internet and World Wide Web)

    A. Sergei Zuckerberg and Larry King

    B. Louis Page and Sergei Rockmonanov

    C. Larry Page and Sergei Brin

    D. Mark Zuckerberg and Steve Balmer

    E. Louis Page and Steve Balmer

31. Which of the following tags allows loading malicious code (often in the form of JavaScript applet) onto an otherwise trusted page?
    (Social and Ethical Implications and Issues)

    A. <script>

    B. <!-->

    C. <iframe>

    D. <section>

    E. <header>

32. Data management technology consists of the
    (Programming Concepts and Data Management)

    A. physical hardware and media used by an organization for storing data.

    B. detailed, preprogrammed instructions that control and coordinate the computer hardware components in an information system.

    C. software governing the organization of data on physical storage media.

    D. hardware and software used to transfer data.

    E. hardware that connects the user to the data.

INFORMATION SYSTEMS

33. **The hardware and software used to transfer data in an organization is called**
    (Hardware and Systems Technology)

    A. data management technology.

    B. networking and data management technology.

    C. data and telecommunications technology.

    D. networking and telecommunications technology.

    E. data management and hardware management.

34. **Sociologists study information systems with an eye to understanding**
    (Social and Ethical Implications and Issues)

    A. how systems affect individuals, groups and organizations.

    B. how human decision makers perceive and use formal information.

    C. how new information system changes the control and cost structures within the firm.

    D. the production of digital goods.

    E. why consumers buy products.

35. **Which of the following would NOT be used as an input for an information system?**
    (Hardware and Systems Technology)

    A. digital dashboard

    B. handheld computer

    C. bar-code scanner

    D. cell phone

    E. iPad

36. **Which field of study focuses on both a behavior and technical understanding of information systems?**
    (Social and Ethical Implications and Issues)

    A. sociology

    B. operations research

    C. economics

    D. management information systems

    E. research management

37. **The computer's hardware is controlled by the**
    (Hardware and Systems Technology)

    A. CPU

    B. random access memory (RAM)

    C. operating system

    D. keyboard

    E. mouse

INFORMATION SYSTEMS

38. Which of the following is not an example of a digital modem?
    (Hardware and Systems Technology)

    A. modem connected to a television cable

    B. modem connecting to a wireless network

    C. modem connecting to a public telephone network

    D. modem connecting to a DSL telephone line

    E. modem connecting to an Ethernet cable.

39. The first application in what came to be called office automation was
    (Office Applications)

    A. word processing.

    B. email.

    C. facsimile (fax).

    D. electronic calendaring.

    E. database management

40. What is WPA/WPA-2 PSK?
    (Hardware and Systems Technology)

    A. WPA/WPA2 PSK uses a pre-shared key for access to he wireless network.

    B. A protection check that validates the connecting client.

    C. A special attack on WPA/WPA-2 wireless networks.

    D. A method to protect wireless access points from DoS (denial of service) attacks.

    E. A new encryption method that will replace AES.

41. Malicious software performing unwanted and harmful actions in disguise of a legitimate and useful program is know as
    (Social and Ethical Implications and Issues)

    A. adware

    B. a computer worm

    C. a Trojan horse

    D. spyware

    E. hoax

INFORMATION SYSTEMS

42. **Systems analysts are**
    (Social and Ethical Implications and Issues)

    A. highly trained technical specialists who write computer software instructions.

    B. specialists who translate business problems and requirements into information requirements and systems.

    C. employees who head the formal security function for an organization.

    D. senior managers in charge of the information systems function in a firm.

    E. employees who oversee programmers.

43. **_____ are online communities for expanding users' business or social contacts by making connections through their mutual business or personal connections.**
    (Social and Ethical Implications and Issues)

    A. Wikis

    B. Virtual worlds

    C. Social networking

    D. Email

    E. Bookmarking tools

44. **Buying or selling goods over the Internet is called**
    (Technology Applications)

    A. e-commerce

    B. e-business

    C. an intranet

    D. an extranet

    E. computer business

45. **A _____ allows individuals at two or more locations to communicate simultaneously through two-way video and audio transmissions.**
    (Office Applications)

    A. videotape

    B. wiki

    C. blog

    D. videoconference

    E. social media account

INFORMATION SYSTEMS

46. **Because the Internet lowers barriers to entry in most industries, it**
    (Technology Applications)

    A. decreases the threat of new entrants.

    B. increases the threat of new entrants.

    C. makes it easier to build customer loyalty.

    D. increases supplier power.

    E. increases the number of brick and mortar stores.

47. **Gathering "competitive intelligence"**
    (Technology Applications)

    A. is good business practice.

    B. is illegal.

    C. is considered unethical.

    D. minimizes the need to obtain information in the public domain.

    E. is a waste of time.

48. **Which of the following is considered to be social software?**
    (Social and Ethical Implications and Issues)

    A. an iPad

    B. Google Alerts

    C. a Dell PC

    D. an iPhone

    E. Mac computers

49. **An app on a smartphone is labeled as _____.**
    (Social and Ethical Implications and Issues)

    A. a device

    B. social software

    C. a wiki

    D. a connection

    E. hardware

50. **Which of the following constitutes four types of social publishing sites?**
    (Internet and World Wide Web)

    A. social networking sites, message boards, forums, and wikis

    B. microsharing sites, media sharing sites, and social bookmarking and news sites

    C. reviews and ratings, deal sites and deal aggregators, social shopping markets and social storefronts

    D. the Internet, social software, devices and social media users

    E. blogs, smart phones, news sites, forums

INFORMATION SYSTEMS

51. **Which of the following is considered to be social software?**
    (Social and Ethical Implications and Issues)

    A. an app

    B. an iPad

    C. a Sony digital camera

    D. an iPhone

    E. a Dell computer

52. **To which of the following zones of social media do Facebook applications apply?**
    (Social and Ethical Implications and Issues)

    A. social community only

    B. social publishing only

    C. social entertainment and social commerce

    D. social commerce and social publishing

    E. social community, publishing, entertainment and commerce

53. **In computer security, the part of malware code responsible for performing malicious action is referred to as**
    (Social and Ethical Implications and Issues)

    A. payload

    B. header

    C. frame

    D. preamble

    E. footer

54. **The _____ includes esteem in its measure of the value that people exchange.**
    (Social and Ethical Implications and Issues)

    A. horizon revolution

    B. digital native

    C. reputation economy

    D. network effect

    E. network revolution

INFORMATION SYSTEMS

55. The process social media users undergo to categorize content according to their own folksonomy is labeled as _____.
(Social and Ethical Implications and Issues)

    A. crowdsourcing

    B. tagging

    C. cloud computing

    D. blogging

    E. E-chatting

56. Web 2.0:
(Social and Ethical Implications and Issues)

    A. is a one-way communications device.

    B. provides limited availability to users.

    C. is an interactive social system of users and senders.

    D. cannot be accessed on devices like smartphones.

    E. is outdated technology.

57. A _____ protects against an attack in which one party generates a message for another party to sign.
(Social and Ethical Implications and Issues)

    A. data authenticator

    B. strong hash function

    C. weak hash function

    D. digital signature

    E. data signature

58. Harnessing collective knowledge to solve problems and complete tasks is labeled as _____.
(Technology Applications)

    A. crowdsourcing

    B. tagging

    C. cloud computing

    D. blogging

    E. face timing

INFORMATION SYSTEMS

59. **Social media are:**
    (Social and Ethical Implications and Issues)

    A. anything that involves delivering hosted services online.

    B. the means to harness the collective knowledge of a crowd to solve problems and complete tasks;

    C. the online means of communication, conveyance, collaboration, and cultivation among interconnected and interdependent networks.

    D. people who share their views about a product or service even though they're not affiliated with the company.

    E. a one-way communication device.

60. **On average, _____ of all possible keys must be tried in order to achieve success with a brute-force attack.**
    (Technology Applications)

    A. one-fourth

    B. half

    C. wo-thirds

    D. three-fourths

    E. four-fifths

61. **The purpose of a _____ is to produce a "fingerprint" of a file, message, or other block of data.**
    (Technology Applications)

    A. secret key

    B. digital signature

    C. keystream

    D. hash function

    E. digital file

62. **The idea that the program instructions and data are both stored in memory while being processed is known as the**
    (Technology Applications)

    A. processing concept.

    B. stored program concept

    C. data-instruction concept

    D. memory-data-instruction concept

    E. memory-processing concept.

INFORMATION SYSTEMS

63. As a matter of necessity, network interfaces must conform to standard agreements, known as _____, for messages to be understood by both computers during a message exchange between a pair of computers.
    (Software Development)

    A. protocols

    B. I/O services

    C. device controllers

    D. Ethernet standards

    E. networks

64. The components of an individual computer system consist of processing hardware, input devices, output devices, storage devices,
    (Hardware and System Technology)

    A. and application programs.

    B. and operating system software.

    C. application software and operating system software.

    D. application software, file storage, and data processing.

    E. file storage and data processing.

65. What is the only requirement for data to be manipulated and processed by a computer?
    (Office Applications)

    A. The data type must be numeric.

    B. The data must be represented in binary form.

    C. The data type must be alphanumeric, graphic, sound or color.

    D. The size of the data must be smaller than the capacity of the hard drive.

    E. The data type must be alphanumeric.

INFORMATION SYSTEMS

66. The main memory, often known as primary storage, working storage, or RAM (for random access memory), holds
    (Software Development)

    A. data.

    B. program instructions.

    C. program instructions and data.

    D. program instructions, data, and instructions for booting the computer.

    E. None of the above.

67. Many of the internal OS services are provided by the _____ module, which contains the most important operating system processing functions.
    (Hardware and Systems Technology)

    A. CPU

    B. root

    C. kernel

    D. central

    E. functioning

68. A development methodology that focuses on the processes as the core of the system is said to be _____.
    (Programming Concepts and Data Management)

    A. action-oriented

    B. structure-oriented

    C. process-centered

    D. object-oriented

    E. nature-oriented

69. Which of the following computer applications would best help a teacher keep records of students' academic information in a format that would allow complex searches using logical operators such as AND, OR, and NOT?
    (Office Applications)

    A. utility

    B. database

    C. spreadsheet

    D. word processing

    E. text file

95

INFORMATION SYSTEMS

70. **The primary advantage of defining styles when creating a word processing document is that they:**
    (Office Applications)

    A. allow page breaks to be set automatically.

    B. provide a template for the placement of text and images.

    C. automatically create text boxes and allow text to be wrapped.

    D. facilitate formatting of the text elements in the document.

    E. reduce errors in typing.

71. **It is most appropriate to use a vector graphics program rather than a bitmapped graphics program when creating:**
    (Office Applications)

    A. images that will be saved in a file format for the Web.

    B. an image that contains small decorative type.

    C. images that will be used in print products.

    D. an image that can be enlarged with no loss of quality.

    E. the image does not need to be saved.

72. **Which of the following is a function of a plug-in?**
    (Internet and World Wide Web)

    A. allowing a Web browser to execute files that are in formats the Web browser would normally not recognize

    B. decreasing the amount of time required for a Web browser to display multimedia files

    C. providing site visitors with greater control over how the files are displayed

    D. checking multimedia files for viruses before displaying them in the Web browser

    E. allowing users to modify others websites

73. **A person designing a Web page is most likely to use JavaScript for which of the following applications?**
    (Internet and World Wide Web)

    A. to play a sound file when the user clicks on a sound icon

    B. to allow the user to send an email to the Webmaster

    C. to print and save information entered in forms by users

    D. to pause and play video clips and animations

    E. to allow the visitor to leave the site quickly.

INFORMATION SYSTEMS

74. **How can the risk of unauthorized computer system access be reduced?**
    (Technology Applications)

    A. By installing anti-spam software.

    B. By using a firewall.

    C. By setting up a WAN.

    D. By encrypting all data stored in the system.

    E. By creating a password.

75. **A user wants to detect and clean a virus-infected file as it is opened. Which of the following would best achieve this?**
    (Technology Applications)

    A. Schedule a local virus scan.

    B. Utilize a real-time virus scan.

    C. Perform a scheduled network virus scan.

    D. Perform a complete virus scan of all hard disks.

    E. Reinstall virus protection software.

76. **Which of the following is a feature or characteristic of macros?**
    (Office Applications)

    A. They can be hyperlinked to a file.

    B. They can be saved as a separate file.

    C. They can only be used to carry viruses.

    D. They can be embedded in spreadsheet.

    E. They cause viruses to spread.

77. **The _____ provides the physical mechanisms to input and output data, to manipulate and process data, and to electronically control the various input, output and storage components.**
    (Hardware and Systems Technology)

    A. data

    B. network

    C. computer hardware

    D. computer software

    E. Internet

INFORMATION SYSTEMS

78. Which of the following is NOT an HTML container element?
    (Internet and World Wide Web)

    A. <region>

    B. <section>

    C. <footer>

    D. <aside>

    E. <header>

79. Which of the following is the most common operating system used by webservers?
    (Internet and World Wide Web)

    A. Windows

    B. Mac OS

    C. Android

    D. Linux

    E. System 7

80. When does a written work receive protection under U.S. copyright laws?
    (Social and Ethical Implications and Issues)

    A. When the work is written down.

    B. When the author first comes up with the idea for the work.

    C. When the work is published.

    D. When the work is registered with the U.S. Copyright Office.

    E. When the work is notarized.

81. A _____ is created by using a secure hash function to generate a hash value for a message and then encrypting the hash code with a private key.
    (Software Development)

    A. digital signature

    B. keystream

    C. one way hash function

    D. secret key

    E. protected message

82. Web addresses are called Uniform Resource Locators (URLs). A URL is a text string that specifies an Internet address and the method by which the address can be accessed. The protocol component of a URL identifies
    (Internet and World Wide Web)

    A. the name of the server on which the page resides.

    B. the site owner's registered site.

    C. the type of server and Internet service being used.

    D. the organization type.

    E. where the owner resides.

INFORMATION SYSTEMS

83. The work performed by an individual computer system within an IT system can be characterized by
    (Hardware and Systems Technology)

    A. hardware and software.

    B. input, storage and output.

    C. storage, processing and output.

    D. input, processing and output.

    E. input, storage and software.

84. In what ways can cookies be useful for Web site developers?
    (Internet and World Wide Web)

    A. Cookies give developers access to Web site visitors' hard drive files.

    B. Cookies inform the Web site manager about visitors' preferences.

    C. Cookies are dangerous and should never be used in Web development.

    D. Cookies enable developers to convey their preferences to Web site users.

    E. Cookies allow users to access the website's backend.

85. Mike receives an email message from a friend that contains a zip file. He opens the file and later notices that his email application has sent a copy of that zip to each person in his address book without his commanding it to do so. What event has most likely occurred?
    (Technology Applications)

    A. Mike has accidently sent a mass email to everyone on in his address book.

    B. A virus has infected Mike's computer.

    C. A hacker has taken over Mike's computer.

    D. Mike's email application has malfunctioned and must be replaced.

    E. Mike was logged into the wrong email account.

86. Harmful programs used to disrupt computer operation, gather sensitive information, or gain access to private computer systems are commonly referred to as
    (Social and Ethical Implications and Issues)

    A. adware

    B. malware

    C. computer viruses

    D. spyware

    E. worm

87. Which tag must appear within an HTML table?
(Internet and Word Wide Web)

   A. <tr>

   B. <th>

   C. <caption>

   D. <tc>

   E. <tb>

88. What is the correct definition of a block level tag?
(Internet and World Wide Web)

   A. A block level tag is a HTML element that affects one or more paragraphs.

   B. A block level tag affects an individual character or word.

   C. A block level tag does not require a paragraph break before the tag is used.

   D. A block level tag creates a table border.

   E. A block level tag places the paragraph into a block format.

89. Which of the following refers to the characteristic features of an advertising-supported software?
(Social and Ethical Implications and Issues)

   A. Unsolicited or undesired electronic messages

   B. A worm that infiltrates the computer's operating system

   C. Commonly referred to as malware

   D. Malicious program that sends copies of itself to other computers on the network

   E. Commonly referred to as adware

90. This is an application program that provides a way to look at and interact with all the information on the World Wide Web.
(Internet and World Wide Web)

   A. Line Checker

   B. Browser

   C. Access Provider

   D. Avatar

   E. Social Media

INFORMATION SYSTEMS

91. Which technology enables business to create multimedia applications to deliver their messages?
    (Technology Applications)

    A. Push technology

    B. Pull technology

    C. Media access technology

    D. Neo-Web technology

    E. Customer support initiative

92. You are a member of a Web design team. Which member of the team is responsible for developing the overall plan of the Web site?
    (Social and Ethical Implications and Issues)

    A. Web analyst

    B. Web Designer

    C. Web Architect

    D. Web Manager

    E. Systems Manager

93. Which of the following technologies manages the process of resolving URLs to official IP addresses?
    (Internet and World Wide Web)

    A. Domain Name System (DNS)

    B. File Transfer Protocol (FTP)

    C. Internet Service Providers (ISP)

    D. Simple Network Management Protocol (SNMP)

    E. Post Office Protocol (POP3)

94. Which of the following retains the information it's storing when the power to the system is turned off?
    (Hardware and Systems Technology)

    A. RAM

    B. DRAM

    C. DIMM

    D. CPU

    E. ROM

INFORMATION SYSTEMS

95. You are setting up a new email client application, which of the follow pieces of information will you provide that will handle outgoing mail messages?
    (Technology Applications)

    A. Post Office Protocol (POP3)

    B. Simple Mail Transfer Protocol (SMTP)

    C. Internet Message Access Protocol (IMAP)

    D. Transmission Control Protocol (TCP)

    E. File Transfer Protocol (FTP)

96. Which of the following is NOT true about Open Source Software?
    (Social and Ethical Implications and Issues)

    A. Open Source Software is developed primarily by inexperienced students.

    B. Open Source Software is typically developed through a collaborative process.

    C. "Freeware" or "shareware" are not the same as open source software.

    D. Open Source Software is commercial software.

    E. There is a lot of Open Source Software available.

97. Which of the following image types typically supports transparency?
    (Office Applications)

    A. BMP and JPEG

    B. PNG and BMP

    C. PNG and GIF

    D. JPEG and GIF

    E. JPEG and BMP

98. Which of the following do search engines expect you to use when making complex searches for information?
    (Programming Concepts and Data Management)

    A. Radical Inquiries

    B. Spiders

    C. SMS text messages

    D. SQL statements

    E. Boolean values

99. **You have been asked to help implement a Web marketing campaign. Which of the following tools will best help you ensure that this project is completed on time?**
    (Office Applications)

    A. A spreadsheet program

    B. An email application

    C. A Gantt chart

    D. A social networking site such as LinkedIn

    E. A relational database

100. **Who owns the user data found on social networking sites such as Facebook and Twitter?**
    (Social and Ethical Implications and Issues)

    A. The user who created the data

    B. The social networking site

    C. The W3C or similar third party who ensures user privacy

    D. The group of users with whom the user has communicated.

    E. Everyone. It is part of Creative Commons.

INFORMATION SYSTEMS

ANSWER KEY

Question Number	Correct Answer	Your Answer	Question Number	Correct Answer	Your Answer	Question Number	Correct Answer	Your Answer
1	D		35	A		69	B	
2	C		36	A		70	D	
3	B		37	C		71	D	
4	A		38	C		72	A	
5	C		39	A		73	D	
6	A		40	A		74	B	
7	B		41	C		75	B	
8	C		42	B		76	D	
9	E		43	C		77	C	
10	C		44	A		78	D	
11	A		45	D		79	D	
12	B		46	B		80	D	
13	A		47	A		81	A	
14	B		48	B		82	C	
15	B		49	B		83	D	
16	B		50	A		84	B	
17	A		51	A		85	B	
18	B		52	E		86	B	
19	D		53	A		87	A	
20	B		54	C		88	A	
21	A		55	B		89	E	
22	D		56	C		90	B	
23	C		57	D		91	A	
24	E		58	A		92	C	
25	C		59	C		93	A	
26	A		60	B		94	E	
27	A		61	C		95	B	
28	A		62	B		96	A	
29	C		63	A		97	C	
30	C		64	C		98	E	
31	C		65	B		99	C	
32	D		66	C		100	B	
33	A		67	C				
34	A		68	C				

INFORMATION SYSTEMS

RATIONALES

1. What does a .gif picture file stand for?
   (Office Applications)

   A. Graphical Interface Format

   B. Graphics Interior Format

   C. Graphical Interchanging Format

   D. Graphics Interchange Format

   E. Giant Interface Format

The answer is D.
A .gif file stands for Graphics Interchange Format.

2. It allows you to personalize your document, protect your document, and identify the ownership of the document.
   (Social and Ethical Implications and Issues)

   A. Picture background

   B. Confidential

   C. Watermark

   D. Washout

   E. Identity Pin

The answer is C.
To protect your document or image, you place a watermark on it that becomes part of the document or image.

INFORMATION SYSTEMS

3. **The acronym USB stands for?**
   (Hardware and Systems Technology)

   A. Universal Series Bus

   B. Universal Serial Bus

   C. Union Series Bus

   D. Unified Serial Bus

   E. Universal Station Bus

The answer is B.
USB stands for Universal Serial Bus. It is the most popular connection used to connect a computer to devices such as digital cameras, printers, scanners, etc.

4. **There is a huge system of interconnected networks on the Internet. In this context what are *networks*?**
   (Hardware and Systems Technology)

   A. Two or more computers connected together

   B. Programs that go on searches

   C. Groups of programmers

   D. Television stations

   E. A group of software

The answer is A.
When talking about computer networks, the meaning is two or more computers connected together.

INFORMATION SYSTEMS

5. Which of the following is *not* a unique feature of e-commerce technology?
   (Technology Applications)

   A. interactivity

   B. social technology

   C. global broadcasting

   D. richness

   E. Universal standards

The answer is C.
While *global reach* is a unique trait of e-commerce, global broadcasting is not.

6. Inadequate database capacity is an example of the _____ dimension of business problems.
   (Programming Concepts and Data Management)

   A. technology

   B. organizational

   C. people

   D. management

   E. serial

The answer is A.
Having minimal database capacity is a technological problem.

INFORMATION SYSTEMS

7. **When is the best time to secure dedicated backup servers, networks and either hot sites or redundant and independent sites?**
   (Social and Ethical Implications and Issues)

   A. As soon as possible after a disaster declared

   B. Prior to any disaster

   C. Prior to establishing the disaster recovery planning team

   D. Once "business as usual" is established after a disaster is declared.

   E. Once other financial concerns have been taken care of.

The answer is B.
The best time to secure a disaster plan is *before* a disaster hits.

8. **What do online *directories* do?**
   (Internet and World Wide Web)

   A. List the information you search for

   B. List addresses and phone numbers

   C. List information by categories

   D. List information for librarians

   E. Confuse those searching for information.

The answer is C.
Online directories list information by categories for easy search and retrieval of information.

INFORMATION SYSTEMS

9. **Interactivity in the context of e-commerce can be described as the**
   (Technology Applications)

   A. ability to physically touch and manipulate a product.

   B. complexity and content of a message.

   C. ability of consumers to create and distribute content.

   D. establishing of a portal to buy products.

   E. enabling of two-way communication between consumer and merchant.

The answer is E.
When speaking of interactivity in the context of e-commerce the term means the ability for the consumer and merchant to communicate.

10. **Who often performs system testing and acceptance testing respectively?**
    (Software Development)

    A. Senior programmers and professional testers.

    B. Technical system testers and potential customers.

    C. Independent test team and users of the system.

    D. Development team and customers of the system.

    E. Customers of the system and the technical team.

The answer is C.
System testing is usually done by an independent test team, while acceptance testing is performed by users of the system.

INFORMATION SYSTEMS

11. **Which of the problems below best characterizes a result of software failure?**
    (Software Development)

    A. Damaged reputation

    B. Lack of methodology

    C. Inadequate training

    D. Regulatory compliance

    E. Poor management

The answer is A.
This question is looking for the result of the software failure, not the cause or contributing factors. The result is damaged reputation.

12. **_____ computing refers to applications and services that run on a distributed network using virtualized resources.**
    (Internet and World Wide Web)

    A. Distributed

    B. Cloud

    C. Soft

    D. Parallel

    E. Hard

The answer is B.
Cloud computing is the practice of using a network of remote servers hosted on the Internet to store, manage and process data.

INFORMATION SYSTEMS

13. **Which test support tool can be used to enforce coding standards?**
    (Software Development)

    A. Static analysis tool

    B. Performance testing tool

    C. Test comparator

    D. Test management tool

    E. Enforcement tool

The answer is A.
Static analysis tools are used by developers as part of the development and component testing process.

14. **What are the three main search expressions, or operators, recognized by Boolean logic?**
    (Programming Concepts and Data Management)

    A. FROM, TO, WHOM

    B. AND, OR, NOT

    C. SEARCH, KEYWORD, TEXT

    D. AND, OR, BUT

    E. AND, TO, BUT

The answer is B.
Boolean logic is a form of algebra in which all values are reduced to either True or False.

INFORMATION SYSTEMS

15. **Which of the following statements about meta-search engines is NOT true?**
    (Internet and World Wide Web)

    A. Meta-search engines scan multiple search engines simultaneously.

    B. Meta-search engines are a waste of time because they provide very few results.

    C. Meta-search engines provide results based on the keyword(s) submitted.

    D. Meta-search engines can save time, but you shouldn't rely on them exclusively.

    E. Meta-search engines take input from a user and simultaneously send out queries to a third party search engine for results.

The answer is B.
All of the statements are true except B. Meta-search engines provide good results based on the keywords submitted.

16. **This is programming that protects the resources of a private network from users from other networks.**
    (Social and Ethical Implications and Issues)

    A. Cybernetics

    B. Firewall

    C. Server-side include

    D. Intranet

    E. Server protection

The answer is B.
A firewall is a part of a computing system or network that is designed to block unauthorized access while permitting outward communication.

INFORMATION SYSTEMS

17. **What test can be conducted for off-the-shelf software to get market feedback?**
    (Software Development)

    A. Beta testing

    B. Usability testing

    C. Alpha testing

    D. COTS testing

    E. Trial and error testing

The answer is A.
Beta testing is the trial of software or products in the final stages of development, usually carried out by a party unconnected with its development.

18. **When the computer is started, a bootstrap or Initial Program Load (IPL) begins testing the system. Where is this bootstrap program stored?**
    (Hardware and Systems Technology)

    A. RAM

    B. ROM

    C. hard drive

    D. virtual memory

    E. DNS

The answer is B.
The bootstrap program is stored in the Read Only Memory.

INFORMATION SYSTEMS

19. **A software robot that systematically searches the Web is a:**
    (Internet and World Wide Web)

    A. search engine

    B. web rabbit

    C. weblog

    D. spider

    E. net catch

The answer is D.
A spider is a program that visits Web sites and reads their pages in order to create entries for a search engine index.

20. **What principle is best described when test designs are written by a third-party?**
    (Software Development)

    A. Exploratory testing

    B. Independent testing

    C. Integration testing

    D. Interoperability testing

    E. Designer testing

The answer is B.
Independent testing is performed by testing specialists who have not been involved in the system's development to ensure that the delivered software meets both functional and non-functional requirements.

INFORMATION SYSTEMS

21. **What is the purpose of the program counter?**
    (Software Development)

    A. To store the address of the next instruction.

    B. To store the length of the object code.

    C. To count how often a program has been installed.

    D. To count the number of times a program loop is executed.

    E. To determine when to start the program over again.

The answer is A.
The program counter is a special-purpose register that is used by the processor to hold the address of the next instruction to be executed.

22. While compiling a program the following error message occurred:

    unexpected '=' in code line 57

    What is the most likely cause of this message?
    (Programming Concepts and Data Management)

    A. Line 57 causes an incorrect output.

    B. A global variable has not been initialized.

    C. Line 57 was missing.

    D. The syntax rules of the programming language have not been followed.

    E. The incorrect logical or arithmetic operator has been used in a calculation.

The answer is D.
The code is not syntactically correct.

INFORMATION SYSTEMS

23. **Antivirus software**
    (Social and Ethical Implications and Issues)

    A. needs to be installed only when your computer is networked.

    B. needs to be installed once you have detected a virus on your computer.

    C. needs to be updated regularly in order to ensure protection from newly created viruses.

    D. works quickest when you install multiple antivirus programs from different companies.

    E. Needs to be reinstalled daily.

The answer is C.
Antivirus software needs to be updated regularly to be protected from new viruses.

24. **The maximum amount of data that can be transmitted electronically during a given period of time is known as**
    (Programming Concepts and Data Management)

    A. frequency.

    B. broadband.

    C. fiber-optic.

    D. broadwidth

    E. bandwidth.

The answer is E.
In computer networks, bandwidth is used as a synonym for data transfer rate or the amount of data that can be carried from one point to another in a given time period.

INFORMATION SYSTEMS

25. **One of the purposes of software requirements specifications (SRS) is to provide**
    (Software Development)

    A. the breakdown of a problem into its component parts.

    B. instructions for users, describing how to use the new solution.

    C. instructions to programmers that captures a complete description about how the system is expected to perform.

    D. evaluation criteria to ensure solution requirements have been met.

    E. brainstorming of a program's most desired features.

The answer is C.
A software requirements specification is a document that outlines completely how the system is expected to perform.

26. **Which one of the following techniques would capture data to measure the *effectiveness* of a software solution?**
    (Programming Concepts and Data Management)

    A. Surveying users

    B. Measuring average login time

    C. Running the network under load

    D. Timing the execution of a process

    E. Measuring average wait time

The answer is A.
The best way to measure the effectiveness of a software solution is to survey the users of the software.

INFORMATION SYSTEMS

27. **The most appropriate data structure to store information about customer orders on a computer's hard drive is a**
    (Programming Concepts and Data Management)

    A. file.

    B. character.

    C. one-dimensional array.

    D. two-dimensional array.

    E. document

The answer is A.

28. **A validation check used to ensure that entered data is a number is called**
    (Programming Concepts and Data Management)

    A. a type check.

    B. a range check.

    C. a character check.

    D. an existence check.

    E. a calculation check.

The answer is A.
When you begin to set up your new system, you will choose the most appropriate data type for each field. A type check will ensure that the correct type of data is entered into that field.

INFORMATION SYSTEMS

29. Network technicians can use error logs to measure the
(Hardware and Systems Technology)

    A. speed of a network.

    B. usability of a network.

    C. reliability of a network.

    D. maintainability of a network.

    E. redundancy of a network.

The answer is C.
Error logs can be used to check the reliability of a network.

30. Who founded Google?
(Internet and World Wide Web)

    A. Sergei Zuckerberg and Larry King

    B. Louis Page and Sergei Rockmonanov

    C. Larry Page and Sergei Brin

    D. Mark Zuckerberg and Steve Balmer

    E. Louis Page and Steve Balmer

The answer is C.
Larry Page and Sergie Brin founded Google in 1998.

INFORMATION SYSTEMS

31. Which of the following tags allows loading malicious code (often in the form of JavaScript applet) onto an otherwise trusted page?
    (Social and Ethical Implications and Issues)

    A. <script>

    B. <!-->

    C. <iframe>

    D. <section>

    E. <header>

The answer is C.
By using <iframe>, the malicious content is loaded from another site.

32. Data management technology consists of the
    (Programming Concepts and Data Management)

    A. physical hardware and media used by an organization for storing data.

    B. detailed, preprogrammed instructions that control and coordinate the computer hardware components in an information system.

    C. software governing the organization of data on physical storage media.

    D. hardware and software used to transfer data.

    E. hardware that connects the user to the data.

The answer is D.
Data management technology is the skills and equipment used to organize, secure, store and retrieve information.

INFORMATION SYSTEMS

33. The hardware and software used to transfer data in an organization is called
(Hardware and Systems Technology)

    A. data management technology.

    B. networking and data management technology.

    C. data and telecommunications technology.

    D. networking and telecommunications technology.

    E. data management and hardware management.

The answer is A.
Data management technology can refer to a wide range of techniques and database systems used for managing information use and allocating access.

34. Sociologists study information systems with an eye to understanding
(Social and Ethical Implications and Issues)

    A. how systems affect individuals, groups and organizations.

    B. how human decision makers perceive and use formal information.

    C. how new information system changes the control and cost structures within the firm.

    D. the production of digital goods.

    E. why consumers buy products.

The answer is A.
Sociologists study how things affect people. This is true when they look at information systems as well.

INFORMATION SYSTEMS

35. **Which of the following would NOT be used as an input for an information system?**
    (Hardware and Systems Technology)

    A. digital dashboard

    B. handheld computer

    C. bar-code scanner

    D. cell phone

    E. IPad

The answer is A.
A digital dashboard is used to consolidate data, not input data. The other responses could all be used to input data.

36. **Which field of study focuses on both a behavior and technical understanding of information systems?**
    (Social and Ethical Implications and Issues)

    A. sociology

    B. operations research

    C. economics

    D. management information systems

    E. research management

The answer is A.
Sociologists study how external factors, such as technology, impact behavior.

INFORMATION SYSTEMS

37. **The computer's hardware is controlled by the**
    (Hardware and Systems Technology)

    A. CPU

    B. random access memory (RAM)

    C. operating system

    D. keyboard

    E. mouse

The answer is C.
The operating system controls the bulk of the hardware's activity. The operating system works with the CPU and memory management to control the hardware.

38. **Which of the following is not an example of a digital modem?**
    (Hardware and Systems Technology)

    A. modem connected to a television cable

    B. modem connecting to a wireless network

    C. modem connecting to a public telephone network

    D. modem connecting to a DSL telephone line

    E. modem connecting to an Ethernet cable.

The answer is C.
All but C are examples of digital modems.

INFORMATION SYSTEMS

39. The first application in what came to be called office automation was
    (Office Applications)

    A. word processing

    B. email.

    C. facsimile (fax).

    D. electronic calendaring.

    E. database management

The answer is A.
Word processing began in the late 1960s, while email came to be in 1971.

40. What is WPA/WPA-2 PSK?
    (Hardware and Systems Technology)

    A. WPA/WPA2 PSK uses a pre-shared key for access to the wireless network.

    B. A protection check that validates the connecting client.

    C. A special attack on WPA/WPA-2 wireless networks.

    D. A method to protect wireless access points from DoS (denial of service) attacks.

    E. A new encryption method that will replace AES.

The answer is A.
PSK stands for Pre-Shared Key. It allows all users to connect to the network using the same password or passphrase.

INFORMATION SYSTEMS

41. Malicious software performing unwanted and harmful actions in disguise of a legitimate and useful program is known as
(Social and Ethical Implications and Issues)

A. adware

B. a computer worm

C. a Trojan horse

D. spyware

E. hoax

The answer is C.
A Trojan horse is software that performs unwanted and harmful actions in disguise of a legitimate program. Adware automatically displays advertising material, spyware enables a user to obtain cover information about another computer's activities and a worm is malware the replicates itself in order to spread to other computers.

42. Systems analysts are
(Social and Ethical Implications and Issues)

A. highly trained technical specialists who write computer software instructions.

B. specialists who translate business problems and requirements into information requirements and systems.

C. employees who head the formal security function for an organization.

D. senior managers in charge of the information systems function in a firm.

E. employees who oversee programmers.

The answer is B.
A systems analyst analyzes complex processes or operations in order to improve the efficiency.

INFORMATION SYSTEMS

43. _____ are online communities for expanding users' business or social contacts by making connections through their mutual business or personal connections.
    (Social and Ethical Implications and Issues)

    A. Wikis

    B. Virtual worlds

    C. Social networks

    D. Email

    E. Bookmarking tools

The answer is C.
Social networks allow for information and knowledge to flow between people and groups.

44. Buying or selling goods over the Internet is called
    (Technology Applications)

    A. e-commerce

    B. e-business

    C. an intranet

    D. an extranet

    E. computer business

The answer is A.
E-commerce is commercial transactions conducted electronically on the Internet.

INFORMATION SYSTEMS

45. A _____ allows individuals at two or more locations to communicate simultaneously through two-way video and audio transmissions.
    (Office Applications)

    A. videotape

    B. wiki

    C. blog

    D. videoconference

    E. social media account

The answer is D.
Videoconferencing, by a set of telecommunication technologies, allows two or more locations to communicate by simultaneous two-way video and audio transmissions.

46. Because the Internet lowers barriers to entry in most industries, it
    (Technology Applications)

    A. decreases the threat of new entrants.

    B. increases the threat of new entrants.

    C. makes it easier to build customer loyalty.

    D. increases supplier power.

    E. increases the umber of brick and mortar stores.

The answer is B.
Due to the ease and low cost of creating a business online, the Internet increases the threat of new entrants.

INFORMATION SYSTEMS

47. **Gathering "competitive intelligence"**
    (Technology Applications)

    A. is good business practice.

    B. is illegal.

    C. is considered unethical.

    D. minimizes the need to obtain information in the public domain.

    E. Is a waste of time.

The answer is A.
Competitive intelligence is the action of gathering and analyzing intelligence about competitor's products, marketing and customers to help in strategic decision making.

48. **Which of the following is considered to be social software?**
    (Social and Ethical Implications and Issues)

    A. an iPad

    B. Google Alerts

    C. a Dell PC

    D. an iPhone

    E. Mac computers

The answer is B.
Google Alerts is considered to be social software. It is a content change detection and notification service.

INFORMATION SYSTEMS

49. An app on a smartphone is labeled as _____.
(Social and Ethical Implications and Issues)

    A. a device

    B. social software

    C. a wiki

    D. a connection

    E. hardware

The answer is B.
An app on a smartphone is considered social software because it enables users to interact and share data.

50. Which of the following constitutes four types of social publishing sites?
(Internet and World Wide Web)

    A. social networking sites, message boards, forums, and wikis

    B. microsharing sites, media sharing sites, and social bookmarking and news sites

    C. reviews and ratings, deal sites and deal aggregators, social shopping markets and social storefronts

    D. the Internet, social software, devices and social media users

    E. blogs, smart phones, news sites, forums

The answer is A.
Four types of social publishing sites are social networking sites, message boards, forums and wikis because they all allow users to publish and share content.

INFORMATION SYSTEMS

51. **Which of the following is considered to be social software?**
    (Social and Ethical Implications and Issues)

    A. an app

    B. an iPad

    C. a Sony digital camera

    D. an iPhone

    E. a Dell computer

The answer is A.
An app is considered to be social software because they are communication and interactive tools that are often based on the Internet.

52. **To which of the following zones of social media do Facebook applications apply?**
    (Social and Ethical Implications and Issues)

    A. social community only

    B. social publishing only

    C. social entertainment and social commerce

    D. social commerce and social publishing

    E. social community, publishing, entertainment and commerce

The answer is E.
Facebook applications apply to social community, publishing, entertainment and commerce.

INFORMATION SYSTEMS

53. **In computer security, the part of malware code responsible for performing malicious action is referred to as**
    (Social and Ethical Implications and Issues)

    A. payload

    B. header

    C. frame

    D. preamble

    E. footer

The answer is A.
Payload causes damage to system files. They also enable backdoor access to a user's computer and can steal sensitive data.

54. **The _____ includes esteem in its measure of the value that people exchange.**
    (Social and Ethical Implications and Issues)

    A. horizon revolution

    B. digital native

    C. reputation economy

    D. network effect

    E. network revolution

The answer is C.
Reputation economy has been rapidly growing as a result of e-commerce and social media. People post and find reviews prior to purchasing goods and services.

INFORMATION SYSTEMS

55. The process social media users undergo to categorize content according to their own folksonomy is labeled as _____.
    (Social and Ethical Implications and Issues)

    A. crowdsourcing

    B. tagging

    C. cloud computing

    D. blogging

    E. E-chatting

The answer is B.
Tagging has gained wide popularity due to the growth of social media as a way to manage labels that categorize content using simply keywords.

56. Web 2.0:
    (Social and Ethical Implications and Issues)

    A. is a one-way communications device.

    B. provides limited availability to users.

    C. is an interactive social system of users and senders.

    D. cannot be accessed on devices like smartphones.

    E. is outdated technology.

The answer is C.
Web 2.0 refers to an interactive social system that is characterized by the change from static web pages to user-generated content and the growth of social media.

INFORMATION SYSTEMS

57. A _____ protects against an attack in which one party generates a message for another party to sign.
(Social and Ethical Implications and Issues)

A. data authenticator

B. strong hash function

C. weak hash function

D. digital signature

E. data signature

The answer is D.
A digital signature is a type of electronic signature that encrypts documents with digital codes that are difficult to duplicate, thus protecting the signer.

58. Harnessing collective knowledge to solve problems and complete tasks is labeled as _____.
(Technology Applications)

A. crowdsourcing

B. tagging

C. cloud computing

D. blogging

E. face timing

The answer is A.
Crowdsourcing is the act of obtaining information or input by enlisting the services of a number of people. This has been made easier with social media.

INFORMATION SYSTEMS

59. Social media are:
(Social and Ethical Implications and Issues)

A. anything that involves delivering hosted services online.

B. the means to harness the collective knowledge of a crowd to solve problems and complete tasks;

C. the online means of communication, conveyance, collaboration, and cultivation among interconnected and interdependent networks.

D. people who share their views about a product or service even though they're not affiliated with the company.

E. a one-way communication device.

The answer is C.
Social media enables users to create and share content or to participate in social networking.

60. On average, _____ of all possible keys must be tried in order to achieve success with a brute-force attack.
(Technology Applications)

A. one-fourth

B. half

C. two-thirds

D. three-fourths

E. four-fifths

The answer is B.
Half of all possible keys must be tried in order to achieve brute-force attack success. This is why computers are programmed to do this task.

INFORMATION SYSTEMS

61. The purpose of a _____ is to produce a "fingerprint" of a file, message, or other block of data.
    (Technology Applications)

    A. secret key

    B. digital signature

    C. keystream

    D. hash function

    E. digital file

The answer is C.
A keystream is a string of random or pseudorandom characters that are combined with a plain text message to produce an encrypted message.

62. The idea that the program instructions and data are both stored in memory while being processed is known as the
    (Technology Applications)

    A. processing concept.

    B. stored program concept

    C. data-instruction concept

    D. memory-data-instruction concept

    E. memory-processing concept.

The answer is B.
Proposed by John von Neumann and Alan Turing in 1945, the stored program concept is where machine code instructions are fetched from main memory one at a time, then decoded and executed in the processor.

INFORMATION SYSTEMS

63. As a matter of necessity, network interfaces must conform to standard agreements, known as _____, for messages to be understood by both computers during a message exchange between a pair of computers.
    (Software Development)

    A. protocols

    B. I/O services

    C. device controllers

    D. Ethernet standards

    E. networks

The answer is A.
Protocols are a set of rules governing the exchange of transmission of data between devices.

64. The components of an individual computer system consist of processing hardware, input devices, output devices, storage devices,
    (Hardware and System Technology)

    A. and application programs.

    B. and operating system software.

    C. application software and operating system software.

    D. application software, file storage, and data processing.

    E. file storage and data processing.

The answer is C.
Application and operating system software along with the hardware, input, output and storage devices make up an individual computer system.

INFORMATION SYSTEMS

65. What is the only requirement for data to be manipulated and processed by a computer?
(Office Applications)

   A. The data type must be numeric.

   B. The data must be represented in binary form.

   C. The data type must be alphanumeric, graphic, sound or color.

   D. The size of the data must be smaller than the capacity of the hard drive.

   E. The data type must be alphanumeric.

The answer is B.
In order for data to be manipulated and processed by a computer it must be represented in binary form. This system consists of just two unique numbers, 0 and 1.

66. The main memory, often known as primary storage, working storage, or RAM (for random access memory), holds
(Software Development)

   A. data.

   B. program instructions.

   C. program instructions and data.

   D. program instructions, data, and instructions for booting the computer.

   E. None of the above.

The answer is C.
RAM holds the program instructions and data.

INFORMATION SYSTEMS

67. Many of the internal OS services are provided by the _____ module, which contains the most important operating system processing functions.
    (Hardware and Systems Technology)

    A. CPU

    B. root

    C. kernel

    D. central

    E. functioning

The answer is C.
The kernel is a fundamental part of a computer's operating system, managing input/output requests from software and translating them into data processing instructions for the central processing unit and other electronic components of the computer.

68. A development methodology that focuses on the processes as the core of the system is said to be _____.
    (Programming Concepts and Data Management)

    A. action-oriented

    B. structure-oriented

    C. process-centered

    D. object-oriented

    E. nature-oriented

The answer is C.
Object-oriented programming focuses on objects rather than actions, and data rather than logic. Process-centered focuses on the processes rather than

INFORMATION SYSTEMS

69. **Which of the following computer applications would best help a teacher keep records of students' academic information in a format that would allow complex searches using logical operators such as AND, OR, and NOT?**
    (Office Applications)

    A. utility

    B. database

    C. spreadsheet

    D. word processing

    E. text file

The answer is B.
One uses searches using logical operators within databases.

70. **The primary advantage of defining styles when creating a word processing document is that they:**
    (Office Applications)

    A. allow page breaks to be set automatically.

    B. provide a template for the placement of text and images.

    C. automatically create text boxes and allow text to be wrapped.

    D. facilitate formatting of the text elements in the document.

    E. reduce errors in typing.

The answer is D.
Defining styles allow for ease and speed in formatting the text elements in a document.

INFORMATION SYSTEMS

71. **It is most appropriate to use a vector graphics program rather than a bitmapped graphics program when creating:**
    (Office Applications)

    A. images that will be saved in a file format for the Web.

    B. an image that contains small decorative type.

    C. Images that will be used in print products.

    D. an image that can be enlarged with no loss of quality.

    E. the image does not need to be saved.

The answer is D.
With vector graphics the image can be magnified infinitely without loss of quality.

72. **Which of the following is a function of a plug-in?**
    (Internet and World Wide Web)

    A. allowing a Web browser to execute files that are in formats the Web browser would normally not recognize

    B. decreasing the amount of time required for a Web browser to display multimedia files

    C. providing site visitors with greater control over how the files are displayed

    D. checking multimedia files for viruses before displaying them in the Web browser

    E. allowing users to modify others websites.

The answer is A.
Plug-in applications are programs that can easily be installed and used to install, define and perform other functions.

INFORMATION SYSTEMS

73. **A person designing a Web page is most likely to use JavaScript for which of the following applications?**
    (Internet and World Wide Web)

    A. to play a sound file when the user clicks on a sound icon

    B. to allow the user to send an email to the Webmaster

    C. to print and save information entered in forms by users

    D. to pause and play video clips and animations

    E. to allow the visitor to leave the site quickly.

The answer is D.
JavaScript can be used to create a simple controller that would enable the person to change the size of a movie dynamically, display a progress indicator while the media is loading, replace one movie with another, etc.

74. **How can the risk of unauthorized computer system access be reduced?**
    (Technology Applications)

    A. By installing anti-spam software.

    B. By using a firewall.

    C. By setting up a WAN.

    D. By encrypting all data stored in the system.

    E. By creating a password.

The answer is B.
A firewall is a network security system that monitors and controls the incoming and outgoing network traffic based on predetermined security rules.

INFORMATION SYSTEMS

75. A user wants to detect and clean a virus-infected file as it is opened. Which of the following would best achieve this?
    (Technology Applications)

    A. Schedule a local virus scan.

    B. Utilize a real-time virus scan.

    C. Perform a scheduled network virus scan.

    D. Perform a complete virus scan of all hard disks.

    E. Reinstall virus protection software.

The answer is B.
By using a real-time virus scan, the user will be able to detect and clean the virus immediately and not in the future.

76. Which of the following is a feature or characteristic of macros?
    (Office Applications)

    A. They can be hyperlinked to a file.

    B. They can be saved as a separate file.

    C. They can only be used to carry viruses.

    D. They can be embedded in spreadsheet.

    E. They cause viruses to spread.

The answer is D.
A macro is a single instruction that expands automatically into a set of instructions to perform a particular task and be embedded into a spreadsheet.

INFORMATION SYSTEMS

77. The _____ provides the physical mechanisms to input and output data, to manipulate and process data, and to electronically control the various input, output and storage components.
    (Hardware and Systems Technology)

    A. data

    B. network

    C. computer hardware

    D. computer software

    E. Internet

The answer is C.
It is the computer's hardware that provides the physical mechanisms needed to input and output data and manipulate and process data.

78. Which of the following is NOT an HTML container element?
    (Internet and World Wide Web)

    A. <region>

    B. <section>

    C. <footer>

    D. <aside>

    E. <header>

The answer is D.
<aside> is not an HTML container element while the others are.

INFORMATION SYSTEMS

79. **Which of the following is the most common operating system used by webservers?**
    (Internet and World Wide Web)

    A. Windows

    B. Mac OS

    C. Android

    D. Linux

    E. System 7

The answer is D.
Linux is the most common operating system used by webservers.

80. **When does a written work receive protection under U.S. copyright laws?**
    (Social and Ethical Implications and Issues)

    A. When the work is written down.

    B. When the author first comes up with the idea for the work.

    C. When the work is published.

    D. When the work is registered with the U.S. Copyright Office.

    E. When the work is notarized.

The answer is D.
A written work receives protection under the U.S. copyright laws when the work is registered with the U.S. Copyright Office.

INFORMATION SYSTEMS

81. A _____ is created by using a secure hash function to generate a hash value for a message and then encrypting the hash code with a private key.
    (Software Development)

    A. digital signature

    B. keystream

    C. one way hash function

    D. secret key

    E. protected message

The answer is A.

82. Web addresses are called Uniform Resource Locators (URLs). A URL is a text string that specifies an Internet address and the method by which the address can be accessed. The protocol component of a URL identifies
    (Internet and World Wide Web)

    A. the name of the server on which the page resides.

    B. the site owner's registered site.

    C. the type of server and Internet service being used.

    D. the organization type.

    E. where the owner resides.

The answer is C.
The protocol component in the URL http://example.com is http. The resource name is example.com.

INFORMATION SYSTEMS

83. **The work performed by an individual computer system within an IT system can be characterized by**
    (Hardware and Systems Technology)

    A. hardware and software.

    B. input, storage and output.

    C. storage, processing and output.

    D. input, processing and output.

    E. input, storage and software.

The answer is D.
A computer system's function is input, process and output.

84. **In what ways can cookies be useful for Web site developers?**
    (Internet and World Wide Web)

    A. Cookies give developers access to Web site visitors' hard drive files.

    B. Cookies inform the Web site manager about visitors' preferences.

    C. Cookies are dangerous and should never be used in Web development.

    D. Cookies enable developers to convey their preferences to Web site users.

    E. Cookies allow users to access the website's backend.

The answer is B.
Cookies are arbitrary pieces of data, usually chosen by the web server, and stored on the client computer by the browser.

INFORMATION SYSTEMS

85. Mike receives an email message from a friend that contains a zip file. He opens the file and later notices that his email application has sent a copy of that zip to each person in his address book without his commanding it to do so. What event has most likely occurred?
    (Technology Applications)

    A. Mike has accidently sent a mass email to everyone on in his address book.

    B. A virus has infected Mike's computer.

    C. A hacker has taken over Mike's computer.

    D. Mike's email application has malfunctioned and must be replaced.

    E. Mike was logged into the wrong email account.

The answer is B.
A virus has infected Mike's computer through the email attachment that Mike opened.

86. Harmful programs used to disrupt computer operation, gather sensitive information, or gain access to private computer systems are commonly referred to as
    (Social and Ethical Implications and Issues)

    A. adware

    B. malware

    C. computer viruses

    D. spyware

    E. worm

The answer is B.
Adware is software that automatically displays or downloads advertising material. Spyware enables a user to obtain covert information about another's computer activities by transmitting data covertly from their hard drive. Malware is software that is intended to damage or disable computers and computer systems.

INFORMATION SYSTEMS

87. **Which tag must appear within an HTML table?**
    (Internet and Word Wide Web)

    A. <tr>

    B. <th>

    C. <caption>

    D. <tc>

    E. <tb>

The answer is A.
The HTML tag that must appear is <tr> which is used to establish the table rows.

88. **What is the correct definition of a block level tag?**
    (Internet and World Wide Web)

    A. A block level tag is a HTML element that affects one or more paragraphs.

    B. A block level tag affects an individual character or word.

    C. A block level tag does not require a paragraph break before the tag is used.

    D. A block level tag creates a table border.

    E. A block level tag places the paragraph into a block format.

The answer is A.
Block level elements act like separate paragraphs and everything that is done to them applies to the entire paragraph.

INFORMATION SYSTEMS

89. **Which of the following refers to the characteristic features of an advertising-supported software?**
    (Social and Ethical Implications and Issues)

    A. Unsolicited or undesired electronic messages

    B. A worm that infiltrates the computer's operating system

    C. Commonly referred to as malware

    D. Malicious program that sends copies of itself to other computers on the network

    E. Commonly referred to as adware

The answer is E.
Adware is software that automatically displays or downloads advertising material when a user is online.

90. **This is an application program that provides a way to look at and interact with all the information on the World Wide Web.**
    (Internet and World Wide Web)

    A. Line Checker

    B. Browser

    C. Access Provider

    D. Avatar

    E. Social Media

The answer is B.
A browser is software that accesses and displays pages and files on the web.

INFORMATION SYSTEMS

91. **Which technology enables business to create multimedia applications to deliver their messages?**
    (Technology Applications)

    A. Push technology

    B. Pull technology

    C. Media access technology

    D. Neo-Web technology

    E. Customer support initiative

The answer is A.
Push technology is a means for automating the delivery of news and information to devices on the Internet.

92. **You are a member of a Web design team. Which member of the team is responsible for developing the overall plan of the Web site?**
    (Social and Ethical Implications and Issues)

    A. Web analyst

    B. Web Designer

    C. Web Architect

    D. Web Manager

    E. Systems Manager

The answer is C.
The Web Architect designs and plans the website and focuses on the user and user requirements.

INFORMATION SYSTEMS

93. **Which of the following technologies manages the process of resolving URLs to official IP addresses?**
    (Internet and World Wide Web)

    A. Domain Name System (DNS)

    B. File Transfer Protocol (FTP)

    C. Internet Service Providers (ISP)

    D. Simple Network Management Protocol (SNMP)

    E. Post Office Protocol (POP3)

The answer is A.
The Domain Name System is used to resolve human-readable hostnames into machine-readable IP addresses.

94. **Which of the following retains the information it's storing when the power to the system is turned off?**
    (Hardware and Systems Technology)

    A. RAM

    B. DRAM

    C. DIMM

    C. CPU

    E. ROM

The answer is E.
The ROM retains the information it's storing when the power to the system is turned off.

151

INFORMATION SYSTEMS

95. **You are setting up a new email client application, which of the follow pieces of information will you provide that will handle outgoing mail messages?**
    (Technology Applications)

    A. Post Office Protocol (POP3)

    B. Simple Mail Transfer Protocol (SMTP)

    C. Internet Message Access Protocol (IMAP)

    D. Transmission Control Protocol (TCP)

    E. File Transfer Protocol (FTP)

The answer is B.
SMTP is the protocol that all computers use to send traffic an email and it's the protocol that email servers use to send messages across the TCP/IP network.

96. **Which of the following is NOT true about Open Source Software?**
    (Social and Ethical Implications and Issues?)

    A. Open Source Software is developed primarily by inexperienced students.

    B. Open Source Software is typically developed through a collaborative process.

    C. "Freeware" or "shareware" are not the same as open source software.

    D. Open Source Software is commercial software.

    E. There is a lot of Open Source Software available.

The answer is A.
Open Source Software is not primarily developed by inexperienced students.

INFORMATION SYSTEMS

97. **Which of the following image types typically supports transparency?**
    (Office Applications)

    A. BMP and JPEG

    B. PNG and BMP

    C. PNG and GIF

    D. JPEG and GIF

    E. JPEG and BMP

The answer is C.
PNG and GIF support transparency.

98. **Which of the following do search engines expect you to use when making complex searches for information?**
    (Programming Concepts and Data Management)

    A. Radical Inquiries

    B. Spiders

    C. SMS text messages

    D. SQL statements

    E. Boolean values

The answer is E.
Search engines expect Boolean values when making complex searches for information.

INFORMATION SYSTEMS

99. **You have been asked to help implement a Web marketing campaign. Which of the following tools will best help you ensure that this project is completed on time?**
    (Office Applications)

    A. A spreadsheet program

    B. An email application

    C. A Gantt chart

    D. A social networking site such as LinkedIn

    E. A relational database

The answer is C.
A Gantt chart is a series of horizontal lines that show the amount of work done or production completed in certain periods of time in relation to the amount planned for those periods.

100. **Who owns the user data found on social networking sites such as Facebook and Twitter?**
     (Social and Ethical Implications and Issues)

    A. The user who created the data

    B. The social networking site

    C. The W3C or similar third party who ensures user privacy

    D. The group of users with whom the user has communicated.

    E. Everyone. It is part of Creative Commons.

The answer is B.
The social networking site owns the data on the site.

BUSINESS LAW

Description of the Examination

The Introductory Business Law examination covers material that is usually taught in an introductory one-semester college course in the subject. The examination places not only major emphasis on understanding the functions of contracts in American business law, but it also includes questions on the history and sources of American law, legal systems and procedures, agency and employment, sales, and other topics.

The examination contains approximately 100 questions to be answered in 90 minutes. Some of these are pretest questions that will not be scored. Any time candidates spend on tutorials or providing personal information is in addition to the actual testing time.

Knowledge and Skills Required

Questions on the test require candidates to demonstrate one or more of the following abilities in the approximate proportions indicated.

- Knowledge of the basic facts and terms (about 30-35 percent of the examination)

- Understanding of concepts and principles (about 30-35 percent of the examination)

- Ability to apply knowledge to specific case problems (about 30 percent of the examination)

The subject matter of the Introductory Business Law examination is drawn from the following topics. The percentages next to the main topics indicate the approximate percentages of exam questions on those topics.

5%–10% History and Sources of American Law/Constitutional Law

5%–10% American Legal Systems and Procedures

25%–35% Contracts
- Meanings of terms
- Formation of contracts
- Capacity
- Consideration
- Joint obligations
- Contracts for the benefit of third parties
- Assignment/delegation
- Statute of frauds
- Scopes and meanings of contracts
- Breach of contract and remedies
- Bar to remedies for breach of contract
- Discharge of contracts
- Illegal contracts
- Other

25%–30% Legal Environment
- Ethics
- Social responsibility of corporations
- Government regulation/administrative agencies
- Environmental law
- Securities and antitrust law
- Employment law
- Creditors' rights
- Product liability
- Consumer protection
- International business law

BUSINESS LAW

10%–15% **Torts**

5%–10% **Miscellaneous**
- Agency, partnerships, and corporations
- Sales

BUSINESS LAW

SAMPLE TEST

DIRECTIONS: Read each item and select the best response.

1. **What is the "supreme law of the land?"**

   A. Congress

   B. The Supreme Court

   C. The President

   D. The Constitution

   E. The Senate

2. **Legislative law is called _____ law.**

   A. statutory

   B. common

   C. judge-made

   D. executive

   E. codified

3. **What part of the government makes rules and regulations that have the force and effect of law?**

   A. Congress

   B. The President

   C. The Supreme Court

   D. Administrative agencies

   E. The House of Representatives

4. **Court-made law is called _____.**

   A. legal law

   B. common law

   C. administrative law

   D. legislative law

   E. codified law

5. **Stare decisis means _____.**

   A. "let the decision stand"

   B. precedent

   C. codification

   D. "jurisdictional authority"

   E. the authority of the court to hear a case

6. **An ordinance is an example of _____ law.**

   A. federal

   B. state

   C. local

   D. territorial

   E. global

BUSINESS LAW

7. Colonists settled Plymouth, Jamestown, and Massachusetts Bay Colony in the 1600s. They brought with them the concepts of laws from their home country. From which country is our common law derived?

   A. France

   B. Holland

   C. England

   D. Spain

   E. Germany

8. The criminal code is an example of _____.

   A. statutory law

   B. executive law

   C. common law

   D. civil law

   E. judicial law

9. What is the source of law that results when Congress approved an agreement with another country?

   A. Civil law

   B. Treaty

   C. Criminal law

   D. Administrative law

   E. International

10. Pedestrian is injured when crossing a street. The driver insists that the pedestrian crossed the street while the light was red. Pedestrian claims the light was green. Pedestrian suffers a broken leg and back injuries and misses a month of work. In order to resolve the issue, pedestrian sues driver. Which type of law will be applied to the case?

    A. Administrative law

    B. Civil law

    C. Criminal law

    D. Statutory law

    E. Agency law

11. What is the trial court for the federal court system called?

    A. Circuit court

    B. Appeals court

    C. District court

    D. Chancery court

    E. Criminal court

12. For how long are federal judges appointed?

    A. Five years

    B. Life

    C. Ten years

    D. Two years

    E. During good behavior

BUSINESS LAW

13. **Which court will first hear a dispute between two states?**

    A. State trial court

    B. Federal trial court

    C. State appellate court

    D. Federal court of appeals

    E. U.S. Supreme Court

14. **The state's highest court of appeals ruled against a defendant on his claim that his constitutional rights were violated. If he wants to take the case to the U.S. Supreme court, what is the first filing his attorney must make?**

    A. Complaint

    B. Writ of Certiorari

    C. Writ of Mandamus

    D. Counterclaim

    E. Reply

15. **Store owner wants to collect an unpaid account. What is the first pleading the owner must file in court?**

    A. Cross-claim

    B. Deposition

    C. Answer

    D. Complaint

    E. Summons

16. **What is the burden of proof for the prosecution in a criminal case?**

    A. Precedent

    B. Beyond a Reasonable Doubt

    C. Stare Decisis

    D. Nolo contendre

    E. Preponderance of the evidence

17. **What is the term for the power of a court to hear a case?**

    A. Venue

    B. Jurisdiction

    C. Arraignment

    D. Docketing

    E. Voir Dire

18. **When is a summary judgment granted?**

    A. When the plaintiff fails to appear

    B. When the defendant fails to appear

    C. When interrogatories are not answered

    D. When there is no genuine issue of material fact

    E. When all issues have been decided

BUSINESS LAW

19. What is another name for jury selection?

    A. Voir dire

    B. Stare decisis

    C. Depositions

    D. The appellate process

    E. Subpoena duces tecum

20. What are written questions propounded by one party to another party to be answered by the second party under oath prior to trial?

    A. Depositions

    B. Interrogatories

    C. Voir Dire

    D. Cross-claims

    E. Counterclaims

21. What is the rule that states a common law acceptance must be identical in reverse to a common law offer?

    A. Identical Rule

    B. Common Law Offer Rule

    C. Common Law Acceptance Rule

    D. Mirror Image Rule

    E. Exactness Rule

22. What is the term that indicates the parties have the legal ability to enter into a contract?

    A. Capacity

    B. Competency

    C. Adulthood

    D. Intent

    E. Majority

23. What is the term that defines a situation in which a landlord gives to a relative the power to receive rents that are normally paid to the landlord?

    A. Delegation

    B. Authorization

    C. Assignment

    D. Transfer

    E. Intent

24. Which statue requires transactions involving real estate to be in writing?

    A. Parol Evidence Rule

    B. Doctrine of Promissory Estoppel

    C. Doctrine of Plain Meaning

    D. Statute of Limitations

    E. Statute of Frauds

25. What is the person making an offer called?

    A. Offeree

    B. Offeror

    C. Beneficiary

    D. Assignor

    E. Assignee

26. Who is the delegee?

    A. The person to whom a contractual duty is delegated

    B. The person who delegates a contractual duty

    C. The person who assigns a contract.

    D. The person to whom a contract is assigned.

    E. The person to whom the mirror image rule applies.

27. What is the benefit that must be bargained for in contract law?

    A. Offer

    B. Consideration

    C. Acceptance

    D. Mutual promises

    E. Remedies

28. Which element listed below is NOT applicable to a misrepresentation?

    A. Reliance

    B. Knowledge of falsity

    C. Material fact

    D. Statement of fact

    E. Intent to deceive

29. What does "force majure" mean?

    A. Commercial frustration of a contract

    B. The impossibility of performing a contract

    C. A reason for imposing damages

    D. An unexpected event of nature that allows parties not to perform a contract

    E. A major reason for requiring the performance of a contract

30. Which of the following is NOT an element of undue influence?

    A. A superior and subservient relationship

    B. An opportunity to influence

    C. Duress

    D. Vulnerable person

    E. Suspicious transaction

BUSINESS LAW

31. Buyer has always wanted to purchase Seller's farm and has made offers to purchase several times. However, Seller has always turned Buyer down. Both are at a party, enjoying the refreshments. Seller tells Buyer to write out an agreement. Buyer writes out the terms on a paper napkin. Seller and Buyer sign the napkin. Buyer takes the money (in cash) to Seller. Seller refuses to deliver the property and says he did not have any intent to sell his family farm and that the "agreement" was a joke. What element of contract law is applicable to the "agreement"?

    A. Offer

    B. Acceptance

    C. Formation

    D. Consideration

    E. Capacity

32. Owner of property has drawn up plans for a subdivision. He has complied with all government requirements. He advertises the acre lots as "ready for well-drilling and building" upon signing closing papers. Buyer of lot contracts with well-driller who, after doing some testing, finds the water table too low for a well. Buyer wants his money back. On what basis would a refund be proper?

    A. Unilateral mistake

    B. Mutual mistake

    C. Lack of consideration

    D. No meeting of the minds

    E. Undue influence

33. What is the purpose of awarding contract damages?

    A. To put the person in a better position than he was in before the breach

    B. To put the person in the position he would have been in had the breach not occurred

    C. To punish the person causing the harmful breach

    D. To order the breaching party to specifically perform

    E. To halt the harmful behavior

34. What type of remedy is available to a purchaser who wants a court to order the seller to deliver property that he/she sold to the buyer?

    A. Injunction

    B. Damages

    C. Specific Performance

    D. Recission

    E. Liquidated damages

35. Which statement is NOT correct about liquidated damages?

    A. They must be reasonable.

    B. The parties need to agree that liquidated damages will be awarded.

    C. Liquidated damages are awarded for anticipatory breach.

    D. They must be stated as a specific amount.

    E. They may be determined by a percentage or by another agreed-upon method.

36. For which type of remedy must irreparable harm be shown?

    A. Liquidated damages

    B. Damages at law

    C. Specific performance

    D. Recission

    E. Injunction

37. According to the common law "mailbox rule" when is an offer accepted?

    A. When the offer is sent

    B. When the offer is received

    C. When the time is agreed upon

    D. When any method of acceptance is used

    E. When the acceptance is delivered by the agreed upon method

38. All of the following are examples of termination of a contract sale of real estate EXCEPT:

    A. completion

    B. breach

    C operation of law

    D. recission

    E. death of a party

39. Buyer and Seller sign a purchase agreement for the sale/purchase of a house that sits on ½ acre. Buyer moves into the house and begins to use the shed that is on the property at the edge of the property line. Seller tells buyer to stop using the shed because the shed had not been part of the deal. What rule of law would prevent the buyer from arguing that the parties had meant to include the shed in the real estate transaction?

    A. mutual mistake

    B. parol evidence

    C. specific performance

    D. promissory estoppel

    E. injunction

40. Builder and homeowner enter into a contract for builder to construct an addition to a home that includes a 16' x 24' family room. Builder sends homeowner his last invoice for ½ the agreed-upon price. Homeowner refuses to pay because he argues that contractor breached their contract. Homeowner shows builder that the size of the family room is only 15'5" x 23'9". What doctrine would permit builder to be paid?

    A. Substantial performance

    B. Substantial breach

    C. No meeting of the minds

    D. Promissory estoppel

    E. Mutual mistake

41. Bob has his Rav 4 for sale. Sue offers him $9,000. Bob says, "No, but I will take $11,000." What is Bob's response?

    A. A revocation

    B. A rejection

    C. An offer

    D. A counter-offer

    E. Agreement

42. Jim, a college student, began selling used vehicles. A customer looks at a 1990 Ford Mustang convertible. Jim tells the customer that the car is in A-1 condition. How would you classify Jim's statement?

    A. Puffing

    B. Misrepresentation

    C. Fraudulent

    D. A statement made under duress

    E. A mistake

43. Daughter tells her elderly parents that she will move into their house care for them if they give her the house. A few days later, the parents contact their lawyer and add a codicil to their will, bequeathing the house to their daughter when they die. One week later, daughter has not moved in but her parents are killed in an airplane crash. She is devastated about their deaths but begins moving into the house. Her brother objects to her being given the house and argues that the house should be sold and proceeds divided equally as they are the only heirs. What is his argument?

    A. Fraud on the part of his sister

    B. Duress caused by his sister

    C. Undue influence of his sister

    D. Misrepresentation by his sister

    E. She should be promissorily estopped from getting the house.

44. A racing enthusiast purchases a horse to enter races. When he gets the horse to the stable, he learns the horse is great with foal (pregnant). Pregnant horses don't race. Seller learns of the pregnancy and wants the horse returned because pregnant horses are more valuable and expensive than racing horses. What will seller argue to try to get the horse returned?

    A. Benefit of the bargain

    B. Illegal contract

    C. Void contract

    D. Mutual mistake

    E. Unilateral mistake

45. Pet owner hired an artist to paint a portrait of her cat. Artist has an opportunity to go on vacation and wants a friend, who is also a painter, to finish the portrait. Cat owner objects. Can the artist have the friend finish the picture?

    A. Yes, if the painter agrees.

    B. Yes, regardless of whether the cat owner agrees. The task is assignable

    C. Yes, regardless of whether the cat owner agrees. The task is delegable

    D. No, because the pet hisses at the substitute painter

    E. No, because it is a personal service contract that is not delegable without approval

BUSINESS LAW

46. **Aimee enters into a contract to purchase a $35,000.00 car. She is 17 years old but looks like she is 18 (an adult). She drives the car twice and decides she does not like the car. Can she avoid the contract?**

    A. Yes, because she is a minor

    B. Yes, because she does not like the way the car handles

    C. No, because she looks like an adult

    D. No, because she has ratified the contract by driving the car

    E. No, if the car is a necessary

47. **Which of the following is an example of an illegal contract?**

    A. A contract a merchant enters into with a malt manufacturer for the purchase of alcoholic beverages during Prohibition

    B. A contract a merchant enters into for the purchase of alcoholic beverages to be sold in a county that, before delivery of the product, declares the products may not be sold in the county.

    C. A contract entered into that requires shipment of items to be delivered to a non-existent street number

    D. A contract entered into for delivery of hazardous products that are not permitted to be shipped by rail, as the contract provides.

    E. A contract to purchase an item that becomes illegal to manufacture after the date of the agreement.

48. **What is another term for an illegal contract?**

    A. Enforceable

    B. Unenforceable

    C. Avoidable

    D. Voidable

    E. Void

49. **Which of the following is an example of a third-party beneficiary contract?**

    A. One party to a contract delegates performance to a third party

    B. One party to a contract asks the advice of a third party before signing the contract

    C. One party to a contract purchases a life insurance policy and names a relative as beneficiary

    D. One party leases a property with a right of first refusal to purchase the property from a subsequent purchaser

    E. One party donates the proceeds of a contract to a charity after receiving payment under the contract

50. **To what does the "plain meaning" rule apply?**

    A. Statutory construction

    B. Offers

    C. Acceptances

    D. Consideration

    E. Damages

51. **Which of the following is an example of a violation of business ethics?**

    A. Making a mistake in the addition of business expenses

    B. Charging a customer a price from a two-year-old price guide that is less than the price stated for a product on an updated guideline sent the day before the sale

    C. Exercising your judgment for a "return policy" for an outdated item where the company has no stated policy

    D. Submitting an "hours worked" sheet that included thirty-additional minutes because you forgot to time one of your work days.

    E. Contacting your manager to assist in solving a business-related issue when you have the authority to solve such problems on your own.

BUSINESS LAW

52. When might "moonlighting" be an ethical violation for a business employee?

   A. It is not an ethical violation.

   B. It is an ethical violation if the employee exceeds 40 work hours per week.

   C. It is an ethical violation if the employee arrives only five minutes ahead of the required time to begin work for the second job.

   D. It is an ethical violation if the employee's work performance becomes poor.

   E. It is only a violation if both employers raise the issue.

53. What does "corporate social responsibility" mean?

   A. A company must provide its employees breaks during the day for social gatherings.

   B. A company's officers are responsible for helping new employees find housing and community information.

   C. A company must provide scheduled times for employees to take "personal days" off work.

   D. A company has a duty to maintain a balance between the economy and the ecosystems.

   E. A company must communicate, through its officers, to its employees new laws regarding workplace safety.

54. Which of the following statements about corporate social responsibility is INCORRECT?

   A. It is an ethical framework.

   B. The concept applies to society as a whole.

   C. Active social responsibility is acting in a way to avoid engaging in socially harmful acts.

   D. Active social responsibility is performing activities that directly advance social goals

   E. Social responsibility can be either active or passive.

55. What is considered the "fourth" branch of government?

   A. Congress

   B. Executive Branch

   C. Administrative Agency

   D. Judicial Branch

   E. The Senate

BUSINESS LAW

56. Which of the following statements about administrative agencies is INCORRECT?

    A. Rules and regulations of administrative agencies have the force and effect of law.

    B. Administrative agencies are created by Congress.

    C. The Internal Revenue Service is an example of an administrative agency.

    D. An objection to an administrative rule can be brought in the judicial branch of government.

    E. Administrative law is considered a branch of public law.

57. Which of the following statements about securities law is INCORRECT?

    A. Securities laws are an example of a regulatory scheme.

    B. U.S. corporate securities are regulated at the federal level.

    D. The purpose of securities laws is to inform people about buying and selling stocks.

    E. Securities laws govern the purchase of stock of private corporations.

58. Of what type of law is greenhouse gas regulation an example?

    A. Environmental law

    B. Real estate law

    C. Business law

    D. Mining law

    E. Social responsibility law

59. Which federal agency helps regulate entities in meeting federal environmental requirements?

    A. Department of Justice

    B. Environmental Protection Agency

    C. Federal Trade Commission

    D. Department of Agriculture

    E. Consumer Protection Agency

60. What was the first major federal anti-trust law?

    A. Robinson Patman Act

    B. Sherman Antitrust Act

    C. Clayton Antitrust Act

    D. Federal Trade Commission Act

    E. Celler-Kefauver Antimerger Act

BUSINESS LAW

61. **A company that sells copy machines requires purchasers to buy copy paper from them. This is an example of what kind of antitrust violation?**

    A. Horizontal restraint

    B. Vertical restraint

    C. Merger

    D. Tying arrangement

    E. Price fixing

62. **What rule does a court use to determine whether there has been price-fixing in a restraint of trade case?**

    A. Rule of reason

    B. Per se rule

    C. Collateral estoppel

    D. Promissory estoppel

    E. Cease and desist

63. **Title VII of the Civil Rights of 1964 prohibits unlawful employment discrimination based on all of the following EXCEPT_____.**

    A. race

    B. national origin

    C. age

    D. religion

    E. sex

64. **Which statement is correct about employment law?**

    A. Employment law excludes hours and wages issues and OSHA issues.

    B. Employment law excludes age and disabilities issues.

    C. Employment law excludes family leave issues.

    D. Employment law excludes collective bargaining.

    E. Employment law excludes worker's compensation issues.

65. **Creditors' rights are protected in bankruptcy filings in all of the following ways EXCEPT_____.**

    A. Filing a proof of claim

    B. Attending a meeting of creditors

    C. Objecting to a plan of reorganization

    D. Filing suit against the debtor

    E. Objecting to discharge

BUSINESS LAW

66. **How may creditors protect their rights to collect a judgment if a debtor refuses to pay a judgment?**

    A. Garnishee wages

    B. Apply the Fair Debt Collection Act

    C. File suit

    D. They have no recourse.

    E. File a showing of contempt

67. **To whom is the Fair Debt Collection Act directed?**

    A. Parties collecting their own debts

    B. Collectors of debts of third parties

    C. Creditors

    D. Debtors

    E. Courts

68. **Which of the following is NOT an example of a consumer debt?**

    A. A student loan

    B. Unpaid taxes

    C. Purchase of a refrigerator on a credit card

    D. Car loan

    E. Pledge to charity

69. **Which is one of the more often used ways to resolve issues of international business transactions?**

    A. Mediation

    B. Arbitration

    C. Litigation

    D. The International Court of Justice

    E. The European Union

70. **Which statement is INCORRECT about a defective product?**

    A. The defective product must cause injury.

    B. The defective product must have been defective when it left the manufacturer.

    C. The defective product must have been in the stream of commerce.

    D. The defective product cannot result in liability for a retailer.

    E. The defect in the defective product cannot always be observed.

BUSINESS LAW

71. **What does a warranty of "merchantability" mean?**

    A. The product can be sold on the open market.

    B. The product is fit for a particular purpose.

    C. The product is fit for ordinary purposes.

    D. The warranty is to be written on the box or label before sale.

    E. The warranty is stated to the purchaser.

72. **A product that is dangerous needs to have a warning. What statement is INCORRECT about warnings?**

    A. Failure to warn is a breach of duty.

    B. The warning must be conspicuous.

    C. The warning must be made large enough.

    D. The warning can be spoken.

    E. The warning must be in writing.

73. **Which of the following is an example of an express warranty?**

    A. The fact that a coffee pot is expected to make coffee

    B. The fact that a tool with attachments will perform as thought

    C. The fact that a lawn mower will cut grass

    D. The fact that an electric toothbrush holds size AA batteries

    E. The fact that an electric mixer can be repaired at no cost for a period of sixty days

74. **Why is strict liability imposed on manufacturers in product liability cases?**

    A. Because there has been negligence

    B. Because there has been a breach of warranty

    C. Because there is a deep pocket.

    D. Because of the goal of punishing the manufacturer

    E. Because of the goal of negligence litigation

BUSINESS LAW

75. "Manufacturer will repair or replace item within one year of purchase if a defect or malfunction occurs. Manufacturer will not compensate purchaser for any loss arising from defect or malfunction." The preceding statement is an example of a(n) _____.

    A. Warranty

    B. Implied warranty

    C. Express warranty

    D. Limited Warranty

    E. Breach of warranty

76. What is the "egg shell" theory?

    A. The wrongdoer takes the victim the way he/she finds the victim.

    B. The plaintiff's weaknesses must be exposed.

    C. The defendant's weaknesses must be exposed.

    D. There is a fracture in the plaintiff's case.

    E. The plaintiff has a thin chance of success.

77. Which of the following is NOT an element of battery?

    A. An unconsented to or rude touching

    B. Touching the person or something close to him/her, such as a cane or hat

    C. Intent to touch

    D. Intent to harm

    E. Resulting harm

78. Which of the following is NOT an element of assault?

    A. Putting a person in fear

    B. The element of fear is subjective

    C. An intent to put a person in fear

    D. Touching a person or something close to the person

    E. The fear of imminent harm

79. If you are attending a pool party in the backyard of a friend and you see a two-year-old step into the pool and sink to the bottom, who, sitting around the pool, has a legal duty to try to save the child?

    A. You

    B. A neighbor

    C. A babysitter

    D. A family friend

    E. The caterer

BUSINESS LAW

80. Which of the following is an example of an ultrahazardous or abnormally dangerous activity?

    A. Mink farming

    B. Baseball

    C. Mining

    D. Snow plowing

    E. Reforestation

81. Which of the following is an example of a situation in which vicarious liability is imposed?

    A. Workmen's compensation cases

    B. Intentional torts cases

    C. A driver's negligence due to hitting a pedestrian with the driver's own vehicle

    D. Emotional distress cases

    E. Battery cases

82. Nominal damages are likely to be awarded in which type of case?

    A. Assault

    B. Negligence

    C. Interference with contractual relations

    D. Battery

    E. Trespass

83. Which is NOT an element of negligence?

    A. Duty

    B. Breach of duty

    C. Legal cause

    D. Injury

    E. Damages

84. Upon what does proximate cause depend?

    A. Negligence

    B. Foreseeability

    C. Legal cause

    D. "But for" cause

    E. Respondeat superior

85. Most states would deny a bystander the right to recover damages for the negligent infliction of emotional distress based on what rule?

    A. The foreseeability rule

    B. The impact rule

    C. The privity rule

    D. The proximate cause rule

    E. The Discovery rule

BUSINESS LAW

86. **In which situation might punitive damages be imposed?**

    A. A personal injury case where the driver injured a pedestrian who was crossing the street while the light was red.

    B. A case where a driver on a 'frolic and detour' caused injury to a bicyclist

    C. A case where a person sued for negligent infliction of emotional distress.

    D. A case where a retailer falsely imprisons a suspected shoplifter

    E. A case where a business sells a faulty tool from an overseas manufacturer

87. **In which situation would respondeat superior apply?**

    A. An independent contractor causing damages to a yard while digging a ditch

    B. An employee who, while driving a company truck backs into a car

    C. A driver, driving her own car, injures a pedestrian

    D. A biker who injures a jogger

    E. The owner of a company who damages the company car of her way to work

88. **Which is NOT correct about conversion?**

    A. The owner is deprived of the possession personal property.

    B. The converter deprives the owner of the ownership of the property.

    C. The converter may intend to return the property.

    D. The converter may have also committed a criminal act of conversion.

    E. Converting property is an intentional tort.

89. **Where a lawnmower has no warning about the dangers of use, what element of negligence applies to the lack of warning?**

    A. Injury

    B. Causation

    C. Breach of duty

    D. Duty

    E. Damages

90. What term is applicable when an employee is running an errand for the employer and decides to take her own mail to the post office?

   A. Negligence

   B. Intentional tort

   C. Independent contractor

   D. Respondeat superior

   E. Frolic and detour

91. Which article of the Uniform Commercial Code applies to sales of goods?

   A. Article 2

   B. Article 2A

   C. Article 3

   D. Article 4

   E. Article 9

92. Which of the following statements about "goods" is INCORRECT?

   A. Goods are movable at the time of identification to the contract for sale.

   B. Goods include the unborn young of animals.

   C. Goods may be existing and/or identified before any interest in them can pass.

   D. Specially manufactured goods are defined as "goods."

   E. Money is a "good" that is defined as the "price that is to be paid."

BUSINESS LAW

93. Mark asks Sue to sell his iPod. She agrees. He gives her a plastic grocery bag with the iPod in it. Sue asks Tom if he is interested in buying Mark's iPod. Tom indicates he is. When he looks in the bag, he finds a case for the iPod in addition to the iPod. Tom indicates he is only interested in the purchase/sale if the case is included. If Sue sells both items together and Mark tells her that the case was not to be sold, what is Sue's argument to support the sale of the case?

    A. She had express authority to sell the case.

    B. She had apparent authority to sell the case.

    C. She had implied authority to sell the case.

    D. She had actual authority to sell the case.

    E. She was acting as a gratuitous agent.

94. Which of the following is an example of a fiduciary duty in the area of agency law?

    A. Pay wages

    B. Act on behalf of the principal

    C. Be controlled by the principal

    D. Be loyal

    E. Discharge duties in a timely manner

95. Which is a key element in determining whether a person is an employee or an independent contractor?

    A. Does the employer pay the person doing work for him?

    B. Does the employer have control over how the person's work is done?

    C. Does the employer pay taxes for the worker's income?

    D. Is there an agreement between the parties?

    E. Is there a past work history between the parties?

96. What generally happens to a partnership when a partner dies?

    A. The partnership is dissolved.

    B. The partnership continues with the remaining partners.

    C. The partnership allows a new partner to purchase the deceased partner's shares.

    D. The partnership becomes a sole proprietorship is there is only one remaining partner.

    E. The partnership's future is determined by the remaining partner(s).

97. If a person wants to invest money into a partnership but does not want to be involved in the decision-making process, what type of partnership should that person form?

   A. General partnership

   B. Limited liability company

   C. Limited liability partnership

   D. Limited partnership

   E. Sole proprietorship

98. What is one of the main advantages of a corporate form of business organization?

   A. The tax structure

   B. Owning shares of stock

   C. Having a board of directors

   D. Having a bylaws

   E. Limited liability

99. Which of the following provides the written guidance for the operation of a corporation?

   A. Articles of Incorporation

   B. Bylaws

   C. Board of Directors

   D. Officers

   E. Corporate employee manual

100. What is the type of lawsuit that is filed by an injured party when a corporation is alleged to be an alter-ego of the sole shareholder?

   A. A derivative suit

   B. A suit to dissolve the corporation

   C. A suit for punitive damages

   D. A suit for an accounting

   E. A suit to pierce the corporate veil

BUSINESS LAW

ANSWER KEY

Question Number	Correct Answer	Your Answer	Question Number	Correct Answer	Your Answer	Question Number	Correct Answer	Your Answer
1	D		35	D		69	B	
2	A		36	E		70	D	
3	D		37	B		71	C	
4	B		38	E		72	D	
5	A		39	B		73	E	
6	C		40	A		74	C	
7	C		41	D		75	D	
8	A		42	A		76	A	
9	B		43	C		77	D	
10	B		44	D		78	D	
11	C		45	E		79	C	
12	E		46	E		80	C	
13	E		47	A		81	A	
14	B		48	E		82	E	
15	D		49	C		83	E	
16	B		50	A		84	B	
17	B		51	D		85	B	
18	D		52	D		86	D	
19	A		53	D		87	B	
20	B		54	C		88	B	
21	D		55	C		89	C	
22	A		56	D		90	E	
23	C		57	E		91	A	
24	E		58	A		92	C	
25	B		59	B		93	C	
26	A		60	B		94	D	
27	B		61	D		95	B	
28	E		62	B		96	A	
29	D		63	C		97	D	
30	C		64	D		98	E	
31	C		65	D		99	B	
32	B		66	A		100	E	
33	B		67	B				
34	C		68	B				

BUSINESS LAW

RATIONALE

1. **What is the "supreme law of the land?"**

    A. Congress

    B. The Supreme Court

    C. The President

    D. The Constitution

    E. The Senate

The answer is D.
Congress makes the laws and the president executes the laws. The Supreme Court interprets the law. The Constitution is the "supreme law of the land."

2. **Legislative law is called _____ law.**

    A. statutory

    B. common

    C. judge-made

    D. executive

    E. codified

The answer is A.
Common law is judge-made law and the executive branch issues executive orders. Legislatures pass statutes, thus legislative law is also called statutory law.

BUSINESS LAW

3. **What part of the government makes rules and regulations that have the force and effect of law?**

   A. Congress

   B. The President

   C. The Supreme Court

   D. Administrative agencies

   E. The House of Representatives

The answer is D.
Congressional legislation results in laws if signed by the president. The Supreme Court interprets the laws. Administrative agencies are called the "fourth branch" of government because they make rules and regulations that have the force and effect of law.

4. **Court-made law is called _____.**

   A. legal law

   B. common law

   C. administrative law

   D. legislative law

   E. codified law

The answer is B.
Laws are legal until overturned by the courts or reversed by new legislation of Congress. Administrative law is made by government agencies. Judge-made, or court-made, law is called common law.

BUSINESS LAW

5. **Stare decisis means _____.**

    A. "let the decision stand"

    B. precedent

    C. codification

    D. "jurisdictional authority"

    E. the authority of the court to hear a case

The answer is A.
Rationale: Precedent means something that "came before." Codification means putting laws of one kind into a "code." An example is the criminal code. A court has jurisdiction to hear a case. Stare decisis means "let the (earlier) decision stand."

6. **An ordinance is an example of _____ law.**

    A. federal

    B. state

    C. local

    D. territorial

    E. global

The answer is C.
An ordinance is often the term for the law passed by a local government, such as a city council. States, Congress, and territorial legislatures pass laws but their laws are not called ordinances.

BUSINESS LAW

7. **Colonists settled Plymouth, Jamestown, and Massachusetts Bay Colony in the 1600s. They brought with them the concepts of laws from their home country. From which country is our common law derived?**

    A. France

    B. Holland

    C. England

    D. Spain

    E. Germany

The answer is C.
The colonists that settled the present-day state of Massachusetts came from England. They brought the ideas of English common law with them. Louisiana's basis of law was the French Napoleonic Code. The Dutch settled the areas of the mid-Atlantic states and the Spanish had settlements in Florida.

8. **The criminal code is an example of _____.**

    A. statutory law

    B. executive law

    C. common law

    D. civil law

    E. judicial law

The answer is A.
State legislatures pass laws making certain acts crimes within the states. Congress passes federal criminal legislation. The laws are statutes, and thus statutory law. Civil law involves wrongs against individuals. Criminal law involves wrongs against the state. Common law is the basis of judge-made law. The executive branch of government issues executive orders

BUSINESS LAW

9. What is the source of law that results when Congress approved an agreement with another country?

   A. Civil law

   B. Treaty

   C. Criminal law

   D. Administrative law

   E. International

The answer is B.
Treaties are agreements among nations. When a treaty is approved by Congress (as required by the Constitution) it becomes law. The other choices are types of law but they are not the agreements reached between countries.

10. Pedestrian is injured when crossing a street. The driver insists that the pedestrian crossed the street while the light was red. Pedestrian claims the light was green. Pedestrian suffers a broken leg and back injuries and misses a month of work. In order to resolve the issue, pedestrian sues driver. Which type of law will be applied to the case?

    A. Administrative law

    B. Civil law

    C. Criminal law

    D. Statutory law

    E. Agency law

The answer is B.
Statutory law is passed by legislatures. Criminal law involves wrongs against society. Administrative law is made by agencies such as the Environmental Protection Agency. Civil law involves wrongs against individuals. Here, one individual is suing another individual because of injuries resulting from an alleged wrong act of that person. Thus, civil law is applicable.

11. **What is the trial court for the federal court system called?**

    A. Circuit court

    B. Appeals court

    C. District court

    D. Chancery court

    E. Criminal court

The answer is C.
A circuit court may either be a trial court at the state level or the Circuit Court of Appeals in the federal court system. An appeals court is not a trial court. Chancery courts are state courts, and criminal courts refer to the types of cases heard in a federal or state court. The trial court of the federal court system is called the Federal District Court.

12. **For how long are federal judges appointed?**

    A. Five years

    B. Life

    C. Ten years

    D. Two years

    E. During good behavior

The answer is E.
State court judges are elected for a term of years. Although most federal court judges serve for life, their term of appointment is for good behavior.

BUSINESS LAW

13. **Which court will first hear a dispute between two states?**

    A. State trial court

    B. Federal trial court

    C. State appellate court

    D. Federal court of appeals

    E. U.S. Supreme Court

The answer is E.
The U.S. Supreme Court is the first case to hear disputes between states. The Constitution provides that in matters involving states, the U.S. Supreme Court has original jurisdiction. "Original" means the first place where the case is heard.

14. **The state's highest court of appeals ruled against a defendant on his claim that his constitutional rights were violated. If he wants to take the case to the U.S. Supreme court, what is the first filing his attorney must make?**

    A. Complaint

    B. Writ of Certiorari

    C. Writ of Mandamus

    D. Counterclaim

    E. Reply

The answer is B.
A complaint is filed by a plaintiff to begin a lawsuit. A writ of mandamus is filed to ask a court to order someone to do something. A counterclaim is a claim one party has against the other party that arises out of the transaction that is the subject of the litigation. A Reply is filed by the plaintiff in response to the defendant's Answer. When a criminal decides to appeal the highest state court decision to the U.S. Supreme Court, a writ of certiorari is filed. The writ of certiorari is a writing that asks the high court to hear and decide the case.

BUSINESS LAW

15. **Store owner wants to collect an unpaid account. What is the first pleading the owner must file in court?**

    A. Cross-claim

    B. Deposition

    C. Answer

    D. Complaint

    E. Summons

The answer is D.
The store owner will be the plaintiff because it is the party bringing the cause of action. The first pleading filed by the plaintiff is the Complaint. A summons accompanies the Complaint and orders the defendant to appear and answer or be defaulted. A cross-claim is a claim filed by any party against a non-opposing party. A deposition is one of the forms of Discovery, which is a pre-trial device used to narrow the issues for trial.

16. **What is the burden of proof for the prosecution in a criminal case?**

    A. Precedent

    B. Beyond a Reasonable Doubt

    C. Stare Decisis

    D. Nolo contendre

    E. Preponderance of the evidence

The answer is B.
"Stare decisis" means "let the decision stand" and refers to judges letting an earlier decision stand. "Nolo contender" means "no contest" or a person is not contesting a charge. "Precedent" means that an earlier case is being followed. In order to win in a civil case, a person must prove the case by a preponderance of the evidence. The burden is greater in a criminal case. In a criminal case, the burden is "beyond a reasonable doubt."

BUSINESS LAW

17. What is the term for the power of a court to hear a case?

    A. Venue

    B. Jurisdiction

    C. Arraignment

    D. Docketing

    E. Voir Dire

The answer is B.
Arraignment is a term used in criminal cases. "Docketing" means scheduling a case or putting a case on the court's calendar. "Voir dire" means "speak the truth" and is another term for jury selection. Venue is the place where a trial is held. Jurisdiction refers to the "power" of a court to hear a case.

18. When is a summary judgment granted?

    A. When the plaintiff fails to appear

    B. When the defendant fails to appear

    C. When interrogatories are not answered

    D. When there is no genuine issue of material fact

    E. When all issues have been decided

The answer is D.
A motion for summary judgment is filed before trial by either party that claims there is no genuine material of fact for the court to decide. For example, if a store owner wants to collect a debt owed by a customer and the customer cannot provide proof of payment, then there are no genuine issues of material fact to be decided about whether the customer owes the amount. When there are no genuine issues of material fact, the court may grant a summary judgment.

BUSINESS LAW

19. What is another name for jury selection?

    A. Voir dire

    B. Stare decisis

    C. Depositions

    D. The appellate process

    E. Subpoena duces tecum

The answer is A.
"Stare decisis" means "let the decision stand." Depositions are a form of pre-trial discovery. The appellate process takes place after a judgment is entered by the trial court. A subpoena requires a person to be present. The words "duces tecum" mean that the subpoena requires a person to bring with him/her certain items (usually documents). "Voir dire" means "to speak the truth" and that is what jury selection is about—speaking the truth about being selected for the job of deciding the facts of a case.

20. What are written questions propounded by one party to another party to be answered by the second party under oath prior to trial?

    A. Depositions

    B. Interrogatories

    C. Voir Dire

    D. Cross-claims

    E. Counterclaims

The answer is B.
"Voir dire" refers to jury selection. Cross-claims and counterclaims are pleadings filed before trial. Depositions and interrogatories are both forms of pre-trial Discovery. Depositions are questions asked orally in front of a court reporter. They are answered under oath. Interrogatories are written questions asked by one party of another party and answered by the second party under oath.

BUSINESS LAW

21. **What is the rule that states a common law acceptance must be identical in reverse to a common law offer?**

    A. Identical Rule

    B. Common Law Offer Rule

    C. Common Law Acceptance Rule

    D. Mirror Image Rule

    E. Exactness Rule

The answer is D.
The acceptance of an offer under common law must be identical in reverse to an offer. Because it must be identical AND in reverse, the term that is used is mirror image rule.

22. **What is the term that indicates the parties have the legal ability to enter into a contract?**

    A. Capacity

    B. Competency

    C. Adulthood

    D. Intent

    E. Majority

The answer is A.
Parties must have the intent to enter into a contract. Minors may enter into contracts for "necessaries." The age of majority and adulthood refer to the parties being an adult. The legal term for the ability to enter into a contract is "capacity."

BUSINESS LAW

23. What is the term that defines a situation in which a landlord gives to a relative the power to receive rents that are normally paid to the landlord?

    A. Delegation

    B. Authorization

    C. Assignment

    D. Transfer

    E. Intent

The answer is C.
One may delegate a duty. Here, the transfer is the right to receive a benefit. A landlord intends that his relative has the power to receive rents if he assigns the rents to the relative. The assignment is a transfer of the right.

24. Which statue requires transactions involving real estate to be in writing?

    A. Parol Evidence Rule

    B. Doctrine of Promissory Estoppel

    C. Doctrine of Plain Meaning

    D. Statute of Limitations

    E. Statute of Frauds

The answer is E.
The Parol Evidence Rule applies to situation where a party wants to introduce evidence that was discussed before the contract was entered into and the party believes should have been included in the final contract. Common law provides the rule is that a contract is a final and complete expression of the parties' agreement. The doctrine of promissory estoppel applies when a party should be estopped (or stopped) from arguing that a contract is not enforceable. If a promise has been made, there is reliance on the promise, and economic loss has occurred, then it is necessary to enforce the promise to prevent unjust enrichment. The plain meaning doctrine applies in situations where the intent of the parties must be decided as to the contract they entered into. Statutory construction of a contract means that if the wording is not ambiguous, the plain meaning of the words will be applied. A statute of limitations provides for the time in which a lawsuit must be filed. If a lawsuit is not filed within the specified time, the party has waived his/her right to file suit. An example of a statute of limitations is two years for negligence actions to be filed. Each state has its own statute of limitations for different types of litigation. The Statute of Frauds states that real estate transactions must be in writing. The purpose of the statute is to prevent fraud.

BUSINESS LAW

25. What is the person making an offer called?

A. Offeree

B. Offeror

C. Beneficiary

D. Assignor

E. Assignee

The answer is B.
A beneficiary is a third party to a contract and one who receives a benefit, such as a life insurance beneficiary. An assignor is one who makes an assignment. An assignee is the person who receives the assignment. The offeree is the person to whom an offer is made. An offeror is the person making an offer.

26. Who is the delegee?

A. The person to whom a contractual duty is delegated

B. The person who delegates a contractual duty

C. The person who assigns a contract.

D. The person to whom a contract is assigned.

E. The person to whom the mirror image rule applies.

The answer is A.
The person to whom the mirror image rule applies is the offeree. The person to whom a contract assigned is the assignee. The person who assigns a contract is the assignor. The person who delegates a contractual duty is the delegor. The person to whom a contractual duty is delegated is the delegee.

BUSINESS LAW

27. What is the benefit that must be bargained for in contract law?

    A. Offer

    B. Consideration

    C. Acceptance

    D. Mutual promises

    E. Remedies

The answer is B.
Offer, acceptance, and mutual promises are elements of contract law. Remedies are provided when contracts are breached. Consideration is the benefit that must be bargained for when a contract is entered into.

28. Which element listed below is NOT applicable to a misrepresentation?

    A. Reliance

    B. Knowledge of falsity

    C. Material fact

    D. Statement of fact

    E. Intent to deceive

The answer is E.
A misrepresentation occurs when a statement of material fact is made with the knowledge of the statement's falsity. The person hearing the statement relies on the misrepresentation but the misrepresentation can be made without the intent to deceive. Where fraud is present, the intent to deceive is present.

BUSINESS LAW

29. What does "force majure" mean?

   A. Commercial frustration of a contract

   B. The impossibility of performing a contract

   C. A reason for imposing damages

   D. An unexpected event of nature that allows parties not to perform a contract

   E. A major reason for requiring the performance of a contract

The answer is D.
Impossibility and commercial frustration are reasons that courts excuse the performance of contracts. Force majure is an unexpected event of nature, such as contamination by radioactivity from hazardous materials, that allows parties not to perform a contract. It is not a reason for imposing damages. There can also be political forces, such as war, that constitute a force majure.

30. Which of the following is NOT an element of undue influence?

   A. A superior and subservient relationship

   B. An opportunity to influence

   C. Duress

   D. Vulnerable person

   E. Suspicious transaction

The answer is C.
The presence of undue influence permits a contract or transaction to be set aside. There is often a superior and subservient relationship, such as a lawyer/client or parent/child, where one party has the opportunity to exert influence over the other. There must be a vulnerable person and a suspicious transaction that calls attention to the possibility of undue influence. Duress is not an element of undue influence because the use of duress is the intention use of force, or the threat of force, to get a person to do a specific act or enter into an unfair transaction.

BUSINESS LAW

31. Buyer has always wanted to purchase Seller's farm and has made offers to purchase several times. However, Seller has always turned Buyer down. Both are at a party, enjoying the refreshments. Seller tells Buyer to write out an agreement. Buyer writes out the terms on a paper napkin. Seller and Buyer sign the napkin. Buyer takes the money (in cash) to Seller. Seller refuses to deliver the property and says he did not have any intent to sell his family farm and that the "agreement" was a joke. What element of contract law is applicable to the "agreement"?

    A. Offer

    B. Acceptance

    C. Formation

    D. Consideration

    E. Capacity

The answer is C.
The "agreement" appears to have an offer and acceptance. Seller is not arguing that he did not have the capacity to contract. Consideration is not the issue because the "terms" of the "agreement" provided for an amount, which Buyer took to Seller. The issue is whether a contract was formed. The formation of an otherwise valid contract can be questioned is one party argues joke, undue influence, or lack of intent. Here Seller is arguing that he signed the napkin as a joke.

BUSINESS LAW

32. Owner of property has drawn up plans for a subdivision. He has complied with all government requirements. He advertises the acre lots as "ready for well-drilling and building" upon signing closing papers. Buyer of lot contracts with well-driller who, after doing some testing, finds the water table too low for a well. Buyer wants his money back. On what basis would a refund be proper?

    A. Unilateral mistake

    B. Mutual mistake

    C. Lack of consideration

    D. No meeting of the minds

    E. Undue influence

The answer is B.
The facts indicate there was an "arm's length bargain" and that there was consideration. As a result, there was a meeting of the minds. A unilateral (one-sided) mistake will not permit recission of a contract. Here, both parties believed the lot was buildable. It was not until the Buyer found out the water table was too low that it was learned the lot was not buildable. Therefore, mutual mistake is the basis for Buyer obtaining a refund.

33. What is the purpose of awarding contract damages?

    A. To put the person in a better position than he was in before the breach

    B. To put the person in the position he would have been in had the breach not occurred

    C. To punish the person causing the harmful breach

    D. To order the breaching party to specifically perform

    E. To halt the harmful behavior

The answer is B.
Damages are not awarded to put a person in a better position. Punitive damages are awarded to halt harmful behavior and to punish harmful behavior. Specific performance is ordered in situations where damages at law (money) are not adequate. Contract damages are awarded to put the person in the same position he would have been in if the breach had not occurred.

BUSINESS LAW

34. **What type of remedy is available to a purchaser who wants a court to order the seller to deliver property that he/she sold to the buyer?**

    A. Injunction

    B. Damages

    C. Specific Performance

    D. Recission

    E. Liquidated damages

The answer is C.
Injunctions are issued when there may be irreparable harm. Damages are money damages. Recission means to rescind or undo the contract. Liquidated damages are awarded in cases of anticipatory breach. Specific performance is ordered as an equitable remedy when damages at law are inadequate. Real estate is considered unique and specific performance is an appropriate remedy when one of the parties does not perform.

35. **Which statement is NOT correct about liquidated damages?**

    A. They must be reasonable.

    B. The parties need to agree that liquidated damages will be awarded.

    C. Liquidated damages are awarded for anticipatory breach.

    D. They must be stated as a specific amount.

    E. They may be determined by a percentage or by another agreed-upon method.

The answer is D.
All of the choices are correct except that the fact the damages need to be for a specific amount.

BUSINESS LAW

36. For which type of remedy must irreparable harm be shown?

    A. Liquidated damages

    B. Damages at law

    C. Specific performance

    D. Recission

    E. Injunction

The answer is E.
An injunction is an order by a court to stop certain behavior. A person who requests the court grant an injunction must show the likelihood of irreparable harm.

37. According to the common law "mailbox rule" when is an offer accepted?

    A. When the offer is sent

    B. When the offer is received

    C. When the time is agreed upon

    D. When any method of acceptance is used

    E. When the acceptance is delivered by the agreed upon method

The answer is B.
The question did not ask about the method of delivery of the offer. The question asked about the time of acceptance. According to the mailbox rule, the offer is accepted upon receipt.

BUSINESS LAW

38. All of the following are examples of termination of a contract sale of real estate EXCEPT:

    A. completion

    B. breach

    C. operation of law

    D. recission

    E. death of a party

The answer is E.
A death of a party would not terminate a contract for the sale of real estate. The decedent would have become owner of the real estate during his lifetime. An offer can be terminated upon the death of the offeror, however.

39. Buyer and Seller sign a purchase agreement for the sale/purchase of a house that sits on ½ acre. Buyer moves into the house and begins to use the shed that is on the property at the edge of the property line. Seller tells buyer to stop using the shed because the shed had not been part of the deal. What rule of law would prevent the buyer from arguing that the parties had meant to include the shed in the real estate transaction?

    A. mutual mistake

    B. parol evidence

    C. specific performance

    D. promissory estoppel

    E. injunction

The answer is B.
The parol evidence rule prevents a party to a contract from arguing that something that was not included in the contract had been intended to be in the contract. A contract is the final and complete agreement of the parties.

BUSINESS LAW

40. Builder and homeowner enter into a contract for builder to construct an addition to a home that includes a 16' x 24' family room. Builder sends homeowner his last invoice for ½ the agreed-upon price. Homeowner refuses to pay because he argues that contractor breached their contract. Homeowner shows builder that the size of the family room is only 15'5" x 23'9". What doctrine would permit builder to be paid?

    A. Substantial performance

    B. Substantial breach

    C. No meeting of the minds

    D. Promissory estoppel

    E. Mutual mistake

The answer is A.
There was a meeting of the minds when the contract to build a family room was entered into. Mutual mistake is not applicable, nor is promissory estoppel. There was not a substantial breach because the family room was completed. The size would not be considered a substantial beach. Therefore, the doctrine of substantial performance would permit the recovery of the amount on the invoice.

41. Bob has his Rav 4 for sale. Sue offers him $9,000. Bob says, "No, but I will take $11,000." What is Bob's response?

    A. A revocation

    B. A rejection

    C. An offer

    D. A counter-offer

    E. Agreement

The answer is D.
Bob rejected Sue's offer of $9,000. His statement that he would sell the vehicle for $11,000 is a counteroffer.

BUSINESS LAW

42. Jim, a college student, began selling used vehicles. A customer looks at a 1990 Ford Mustang convertible. Jim tells the customer that the car is in A-1 condition. How would you classify Jim's statement?

    A. Puffing

    B. Misrepresentation

    C. Fraudulent

    D. A statement made under duress

    E. A mistake

The answer is A.
If Jim were a mechanic or person who was aware of the condition of the parts and the actual condition of the car, the statement might be a misrepresentation or fraudulent. Puffing is an act that enhances something by exaggeration. Here, Jim is saying he believes the car is in great condition. Because he is a college student and part-time sales person, the statement can be considered puffing. It is an exaggeration about the qualities of the car but the statement does not go to the mechanics of the vehicle.

43. Daughter tells her elderly parents that she will move into their house care for them if they give her the house. A few days later, the parents contact their lawyer and add a codicil to their will, bequeathing the house to their daughter when they die. One week later, daughter has not moved in but her parents are killed in an airplane crash. She is devastated about their deaths but begins moving into the house. Her brother objects to her being given the house and argues that the house should be sold and proceeds divided equally as they are the only heirs. What is his argument?

    A. Fraud on the part of his sister

    B. Duress caused by his sister

    C. Undue influence of his sister

    D. Misrepresentation by his sister

    E. She should be promissorily estopped from getting the house.

The answer is C.
The facts do not indicate there was fraud, duress, or misrepresentation on the part of the sister. The question does not ask for a remedy. The question asks for the brother's argument. His argument is that his sister unduly influenced their parents when she convinced them to deed the house to her or bequeath the house to her in their Wills.

BUSINESS LAW

44. **A racing enthusiast purchases a horse to enter races. When he gets the horse to the stable, he learns the horse is great with foal (pregnant). Pregnant horses don't race. Seller learns of the pregnancy and wants the horse returned because pregnant horses are more valuable and expensive than racing horses. What will seller argue to try to get the horse returned?**

    A. Benefit of the bargain

    B. Illegal contract

    C. Void contract

    D. Mutual mistake

    E. Unilateral mistake

The answer is D.
Buyer did receive the benefit of the bargain. The horse just can't race until the foal is born. The contract is not illegal or void, and a unilateral mistake will usually not result in a recission of a contract. The seller would argue that there was a mutual mistake because purchaser wanted a race horse and seller thought he was selling a race horse. The seller will argue the transaction was a mistake on his part because the horse cannot race at the present time.

45. **Pet owner hired an artist to paint a portrait of her cat. Artist has an opportunity to go on vacation and wants a friend, who is also a painter, to finish the portrait. Cat owner objects. Can the artist have the friend finish the picture?**

    A. Yes, if the painter agrees.

    B. Yes, regardless of whether the cat owner agrees. The task is assignable

    C. Yes, regardless of whether the cat owner agrees. The task is delegable

    D. No, because the pet hisses at the substitute painter

    E. No, because it is a personal service contract that is not delegable without approval

The answer is E.
A personal service contract, such as the one described in this question, is not delegable without agreement. Reasons for this are many. Some of the reasons are that the person to whom the task is delegated may not be as qualified or suited to the task and the person wanting the work done may have reasons why he/she would not want the delegee to work on the project.

BUSINESS LAW

46. Aimee enters into a contract to purchase a $35,000.00 car. She is 17 years old but looks like she is 18 (an adult). She drives the car twice and decides she does not like the car. Can she avoid the contract?

    A. Yes, because she is a minor

    B. Yes, because she does not like the way the car handles

    C. No, because she looks like an adult

    D. No, because she has ratified the contract by driving the car

    E. No, if the car is a necessary

The answer is E.
The facts do not indicate the minor has ratified the contract. A minor may avoid the contract unless the car is a necessary. Here the vehicle price may be a determining factor. If the price of this car is one that the minor might have been expected to pay, given her background and position in life, then a court might consider the car a necessary.

47. Which of the following is an example of an illegal contract?

    A. A contract a merchant enters into with a malt manufacturer for the purchase of alcoholic beverages during Prohibition

    B. A contract a merchant enters into for the purchase of alcoholic beverages to be sold in a county that, before delivery of the product, declares the products may not be sold in the county.

    C. A contract entered into that requires shipment of items to be delivered to a non-existent street number

    D. A contract entered into for delivery of hazardous products that are not permitted to be shipped by rail, as the contract provides.

    E. A contract to purchase an item that becomes illegal to manufacture after the date of the agreement.

The answer is A.
If the contract was entered into at the time the products could be sold, the contract is valid. The lack of an address, or correct address, does not make a contract illegal. If goods cannot be shipped by one method, other methods can be agreed upon. The illegal agreement is the one for the manufacture and sale of alcoholic beverages during Prohibition, a time when both the sale and manufacture are prohibited.

BUSINESS LAW

48. What is another term for an illegal contract?

    A. Enforceable

    B. Unenforceable

    C. Avoidable

    D. Voidable

    E. Void

The answer is E.
Parties cannot enforce an illegal contract. An unenforceable contract is one that is legal or valid when it is entered into but becomes unenforceable for a reason. An avoidable contract is one that was valid when entered into but can be rescinded. A voidable contract is the same as an avoidable contract An illegal contract is void from the beginning. It is as though the contract does not exist.

49. Which of the following is an example of a third-party beneficiary contract?

    A. One party to a contract delegates performance to a third party

    B. One party to a contract asks the advice of a third party before signing the contract

    C. One party to a contract purchases a life insurance policy and names a relative as beneficiary

    D. One party leases a property with a right of first refusal to purchase the property from a subsequent purchaser

    E. One party donates the proceeds of a contract to a charity after receiving payment under the contract

The answer is C.
Delegation means transferring a duty. Asking the advice of a third party does not make the person giving advice a party to the contract. If one leases a property, the fact a third person is involved in a possible purchase does not make the possible seller a third-party beneficiary. Donating to a charity after receiving the money from a contract does not make the charity a third-party beneficiary. If the contract had been assigned to the charity, it would have been a third-party beneficiary. The beneficiary of a life insurance policy is an example of a third-party beneficiary.

BUSINESS LAW

50. To what does the "plain meaning" rule apply?

A. Statutory construction

B. Offers

C. Acceptances

D. Consideration

E. Damages

The answer is A.
The plain meaning rules applies to the statutory construction or interpretation of the meanings of contracts. The states have statutes that set out the rules of how a contract will be construed or interpreted. If a contract's meaning is plain on its fact, there will not be interpretation. If there are ambiguities, the wording of the contract will be construed against the drafter. If there are ambiguities, the intent of the parties is important in deciding how the language of the contract is construed.

51. Which of the following is an example of a violation of business ethics?

A. Making a mistake in the addition of business expenses

B. Charging a customer a price from a two-year-old price guide that is less than the price stated for a product on an updated guideline sent the day before the sale

C. Exercising your judgment for a "return policy" for an outdated item where the company has no stated policy

D. Submitting an "hours worked" sheet that included thirty-additional minutes because you forgot to time one of your work days.

E. Contacting your manager to assist in solving a business-related issue when you have the authority to solve such problems on your own.

The answer is D.
A single mistake in calculation of expenses is not a violation of ethics. The word "mistake" is the key. There is likely no ethical violation for charging a lesser rate because the guidebook is outdated and there may be reasons you were not aware of the most recent updated guide. When an individual has the authority to make decisions involving judgment, so long as the best interests of the company are considered, there is likely no ethical violation. Contacting a superior to help resolve an issue is an ethical business decision. When a person submits incorrect timesheets intentionally, business ethics have been violated.

BUSINESS LAW

52. **When might "moonlighting" be an ethical violation for a business employee?**

    A. It is not an ethical violation.

    B. It is an ethical violation if the employee exceeds 40 work hours per week.

    C. It is an ethical violation if the employee arrives only five minutes ahead of the required time to begin work for the second job.

    D. It is an ethical violation if the employee's work performance becomes poor.

    E. It is only a violation if both employers raise the issue.

The answer is D.
An employee is hired to be loyal and dedicated to the employer. If the employee takes a second job, and that job adversely affects job performance for the first job, than "moonlighting" can become an ethical violation.

53. **What does "corporate social responsibility" mean?**

    A. A company must provide its employees breaks during the day for social gatherings.

    B. A company's officers are responsible for helping new employees find housing and community information.

    C. A company must provide scheduled times for employees to take "personal days" off work.

    D. A company has a duty to maintain a balance between the economy and the ecosystems.

    E. A company must communicate, through its officers, to its employees new laws regarding workplace safety.

The answer is D.
Legally, a company may be required to provide employee work breaks and communicate new laws regarding workplace safety. However, corporate social responsibility refers to the company's duty to maintain a balance between the economy and ecosystems. For example, a company that is socially responsible will not deplete natural resources of a country where the company is building a new plant to manufacture items that require the use of that country's natural resources.

BUSINESS LAW

54. Which of the following statements about corporate social responsibility is INCORRECT?

   A. It is an ethical framework.

   B. The concept applies to society as a whole.

   C. Active social responsibility is acting in a way to avoid engaging in socially harmful acts.

   D. Active social responsibility is performing activities that directly advance social goals

   E. Social responsibility can be either active or passive.

The answer is C.
All of the statements are correct except for C. Engaging in activities that avoid socially harmful acts is considered passive social responsibility, not active social responsibility.

55. What is considered the "fourth" branch of government?

   A. Congress

   B. Executive Branch

   C. Administrative Agency

   D. Judicial Branch

   E. The Senate

The answer is C.
Administrative agencies are considered the fourth branch of government.

BUSINESS LAW

56. Which of the following statements about administrative agencies is INCORRECT?

A. Rules and regulations of administrative agencies have the force and effect of law.

B. Administrative agencies are created by Congress.

C. The Internal Revenue Service is an example of an administrative agency.

D. An objection to an administrative rule can be brought in the judicial branch of government.

E. Administrative law is considered a branch of public law.

The answer is D.
Objections to administrative rules must be brought before the agency in question. After administration remedies are exhausted, a person may appeal the administrative law decision to a court of law.

57. Which of the following statements about securities law is INCORRECT?

A. Securities laws are an example of a regulatory scheme.

B. U.S. corporate securities are regulated at the federal level.

D. The purpose of securities laws is to inform people about buying and selling stocks.

E. Securities laws govern the purchase of stock of private corporations.

The answer is E.
All of the statements except E are correct. Securities laws govern the sale and purchase of stocks of public corporations.

BUSINESS LAW

58. Of what type of law is greenhouse gas regulation an example?

    A. Environmental law

    B. Real estate law

    C. Business law

    D. Mining law

    E. Social responsibility law

The answer is A.
Greenhouse gas is an atmospheric gas that contributes to the greenhouse effect. The greenhouse effect is the warming of the earth's atmosphere by air pollution. Greenhouse gas regulation is an example of environmental law.

59. Which federal agency helps regulate entities in meeting federal environmental requirements?

    A. Department of Justice

    B. Environmental Protection Agency

    C. Federal Trade Commission

    D. Department of Agriculture

    E. Consumer Protection Agency

The answer is B.
The Environmental Protection Agency is the administrative agency responsible for helping entities in meeting federal environmental requirements.

BUSINESS LAW

60. What was the first major federal anti-trust law?

A. Robinson Patman Act

B. Sherman Antitrust Act

C. Clayton Antitrust Act

D. Federal Trade Commission Act

E. Celler-Kefauver Antimerger Act

The answer is B.
In 1890 Congress passed the Sherman Antitrust Act. The law was an attempt to ban combinations in restraint of trade (trusts) and to stop the monopolization by large companies. Violations were punishable by fines and imprisonment.

61. A company that sells copy machines requires purchasers to buy copy paper from them. This is an example of what kind of antitrust violation?

A. Horizontal restraint

B. Vertical restraint

C. Merger

D. Tying arrangement

E. Price fixing

The answer is D.
When the purchase of copy paper is a requirement that is connected to the purchase of a copy machine, the requirement is a typing arrangement. A tying arrangement is the selling of one product as a mandatory addition to the purchase of the other product.

62. **What rule does a court use to determine whether there has been price-fixing in a restraint of trade case?**

    A. Rule of reason

    B. Per se rule

    C. Collateral estoppel

    D. Promissory estoppel

    E. Cease and desist

The answer is B.
In cases involving the restraint of trade, courts use either the rule of reason or the per se rule to decide cases.

63. **Title VII of the Civil Rights of 1964 prohibits unlawful employment discrimination based on all of the following EXCEPT_____.**

    A. race

    B. national origin

    C. age

    D. religion

    E. sex

The answer is C.
Title VII of the 1964 Civil Rights Act does not include age as a basis for unlawful discrimination.

BUSINESS LAW

64. Which statement is correct about employment law?

A. Employment law excludes hours and wages issues and OSHA issues.

B. Employment law excludes age and disabilities issues.

C. Employment law excludes family leave issues.

D. Employment law excludes collective bargaining.

E. Employment law excludes worker's compensation issues.

The answer is D.
Employment law covers all areas of the employer/employee relationship with few exceptions. Two of those exceptions are collective bargaining and the negotiation process covered by labor law.

65. Creditors' rights are protected in bankruptcy filings in all of the following ways EXCEPT_____.

A. Filing a proof of claim

B. Attending a meeting of creditors

C. Objecting to a plan of reorganization

D. Filing suit against the debtor

E. Objecting to discharge

The answer is D.
A creditor may not proceed to file a suit against the debtor who has filed bankruptcy. Once a bankruptcy petition is filed there is an automatic stay, which means no further action can be taken by a creditor without permission of the bankruptcy court.

BUSINESS LAW

66. How may creditors protect their rights to collect a judgment if a debtor refuses to pay a judgment?

    A. Garnishee wages

    B. Apply the Fair Debt Collection Act

    C. File suit

    D. They have no recourse.

    E. File a showing of contempt

The answer is A.
According to the facts, a suit has already been filed and a judgment has been entered by the court. The Fair Debt Collection Act applies to debt collectors. This act applies to debts being collected before litigation. A contempt citation is filed when a defendant does not comply with a court order. A method of collecting a judgment is to file a garnishment order to have the judgment paid out of the judgment debtor's wages.

67. To whom is the Fair Debt Collection Act directed?

    A. Parties collecting their own debts

    B. Collectors of debts of third parties

    C. Creditors

    D. Debtors

    E. Courts

The answer is B.
The Fair Debt Collection Act was passed to protect debtors from bill collectors. The term "collectors" the Act refers to ae those collecting the debts of third parties. Creditors collecting their own debts are not the subject of the act. The courts can enforce violations of the Act.

BUSINESS LAW

68. Which of the following is NOT an example of a consumer debt?

    A. A student loan

    B. Unpaid taxes

    C. Purchase of a refrigerator on a credit card

    D. Car loan

    E. Pledge to charity

The answer is B.
Taxes are imposed by government and, while debts, are not consumer debts because a consumer debt results from the purchase of a good that is consumable and/or is not appreciable.

69. Which is one of the more often used ways to resolve issues of international business transactions?

    A. Mediation

    B. Arbitration

    C. Litigation

    D. The International Court of Justice

    E. The European Union

The answer is B.
The European Union is concerned with issues involving its member nations. The International Court of Justice is the main judicial branch of the United Nations and settles legal disputes between states, not individuals. Arbitration is usually more effective resolving international business issue than mediation or litigation. Arbitration is conducted by one or more individuals who serve as decision makers. International arbitration can be very expensive.

BUSINESS LAW

70. **Which statement is INCORRECT about a defective product?**

    A. The defective product must cause injury.

    B. The defective product must have been defective when it left the manufacturer.

    C. The defective product must have been in the stream of commerce.

    D. The defective product cannot result in liability for a retailer.

    E. The defect in the defective product cannot always be observed.

The answer is D.
A defective product must have been defective when it left the manufacturer, been involved in the stream of commerce, and caused injury. The defect in the product may not always be observable. For example, a soft drink bottle that explodes while being held may be a defective product or the explosion would not have happened. A retailer may be held responsible for product liability if the retailer provided a warranty of a product that later was found to be defective.

71. **What does a warranty of "merchantability" mean?**

    A. The product can be sold on the open market.

    B. The product is fit for a particular purpose.

    C. The product is fit for ordinary purposes.

    D. The warranty is to be written on the box or label before sale.

    E. The warranty is stated to the purchaser.

The answer is C.
Implied warranties are the warranty of merchantability and the warranty that a product is fit for a particular purpose. The warranty of merchantability means that a product is fit for ordinary purposes.

BUSINESS LAW

72. **A product that is dangerous needs to have a warning. What statement is INCORRECT about warnings?**

    A. Failure to warn is a breach of duty.

    B. The warning must be conspicuous.

    C. The warning must be made large enough.

    D. The warning can be spoken.

    E. The warning must be in writing.

The answer is D.
The failure to warn is a breach of duty, must be conspicuous, in large enough print, and must be in writing. The incorrect choice is that the warning can be spoken.

73. **Which of the following is an example of an express warranty?**

    A. The fact that a coffee pot is expected to make coffee

    B. The fact that a tool with attachments will perform as thought

    C. The fact that a lawn mower will cut grass

    D. The fact that an electric toothbrush holds size AA batteries

    E. The fact that an electric mixer can be repaired at no cost for a period of sixty days

The answer is E.
An express warranty is written or spoken and states a promise or guarantee from the seller to the buyer that a buyer can rely on when the buyer purchases the product. The statement that an electric mixer can be repaired at no cost for a period of sixty days is an example of an express warranty.

BUSINESS LAW

74. **Why is strict liability imposed on manufacturers in product liability cases?**

    A. Because there has been negligence

    B. Because there has been a breach of warranty

    C. Because there is a deep pocket.

    D. Because of the goal of punishing the manufacturer

    E. Because of the goal of negligence litigation

The answer is C.
Strict liability is imposed on manufacturers because they are in a better position to correct problems that result in defective products and they have a deep pocket and are better able to absorb the costs for injuries caused by defective products.

75. **"Manufacturer will repair or replace item within one year of purchase if a defect or malfunction occurs. Manufacturer will not compensate purchaser for any loss arising from defect or malfunction." The preceding statement is an example of a(n) _____.**

    A. Warranty

    B. Implied warranty

    C. Express warranty

    D. Limited Warranty

    E. Breach of warranty

The answer is D.
The statement is an example of a limited warranty. A limited warranty limits what the manufacture will do in the event of a defective product or malfunction of a product. The statement indicates the manufacturer will not pay for loss but will repair or replace the product for twelve months from purchase if the product malfunctions or is defective.

BUSINESS LAW

76. **What is the "egg shell" theory?**

    A. The wrongdoer takes the victim the way he/she finds the victim.

    B. The plaintiff's weaknesses must be exposed.

    C. The defendant's weaknesses must be exposed.

    D. There is a fracture in the plaintiff's case.

    E. The plaintiff has a thin chance of success.

The answer is A.
The theory states that the wrongdoer takes the victim as the wrongdoer finds the victim. For example, if the victim has pre-existing conditions at the time of the injury, the victim must accept the plaintiff's condition as one with pre-existing conditions.

77. **Which of the following is NOT an element of battery?**

    A. An unconsented to or rude touching

    B. Touching the person or something close to him/her, such as a cane or hat

    C. Intent to touch

    D. Intent to harm

    E. Resulting harm

The answer is D.
The intent is in the act, not the result. The result may be unintended.

BUSINESS LAW

78. **Which of the following is NOT an element of assault?**

    A. Putting a person in fear

    B. The element of fear is subjective

    C. An intent to put a person in fear

    D. Touching a person or something close to the person

    E. The fear of imminent harm

The answer is D.
Assault is the causing of a person to fear imminent harm. Assault does not require touching.

79. **If you are attending a pool party in the backyard of a friend and you see a two-year-old step into the pool and sink to the bottom, who, sitting around the pool, has a legal duty to try to save the child?**

    A. You

    B. A neighbor

    C. A babysitter

    D. A family friend

    E. The caterer

The answer is C.
Although there may be a moral duty to try to save the child, the question asked who had a *legal* duty to save the child. There must be a special relationship before a legal duty arises. In the choices that were provided, the babysitter had a legal duty to try to save the child.

BUSINESS LAW

80. **Which of the following is an example of an ultrahazardous or abnormally dangerous activity?**

    A. Mink farming

    B. Baseball

    C. Mining

    D. Snow plowing

    E. Reforestation

The answer is C.
An ultrahazardous activity has also been called an abnormally dangerous activity. It is so inherently dangerous that the person engaged in the activity can be held strictly liable for injuries to a person even though every reasonable precaution was taken. Mining is an example of an ultrahazardous activity.

81. **Which of the following is an example of a situation in which vicarious liability is imposed?**

    A. Workmen's compensation cases

    B. Intentional torts cases

    C. A driver's negligence due to hitting a pedestrian with the driver's own vehicle

    D. Emotional distress cases

    E. Battery cases

The answer is A.
Vicarious liability is a form of strict liability. A person who is responsible for the acts of a third party who had the right, duty, or ability to control the activities is often found to be vicariously liable for injuries. Worker's compensations laws impose vicarious liability on the employer because the employer has the ability to make the work environment safe.

BUSINESS LAW

82. Nominal damages are likely to be awarded in which type of case?

   A. Assault

   B. Negligence

   C. Interference with contractual relations

   D. Battery

   E. Trespass

The answer is E.
Normally there is little damage in situations where someone trespasses. The other examples usually result in higher amounts of damages.

83. Which is NOT an element of negligence?

   A. Duty

   B. Breach of duty

   C. Legal cause

   D. Injury

   E. Damages

The answer is E.
The elements of damages are duty, breach of duty, causation, and injury. Damages result from negligence; however, damages are not an element of negligence.

BUSINESS LAW

84. Upon what does proximate cause depend?

A. Negligence

B. Foreseeability

C. Legal cause

D. "But for" cause

E. Respondeat superior

The answer is B.
Actual cause is legal cause. "But for" defendant's actions, plaintiff would not have sustained injury. Proximate cause depends upon the foreseeability of a remote injury happening. Proximate cause is the justification for limiting liability at some point.

85. Most states would deny a bystander the right to recover damages for the negligent infliction of emotional distress based on what rule?

A. The foreseeability rule

B. The impact rule

C. The privity rule

D. The proximate cause rule

E. The Discovery rule

The answer is B.
Most states require that there be physical impact before someone can collect damages for the negligent infliction of emotional distress.

BUSINESS LAW

86. In which situation might punitive damages be imposed?

   A. A personal injury case where the driver injured a pedestrian who was crossing the street while the light was red.

   B. A case where a driver on a 'frolic and detour' caused injury to a bicyclist

   C. A case where a person sued for negligent infliction of emotional distress.

   D. A case where a retailer falsely imprisons a suspected shoplifter

   E. A case where a business sells a faulty tool from an overseas manufacturer

The answer is D.
Punitive damages are imposed to deter people from acting in an injurious way and to prevent harm. Of the examples provided, the one that might result in punitive damages is the situation where a shopkeeper exceeds the boundaries of detaining a person for questioning if the person is suspected of shoplifting.

87. In which situation would respondeat superior apply?

   A. An independent contractor causing damages to a yard while digging a ditch

   B. An employee who, while driving a company truck backs into a car

   C. A driver, driving her own car, injures a pedestrian

   D. A biker who injures a jogger

   E. The owner of a company who damages the company car of her way to work

The answer is B.
Respondeat superior applies to "master-servant" relationships. The employee who is driving a company truck and backs into a car is an example of where *respondeat superior* is applicable, if the employee was in the scope of his/her employment when the accident happened.

BUSINESS LAW

88. **Which is NOT correct about conversion?**

    A. The owner is deprived of the possession personal property.

    B. The converter deprives the owner of the ownership of the property.

    C. The converter may intend to return the property.

    D. The converter may have also committed a criminal act of conversion.

    E. Converting property is an intentional tort.

The answer is B.
The converter does not obtain ownership of the property. The converter deprives the owner of the possession, not the ownership, of the property.

89. **Where a lawnmower has no warning about the dangers of use, what element of negligence applies to the lack of warning?**

    A. Injury

    B. Causation

    C. Breach of duty

    D. Duty

    E. Damages

The answer is C.
A manufacturer has a duty to warn users of possible dangers. When the warning is not on the product, the manufacturer has breached the duty of care.

BUSINESS LAW

90. What term is applicable when an employee is running an errand for the employer and decides to take her own mail to the post office?

   A. Negligence

   B. Intentional tort

   C. Independent contractor

   D. Respondeat superior

   E. Frolic and detour

The answer is E.
When an employee deviates from a path or course for an employer, the deviation is called a frolic and detour.

91. Which article of the Uniform Commercial Code applies to sales of goods?

   A. Article 2

   B. Article 2A

   C. Article 3

   D. Article 4

   E. Article 9

The answer is A.
Article 9 applies to secured transactions. Article 4 applies to bank deposits and collections. Article 3 applies to negotiable instruments. Article 2A involves leases. Article 2 applies to the sale of goods.

BUSINESS LAW

92. Which of the following statements about "goods" is INCORRECT?

   A. Goods are movable at the time of identification to the contract for sale.

   B. Goods include the unborn young of animals.

   C. Goods may be existing and/or identified before any interest in them can pass.

   D. Specially manufactured goods are defined as "goods."

   E. Money is a "good" that is defined as the "price that is to be paid."

The answer is C.
All of the statements are correct about "goods" except choice C. Goods MUST be existing AND identified before any interest in them can pass. Goods that are not both existing and identified are "future" goods.

93. Mark asks Sue to sell his iPod. She agrees. He gives her a plastic grocery bag with the iPod in it. Sue asks Tom if he is interested in buying Mark's iPod. Tom indicates he is. When he looks in the bag, he finds a case for the iPod in addition to the iPod. Tom indicates he is only interested in the purchase/sale if the case is included. If Sue sells both items together and Mark tells her that the case was not to be sold, what is Sue's argument to support the sale of the case?

   A. She had express authority to sell the case.

   B. She had apparent authority to sell the case.

   C. She had implied authority to sell the case.

   D. She had actual authority to sell the case.

   E. She was acting as a gratuitous agent.

The answer is C.
Mark did not expressly authorize Sue to sell the case; therefore, she did not have actual authority to sell it. The facts do not indicate whether she was acting as a gratuitous agent, but the status as to her type of agency does not have an effect on the result. Apparent authority is the authority a third party believes an agent has. If Mark asked Tom to return the case, Tom's argument would be that he believed Sue had apparent authority to sell the case. Sue's argument is that she had implied authority to sell the case. She had express authority to sell the iPod. A case usually goes with the iPod, and a case was in the plastic bag Mark gave her. Implied authority flows from express authority. In this case, Sue had implied authority to sell the case with the iPod.

BUSINESS LAW

94. Which of the following is an example of a fiduciary duty in the area of agency law?

   A. Pay wages

   B. Act on behalf of the principal

   C. Be controlled by the principal

   D. Be loyal

   E. Discharge duties in a timely manner

The answer is D.
The duty of loyalty is an example of a fiduciary duty. The principal and agent need to be loyal to each other in the scope of the agency relationship. Each must act in the other's best interest.

95. Which is a key element in determining whether a person is an employee or an independent contractor?

   A. Does the employer pay the person doing work for him?

   B. Does the employer have control over how the person's work is done?

   C. Does the employer pay taxes for the worker's income?

   D. Is there an agreement between the parties?

   E. Is there a past work history between the parties?

The answer is B.
The key element in determining whether a worker is an employee or an independent contractor is whether the principal has supervision and control over how the work is done. If there is supervision and control, it is more likely that the worker is an employee. If there is not supervision and control, then it is more likely the worker is an independent contractor.

BUSINESS LAW

96. **What generally happens to a partnership when a partner dies?**

    A. The partnership is dissolved.

    B. The partnership continues with the remaining partners.

    C. The partnership allows a new partner to purchase the deceased partner's shares.

    D. The partnership becomes a sole proprietorship is there is only one remaining partner.

    E. The partnership's future is determined by the remaining partner(s).

The answer is A.
When a partner dies, or leaves the partnership, the partnership generally is dissolved. The winding up of the partnership then begins. However, if the partnership agreement provides otherwise, the partnership will continue.

97. **If a person wants to invest money into a partnership but does not want to be involved in the decision-making process, what type of partnership should that person form?**

    A. General partnership

    B. Limited liability company

    C. Limited liability partnership

    D. Limited partnership

    E. Sole proprietorship

The answer is D.
A general partnership is one where the partners share the responsibilities as well as the profits/losses. A limited liability company is a hybrid of a corporation and a partnership. A sole proprietorship is a business owned by a single person. In a limited liability partnership (LLP) there are no general partners. All of the owners have limited liability for the debts of the business. In a limited partnership, there is one general partner who makes the decisions for the partnership and is responsible for the debt of the partnership. The limited partners are investors who do not have control over the operations of the business and are not personally liable for the debts of the partnership.

BUSINESS LAW

98. **What is one of the main advantages of a corporate form of business organization?**

    A. The tax structure

    B. Owning shares of stock

    C. Having a board of directors

    D. Having a bylaws

    E. Limited liability

The answer is E.
The main advantage of the corporation as a form of business organization is the fact that the owners have limited liability.

99. **Which of the following provides the written guidance for the operation of a corporation?**

    A. Articles of Incorporation

    B. Bylaws

    C. Board of Directors

    D. Officers

    E. Corporate employee manual

The answer is B.
The employee manual provides guidelines for the employees but not for the operation of the corporation. The officers are elected by the board of directors to conduct the daily affairs of the corporation. The board of directors manages the corporation. The articles of incorporation are filed with the state office (usually the Secretary of State, or similar department) to organize the corporation. The bylaws establish rules and regulations for the business. They are in writing and identify the roles of the directors, officers, and shareholders.

100. What is the type of lawsuit that is filed by an injured party when a corporation is alleged to be an alter-ego of the sole shareholder?

A. A derivative suit

B. A suit to dissolve the corporation

C. A suit for punitive damages

D. A suit for an accounting

E. A suit to pierce the corporate veil

The answer is E.
The facts indicate there is one shareholder. The injured party would file a suit to ask a court to pierce the corporate veil and find the corporation is the alter ego of the shareholder.

PRINCIPLES OF MANAGEMENT

Description of the Examination

The Principles of Management examination covers material that is usually taught in an introductory course in the essentials of management and organization. The fact that such courses are offered by different types of institutions and in a number of fields other than business has been taken into account in the preparation of this examination. It requires a knowledge of human resources and operational and functional aspects of management.

The examination contains approximately 100 questions to be answered in 90 minutes. Some of these are pretest questions that will not be scored. Any time candidates spend on tutorials and providing personal information is in addition to the actual testing time.

Knowledge and Skills Required

Questions on the Principles of Management examination require candidates to demonstrate one or more of the following abilities in the approximate proportions indicated.

- Specific factual knowledge, recall, and general understanding of purposes, functions, and techniques of management (about 10 percent of the exam)
- Understanding of and ability to associate the meaning of specific terminology with important management ideas, processes, techniques, concepts, and elements (about 40 percent of the exam)
- Understanding of theory and significant underlying assumptions, concepts, and limitations of management data, including a comprehension of the rationale of procedures, methods, and analyses (about 40 percent of the exam)
- Application of knowledge, general concepts, and principles to specific problems (about 10 percent of the exam)

The subject matter of the Principles of Management examination is drawn from the following topics. The percentages next to the main topics indicate the approximate percentage of exam questions on that topic.

15-25% **Organization and Human Resources**
- Personnel Administration
- Human Relations and Motivation
- Training and Development
- Performance Appraisal
- Organizational Development
- Legal Concerns
- Workforce Diversity
- Recruiting and Selecting
- Compensation and Benefits
- Collective Bargaining

10-20% **Operational Aspects of Management**
- Operations Planning and Control
- Work Scheduling
- Quality Management
- Information Processing and Management
- Strategic Planning and Analysis
- Productivity

45-55% **Functional Aspects of Management**
- Planning
- Organizing
- Leading
- Controlling
- Authority

PRINCIPLES OF MANAGEMENT

- Decision Making
- Organization Charts
- Leadership
- Organizational Structure
- Budgeting
- Problem Solving
- Group Dynamics and Team Functions
- Conflict Resolution
- Communication
- Change
- Organizational Theory
- Historical Aspects

10-20% **International Management and Contemporary Issues**
- Value Dimensions
- Regional Economic Integration
- Trading Alliances
- Global Environment
- Social Responsibilities of Business
- Ethics
- Systems
- Environment
- Government Regulation
- Management Theories and Theorists
- E-Business
- Creativity and Innovation

PRINCIPLES OF MANAGEMENT

SAMPLE TEST

DIRECTIONS: Read each item and select the best response.

1. **According to equity theory:**
   (Operational Aspects of Management)

   A. (Employee B's rewards/Employee A's input) = (Employee A's rewards/Employee B's input)

   B. (Employee A's rewards/Employee A's input) = (Employee B's rewards/Employee B's input)

   C. (Employee A's rewards/Employee B's input) = (Employee B's rewards/Employee A's input)

   D. (Employee A's rewards/Employee A's input) > (Employee B's rewards/Employee B's input)

   E. (Employee A's rewards/Employee A's input) < (Employee B's rewards/Employee B's input)

2. **Productivity is:**
   (Operational Aspects of Management)

   A. Input*Output

   B. Input/Output

   C. Output/Input

   D. (Output-Input)/Output

   E. (Input-Output)/Input

3. **The use of a neutral third party tasked with resolving a dispute but who doesn't have the authority to enforce the outcome is known as:**
   (Organization and Human Resources)

   A. Mediation

   B. Conciliation

   C. Arbitration

   D. Bargaining

   E. Litigation

4. **___ is not one of Porter's five forces of environmental scanning:**
   (International Management and Contemporary Issues)

   A. Bargaining power of suppliers

   B. Regulation of governments

   C. Bargaining power of customers

   D. Threat of new entrants

   E. Threat of substitutes

5. ___ is an example of ethnocentrism: *(International Management and Contemporary Issues)*

   A. Opening a wholly-foreign owned enterprise before attempting licensing

   B. Mistranslations of promotional materials

   C. Managing team dynamics in foreign offices as in home offices

   D. Using the same asset management analytics in each global office

   E. Structuring a business by functional division rather than geography

6. ___ is an example of the maintenance group role: *(Functional Aspects of Management)*

   A. Making acquisition decisions for upcoming projects

   B. Collecting feedback on an internal policy change

   C. Alleviating office friction during end of fiscal year

   D. Playing "Devil's Advocate"

   E. Scheduling project milestones in line with final deadline

7. The highest degree of group autonomy is found in ___ groups: *(Functional Aspects of Management)*

   A. Traditional

   B. Semi-autonomous

   C. Cross-functional

   D. Self-managed

   E. Virtual

8. A management method training employees on the operations of the company and the role of their primary function within it: *(Organization and Human Resources)*

   A. Job enlargement

   B. Job rotation

   C. Job enrichment

   D. Job reengineering

   E. Job intensification

9. Equity theory requires the use of objective measurements of input because:
(Operational Aspects of Management)

   A. So that employees know what to expect in their rewards

   B. The endowment effect means each person values their own contributions more than equivalent contributions by others

   C. So that inputs and outputs can be readily calculated

   D. To set a prediction reference point relative to actual outcomes

   E. To set a reference point for negotiations in future exchanges

10. What type of plan is this "Over the next 5 years we will expand the total market by targeting previously untouched demographics":
(Functional Aspects of Management)

    A. Strategic

    B. Tactical

    C. Operational

    D. Project

    E. Contingency

11. Who is in charge of establishing operational plans:
(Functional Aspects of Management)

    A. Middle managers

    B. First-line managers

    C. Executive managers

    D. Financial managers

    E. Shift managers

12. The best contingency plans:
(Functional Aspects of Management)

    A. Deviate from the optimal plan at the point of change, preserving the value of the previous steps

    B. Are fully established plans wholly separate from the optimal plan

    C. Set alternatives for each step which feed back into the optimal plan

    D. Should be pursued simultaneously to the optimal plan

    E. Should only be developed if the optimal plan fails

13. In change management, all the following are part of the unfreezing process except:
    (Functional Aspects of Management)

    A. Surveying employees about their jobs and how they can be improved

    B. Quantify the operational, competitive, and financial impact of elements to be changed

    C. Reinforcing the negative aspects of current methods in the minds of the staff

    D. Communicating controlled isolation of the problem with plans for improvement that doesn't extend into the rest of the organization

    E. Implementing new policies

14. At 6σ, the ideal goal of Six Sigma quality management, there are ____ DPMO with a ____ percentage yield:
    (Operational Aspects of Management)

    A. 0.019, 99.9999981

    B. 3.4, 99.99966

    C. 233, 99.977

    D. 6,210, 99.38

    E. 66,807, 93.3

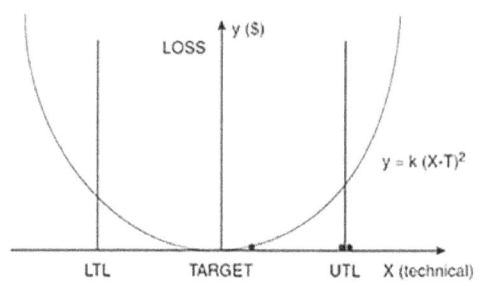

15. The Taguchi Loss Function states:
    (Operational Aspects of Management)

    A. Deviations from target specifications create a loss which increases exponentially and must not exceed upper and lower limits

    B. Quality management operations must be effective enough to be financially viable, but not to the point that its costs exceed its benefits

    C. The defective parts per million opportunities will increase the costs of fixing/reconstructing defective output more than the costs of preventing them

    D. Increasing losses create deviations from planned growth rates which become unsustainable at upper and lower limits

    E. Losses are a function of parabolic curves

16. $100,000 earned at complete project
    Planned 10 week deadline, linear PV
    $60,000 EV at 5 weeks
    What is the SPI:
    (Operational Aspects of Management)

    A. 120%

    B. 83%

    C. 10%

    D. -10%

    E. 100%

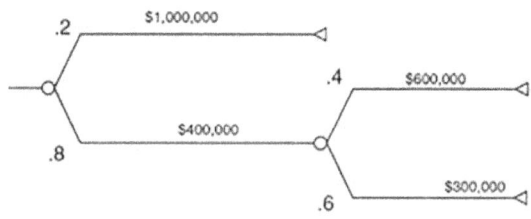

17. The adjusted values at the 2nd node of this decision tree are:
    (Functional Aspects of Management)

    A. -$200,000, $100,000

    B. $240,000, $180,000

    C. $300,000, -$300,000

    D. $200,000, $320,000

    E. $240,000, $300,000

	Probability	Frequent	Likely	Occasional	Seldom	Unlikely
Severity		A	B	C	D	E
Catastrophic	I	E	E	H	H	M
Critical	II	E	H	H	M	L
Moderate	III	H	M	M	L	L
Negligible	IV	M	L	L	L	L

18. In the management of a fire department, the risk to individual staff members is:
    (Functional Aspects of Management)

    A. None

    B. Low (L)

    C. Moderate (M)

    D. High (H)

    E. Extreme (E)

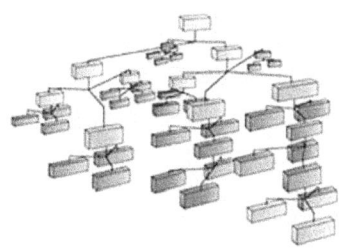

19. Models such as this are most commonly used to depict:
    (Functional Aspects of Management)

    A. Organizational hierarchy

    B. Product portfolio

    C. Subsidiary structure

    D. Capital assets

    E. Team motivation drivers

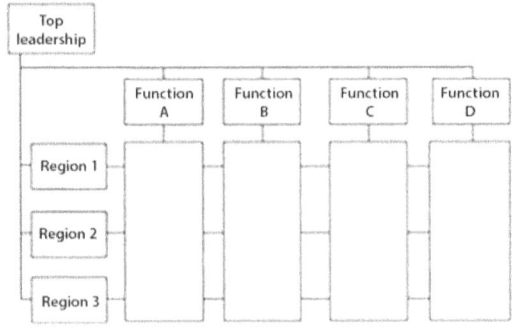

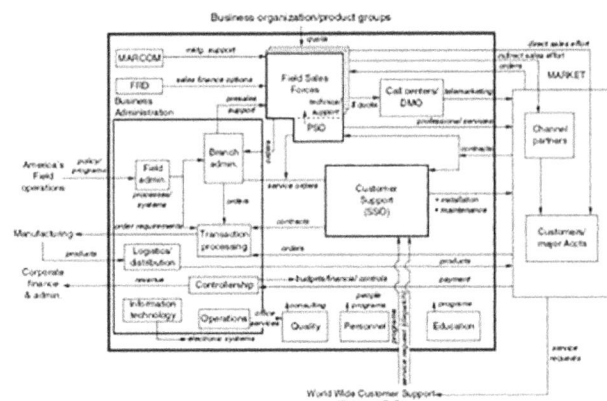

20. **This represents:**
    (Functional Aspects of Management)

    A. Divisional management

    B. Matrix management

    C. Micromanagement

    D. Tight matrix

    E. Organizational spreadsheet

21. **This is called ____ which represents ____:**
    (Functional Aspects of Management)

    A. Process flowchart, dynamic operations of an organization

    B. Organizational structure, management hierarchy

    C. Schematic diagram, an electrical circuit

    D. Organizational structure, dynamic operations of an organization

    E. Process flowchart, management hierarchy

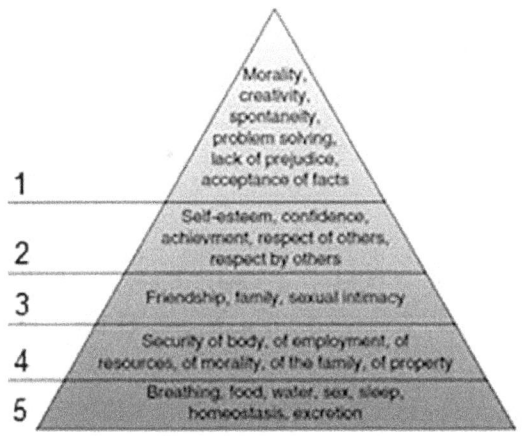

22. **In Maslow's Hierarchy of Needs, self-actualization is found at:** *(Organization and Human Resources)*

   A. 1

   B. 2

   C. 3

   D. 4

   E. 5

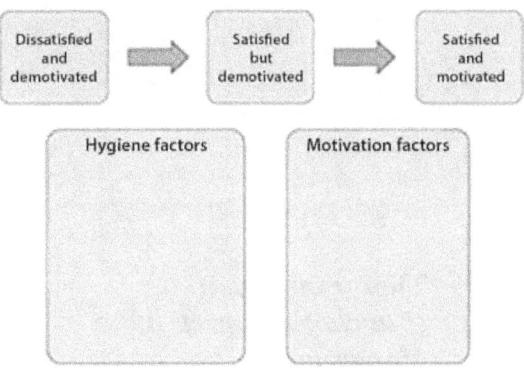

23. **In Herzberg's Two-Factor Theory of Motivation, ____ is a hygiene factor and ___ is a motivator:** *(Organization and Human Resources)*

   A. Wages, prestige

   B. Responsibility, working conditions

   C. Promotions, job security

   D. Sense of purpose, clear expectations

   E. Recognition, professional relationships

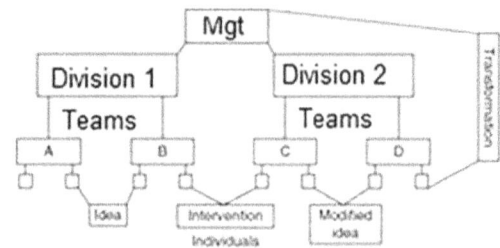

24. This graph illustrates:
(Functional Aspects of Management)

A. Structure of authority

B. Team-based project management

C. Organizational decision making process

D. Bottom-up communication

E. The flow of information in managing continuous improvement

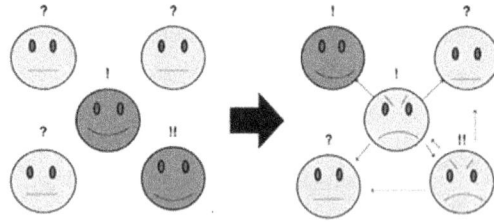

25. This diagram on conflict creation illustrates the need for:
(Functional Aspects of Management)

A. Clear direction and dissemination of information from management

B. The need for arbitration during the decision making process

C. Multiple styles of negotiations

D. Constructive forms of persuasion

E. Team development programs

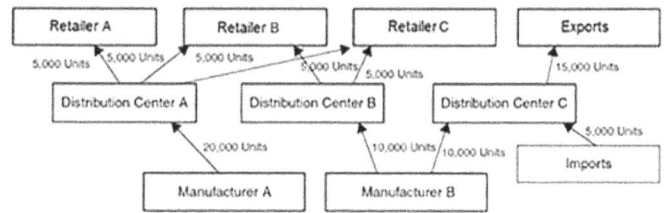

26. Which manufacturer has the lowest-risk supply chain:
(Operational Aspects of Management)

A. Manufacturer B because 100% of their production has multiple channels to the end consumer

B. Manufacturer A because their primary distribution center sells to 50% more retailers than 2nd highest

C. Manufacturer A because they are not competing with foreign imports

D. Manufacturer B because they have domestic and foreign sales

E. Both manufacturers A and B have equal risk of disrupted supply chains

27. ___ is a form of ___ given to first-line managers, though ___ is often reserved for middle management:
(Functional Aspects of Management)

   A. Reward authority, legitimate power, coercive authority

   B. Personal power, legitimate power, positional authority

   C. Referent authority, personal power, coercive authority

   D. Reward authority, personal power, coercive authority

   E. Coercive authority, legitimate power, positional authority

28. ___ is acquired by being charismatic or motivational, rather than having any formal power:
(Functional Aspects of Management)

   A. Expert authority

   B. Referent authority

   C. Positional authority

   D. Reward authority

   E. Coercive authority

29. Compartmentalization of operations to prevent interaction and communication is typically used to:
(Functional Aspects of Management)

   A. This is never done in a healthy organization

   B. To create an immersive environment during job rotation training

   C. To prevent interaction between men and women in some highly orthodox cultures

   D. To prevent conflict with competing individuals or teams

   E. Prevent any person from having access to the whole of proprietary information

30. The point in the team development process in which members conflict with each other as they establish roles and culture is called:
(Functional Aspects of Management)

   A. Forming

   B. Storming

   C. Norming

   D. Performing

   E. Adjourning

31. The point in which a manager will most likely need to validate the credentials of a member is:
    (Functional Aspects of Management)

    A. Adjourning

    B. Forming

    C. Storming

    D. Norming

    E. Performing

32. According to Kohlberg's Stages of Moral Development, how should a manager address an individual at Stage 4:
    (Functional Aspects of Management)

    A. Emphasize conditioning systems of reward and punishment

    B. Emphasize personal gain to be earned in negotiated terms

    C. Emphasize the importance of policies and organizational authority

    D. Emphasize the mutual benefits of constructed operations and dynamics

    E. Emphasize conforming to organizational roles and cultures as a means of acceptance

33. According to Kohlberg's Moral Development, how should a manager address an individual at Stage 3:
    (Functional Aspects of Management)

    A. Emphasize conforming to organizational roles and cultures as a means of acceptance

    B. Emphasize the importance of policies and organizational authority

    C. Emphasize the mutual benefits of constructed operations and dynamics

    D. Emphasize conditioning systems of reward and punishment

    E. Emphasize personal gain to be earned in negotiated terms

34. Motivation is mathematically represented as:
    (Organization and Human Resources)

    A. (Expectancy*Value)/(1+Impulsiveness*Delay)

    B. Expectancy*Value

    C. (Expectancy*Value)/(1+Impulsiveness)

    D. Expected Value – Expected Costs

    E. Expected Value/(Impulsiveness*Delay)

35. The negotiating style which includes offering either fake or inconsequential concessions in order to gain on those things which matter to you is called: *(Functional Aspects of Management)*

    A. Accommodating

    B. Avoiding

    C. Collaborating

    D. Competing

    E. Compromising

36. The negotiating style which involves intentionally keeping negotiations on aspects which are not issues of conflict in order to draw the other person in is called: *(Functional Aspects of Management)*

    A. Collaborating

    B. Competing

    C. Avoiding

    D. Accommodating

    E. Compromising

37. Employees each produce 10 units per day, units sell for $100 each with a total cost of $90 per unit entirely composed of labor. If it takes 5 days to train a new employee, what is the turnover cost: *(Organization and Human Resources)*

    A. $5,000

    B. $4,500

    C. $500

    D. $450

    E. $0

38. Per day, experienced staff produce 500 units and earn $100.
    Per day, new staff produce 300 units and earn $50.
    Training takes 5 days and each unit produced is worth $1
    The calculation to analyze the wage productivity differential is: *(Organization and Human Resources)*

    A. (500/100)n – ((300/50)n-250)

    B. ((300/50)n-250)-(500/100)n

    C. (100/500)n-(300/50)n

    D. (500/100)n-(300/50)n

    E. (500-300)n/100-250

39. Setup costs = $10
    Demand = 100
    Production cost = $20
    Interest rate = 100%
    EOQ is:
    (Operational Aspects of Management)

    A. 5

    B. 10

    C. 50

    D. 100

    E. 500

COSTS	IN-HOUSE	OUTSOURCED
Billing department costs	$118,000	$4,000
Software and hardware costs	$7,500	$500
Direct claim processing costs	$3,600	$122,500
Software and hardware costs	$5,500	$2,000
% of billings collected	60%	70%
Collections	$1,370,900	$1,623,000
Collections costs	$129,100	$127,000
Collections, net of costs		

40. **Decide whether to outsource:**
    (Organization and Human Resources)

    A. Do not outsource to prevent losing $254,200

    B. Outsource to gain $254,200

    C. Do both to gain $254,200

    D. End function completely to prevent losing $254,200

    E. Panic

41. **It is best to use an authoratarian leadership style when:**
    (Functional Aspects of Management)

    A. During skill development programs

    B. When interpersonal conflict begins to hinder basic work functions

    C. When seeking input for revision of internal policies

    D. When managing skilled experts working in creative conditions

    E. During times of crisis when change must be rapid

42. **A pacesetting leadership style intended to facilitate the staff's activities is best used when:**
    (Functional Aspects of Management)

    A. When managing skilled experts working in creative conditions

    B. When seeking input for revision of internal policies

    C. When interpersonal conflict begins to hinder basic work functions

    D. During times of crisis when change must be rapid

    E. During skill development programs

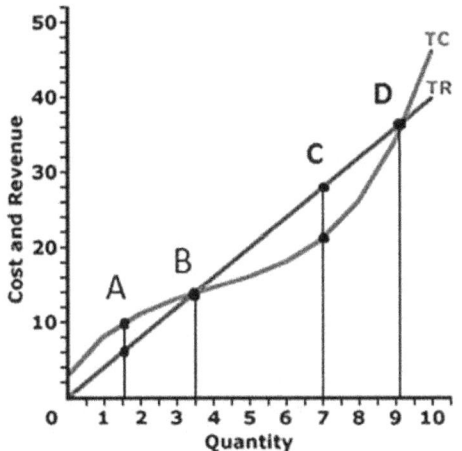

43. For profit-maximizing firms efficiency is optimized at __ and for revenue-maximizing firms at ___:
(Operational Aspects of Management)

   A. B, C

   B. D, C

   C. C, D

   D. C, B

   E. B, D

44. Under generic competitive conditions, productive efficiency is achieved at:
(Operational Aspects of Management)

   A. MC=FC

   B. FC=AC

   C. VC=FC

   D. MC=AC

   E. MC=TC

45. Which is not a type of team dysfunction:
(Functional Aspects of Management)

   A. Groupthink

   B. Interpersonal conflict

   C. Freeriding

   D. Comprehensive input

   E. Lack of individualization

46. Analysis paralysis typically results from:
(Functional Aspects of Management)

   A. Lack of decisive confidence

   B. Too much information

   C. Too little information

   D. Too much or too little information

   E. Rapidly changing business environment

47. **The shareholder wealth maximization model is concerned with:**
    (International Management and Contemporary Issues)

    A. Increasing current profitability

    B. Increasing the value of company equity

    C. Maximizing the value that the company creates for those which it influences

    D. Increasing company revenue growth

    E. Increasing NPV of company investments

48. **Which of the following is not a stakeholder:**
    (International Management and Contemporary Issues)

    A. Competitors

    B. Shareholders

    C. Employees

    D. Customers

    E. Partners

49. **Agency problems result from:**
    (International Management and Contemporary Issues)

    A. Executives who manage a company in a manner contrary to that which benefits the shareholders

    B. Executives who manage a company in a manner contrary to that which benefits the stakeholders

    C. Contradictions between the benefits of the shareholders and stakeholders

    D. Managers who embezzle money from the company

    E. Inefficient functions such as bid rigging and nepotism

50. A short organization is one which has:
    (Functional Aspects of Management)

    A. Few degrees of management with a larger volume of staff per manager

    B. More degrees of management with a lower volume of staff per manager

    C. Few degrees of management with a lower volume of staff per manager

    D. More degrees of management with a with a larger volume of staff per manager

    E. Few degrees of management with higher staff empowerment

51. SIPOC analysis includes each except:
    (Organization and Human Resources)

    A. Competitors

    B. Supplier

    C. Inputs

    D. Processes

    E. Outputs

52. According to Lean-Six Sigma, the 8 sources of waste include everything except:
    (Operational Aspects of Management)

    A. Defects

    B. Overproduction

    C. Non-utilized talent

    D. Overtime

    E. Inventory-in-process

53. The most integrated way to create a direct presence within a foreign market is through:
    (International Management and Contemporary Issues)

    A. WFOE

    B. Licensing

    C. Joint venture

    D. Exporting

    E. Outsourcing

54. In SWOT, ___ is an example of "W" and ___ is an example of "O":
    (Operational Aspects of Management)

    A. Small HR pool in area, small population leading to insufficient revenues

    B. Efficient inventory management, cost-leader strategy from low costs

    C. Low brand recognition, cult following with potential for niche market strategy

    D. High materials costs, price competition

    E. Unique product, lack of sustainable advantage due to no IP registration

55. Something must be ___ and ___ to maintain a sustainable competitive advantage:
    (Operational Aspects of Management)

    A. Valuable, exchangeable

    B. Unsubstitutable, irreplaceable

    C. Rare, inimitable

    D. Rare, exchangeable

    E. Valuable, irreplaceable

56. ___ is the person who influences decisions by using indirect information to guide other to come to the desired conclusion:
    (Functional Aspects of Management)

    A. Idea planters

    B. Predictors

    C. Trend setters

    D. Persuaders

    E. Negotiators

57. According to JIT ___:
    (Functional Aspects of Management)

    A. Reserve inventory should always be held to account for variations from predicted sales volume

    B. The only reserve inventory to be held is that which will be used in the next month

    C. The only reserve inventory to be held is that which will be used biweekly

    D. The only reserve inventory to be held is that which will be used in the next week

    E. No reserve inventory should be held

58. **How is PESTEL different in a global environment than a domestic one:**
(International Management and Contemporary Issues)

A. Economical factors must include a corrective index to account for different economic structures

B. Sociocultural factors become impossible to predict in foreign nations

C. The interaction between nations creates dynamics more complex than both nations by themselves

D. You must include political factors

E. There is no difference

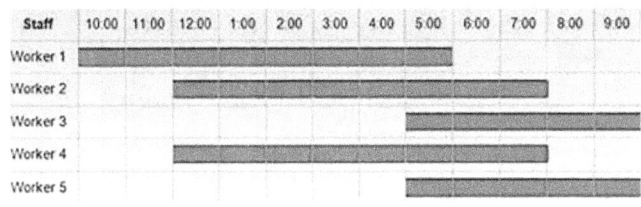

59. **What does this say about operations:**
(Organization and Human resources)

A. Open from 10am-9pm with a shift change at 7pm and mornings are busier than evening

B. Open from 10am-9pm with a shift change at 5pm and mornings are busier than evenings

C. A one-day project starting at 10am with a deadline of 9pm has up to 5 workers on it at any time

D. One person opens at 10am, 2 people close at 9pm, and there are 4 employees to the manager

E. The period of 5pm-7pm is the busiest, requiring the most people

PRINCIPLES OF MANAGEMENT

60. Decentralization requires _____ in order to _____:
    (Organization and Human Resources)

    A. Decreased authority in first-line management, empower employees

    B. Increased authority in middle management, maintain control

    C. Increased authority in first-line management, be responsive to customers

    D. Empowerment of middle management, make decisions

    E. Centralization, maintain order

61. The Foreign Corrupt Practices Act:
    (International Management and Contemporary Issues)

    A. Bans the bribing of domestic officials by US or foreign citizens

    B. Bans the bribing of domestic officials by foreigners, and holds foreign corporations listed domestically to SEC laws

    C. Bans US citizens from banning foreign officials or domestic officials

    D. Bans the bribing of foreign officials, bans the bribing of domestic officials by foreigners

    E. Bans the bribing of foreign officials, and holds foreign corporations listed domestically to SEC laws

62. According to _____, management involves using the scientific method to break-down each function into rigid specializations in a mass-production environment:
    (International Management and Contemporary Issues)

    A. Henri Fayol

    B. David Aaker

    C. FW Taylor

    D. Charon Drotter

    E. Max Weber

63. Henry Ford, founder of the Ford Motor Company, paid twice the standard salary because:
    (Organization and Human Resources)

    A. It allowed employees to purchase the products they were making

    B. Paying standard wages gave people little incentive to stay, creating huge turnover costs

    C. To attract highly-skilled workers

    D. To increase aggregate demand using the income effect

    E. To motivate employees to be more productive

PRINCIPLES OF MANAGEMENT

64. According to ____, management must include participative setting of objectives:
    (International Management and Contemporary Issues)

    A. Frederick Herzberg

    B. Geert Hoftsede

    C. Abraham Maslow

    D. FW Taylor

    E. Peter Drucker

65. Lower wages do not lead to higher employment because:
    (Organization and Human Resources)

    A. Fewer people are willing to work at a given price level despite their need to survive

    B. Companies will never hire more people than they need to meet production demand, regardless of wage level

    C. Lower wages cause greater per-person output

    D. Higher employment requires higher price levels to increase supply

    E. Unions prevent labor negotiations

66. According to Blanchard and Hersey, the ___ management style is used when employees are most developed, and ___ when they are least developed:
    (Functional Aspects of Management)

    A. Coaching, directing

    B. Delegating, supporting

    C. Coaching, supporting

    D. Delegating, directing

    E. Directing, delegating

67. The 20-70-10 rule states:
    (Organization and Human Resources)

    A. Employees in the bottom 70% of productivity must be replaced, those in the top 10% supported, and the remaining 20% coached

    B. Employees get 10% of their skills from training, 70% from working, and the remaining 20% from work socialization

    C. Employees in the bottom 20% of productivity must be replaced, those in the top 10% supported, and the remaining 70% coached

    D. Employees in the bottom 10% of productivity must be replaced, those in the top 20% supported, and the remaining 70% coached

    E. Employees get 70% of their skills from training, 10% from working, and the remaining 20% from work socialization

68. According to Hofstede, the degree to which a culture values gain and achievement over social cohesion is called:
(International Management and Contemporary Issues)

   A. Indulgence

   B. Masculinity

   C. Individualism

   D. Time orientation

   E. Power distance

69. Hofstede and GLOBE share which cultural dimension:
(International Management and Contemporary Issues)

   A. Uncertainty avoidance

   B. Gender egalitarianism

   C. Performance orientation

   D. In-group collectivism

   E. Humane orientation

70. According to the original Civil Rights Act of 1964, it was legal to discriminate employment based on:
(Organization and Human Resources)

   A. Disability

   B. Gender

   C. Race

   D. Religion

   E. Color

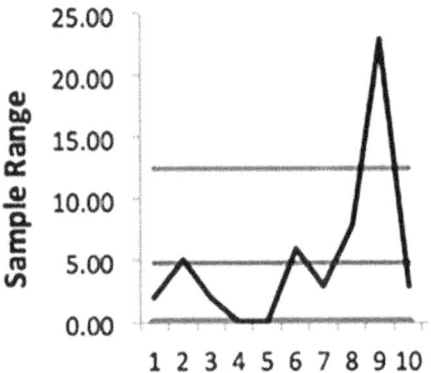

71. In statistical process control, this is typical of:
(Functional Aspects of Management)

   A. A systematic flaw causing consistent variability

   B. An anomalous or temporary flaw in the production cycle

   C. Volatile production growth

   D. Seasonal production variations

   E. Normal production quality

72. **A behavior is considered unlawful harassment when:**
    (Organization and Human Resources)

    A. The behavior is not appropriate in the workplace

    B. An individual perceives the behavior as offensive

    C. It is persistent or severe enough to make the workplace intimidating

    D. The behavior breaks other laws

    E. The behavior is socially inappropriate

73. **A company is held liable for harassment within the workplace when:**
    (Organization and Human Resources)

    A. Companies are never held liable, only people

    B. It fails to act on any harassment brought to its attention

    C. It fails to provide workplace equality training during orientation

    D. It fails to act on harassment brought to its attention, or immediately when supervisors harass

    E. Companies are always immediately liable for what happens

74. **__ is not a type of compensation:**
    (Organization and Human Resources)

    A. Wages

    B. Insurance benefits

    C. Flex time

    D. 401(k) matching

    E. Pensions

75. **Each limits the bargaining power of individual employees except:**
    (Organization and Human Resources)

    A. The high cost of developing new skills relative to low income

    B. Government regulation

    C. The majority of labor does not have the savings to survive for extended negotiations or job search

    D. Low skill requirements for those jobs most vulnerable

    E. Lack of equivalent access to legal and PR resources

76. **Performance appraisals must be all except:**
    (Organization and Human Resources)

    A. Performed regularly

    B. Clear and specific

    C. Objectively measured

    D. Strict

    E. Individualized

77. **Which is not a tool used to create a cohesive virtual environment:**
    (Functional Aspects of Management)

    A. Instant messaging

    B. Cloud computing

    C. Database management systems

    D. Collaborative workspace

    E. Video conferencing

78. **____ is not one of the reasons workplace diversity is important:**
    (Organization and Human Resources)

    A. Different perspectives increases innovation and improves idea pool

    B. Larger labor pools increase total labor potential

    C. Affirmative action requires special consideration for underrepresented groups

    D. Demographic equivalence improves responsiveness to changing markets

    E. Workplace diversity expands market size and/or market share

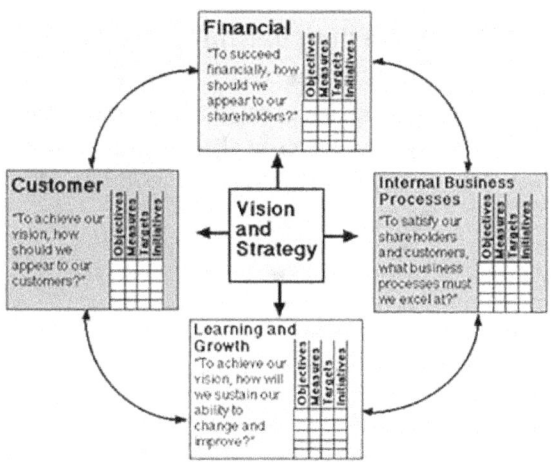

79. This is ____, which _____:
    (Functional Aspects of Management)

    A. Balanced scorecard, evaluates the degree to which different functions are prepared to pursue a strategy initiative before execution

    B. Balanced scorecard, assesses the degree to which operations support the overall strategy

    C. Balanced scorecard, calculates the resource utilization of different functions dedicated to a strategic initiative

    D. Strategic operations chart, defines the way in which organizational operations must function to achieve strategic goals

    E. Strategy control graph, assesses the degree to which operations support the overall strategy

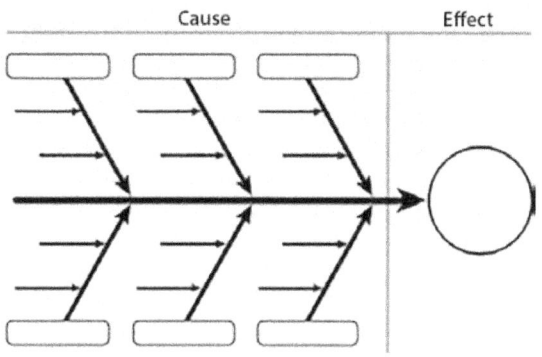

80. This is ____ :
    (Functional Aspects of Management)

    A. Causal loop diagram

    B. Cause-effect graph

    C. Why-because analysis

    D. Ishikawa diagram

    E. Causal diagram

81. In a corporation, top management is hired by:
    (Organization and Human Resources)

    A. Board of directors

    B. Shareholders

    C. Stakeholders

    D. Executives

    E. Front-line management

PRINCIPLES OF MANAGEMENT

82. In a corporation, board of directors is hired by:
    (Organization and Human Resources)

    A. Board of directors

    B. Shareholders

    C. Stakeholders

    D. Executives

    E. Front-line management

83. The four functions of management does not include:
    (Functional Aspects of Management)

    A. Planning

    B. Organizing

    C. Marketing

    D. Leading

    E. Controlling

84. According to Mintzberg, the role of the manager which involves communicating information to people outside the organization is:
    (Functional Aspects of Management)

    A. Disseminator

    B. Spokesperson

    C. Monitor

    D. Figurehead

    E. Liaison

85. According to Mintzberg, the role of the manager which includes networking within and outside the organization is:
    (Functional Aspects of Management)

    A. Liaison

    B. Spokesperson

    C. Figurehead

    D. Disseminator

    E. Monitor

86. According to Mintzberg, the role of the manager which involves defending the interests of the business is:
(Functional Aspects of Management)

   A. Disturbance handler

   B. Entrepreneur

   C. Negotiator

   D. Resource allocator

   E. Leader

87. Which are traditionally listed as part of the managerial skill set:
(Functional Aspects of Management)

   A. Technical skills, human skills

   B. Human skills, marketing skills

   C. Conceptual skills, accounting skills

   D. Technical skills, marketing skills

   E. Human skills, accounting skills

88. ___ refers to those actions and behaviors which people believe to be important:
(Functional Aspects of Management)

   A. Morals

   B. Principles

   C. Beliefs

   D. Values

   E. Ethics

89. Setting goals does not:
(Functional Aspects of Management)

   A. Function has a comprehensive plan

   B. Provide guidance and direction

   C. Create a foundation for organized planning

   D. Establish challenging milestones to motivate staff

   E. Provide a method for evaluating performance

90. The official parameters set by an organization outlining an activity or response is called:
    (Functional Aspects of Management)

    A. Regulations

    B. Rules

    C. Procedures

    D. Laws

    E. Norms

91. Which type of grand strategy can involve selling current business units:
    (Functional Aspects of Management)

    A. Retrenchment

    B. Global

    C. Growth

    D. Stability

    E. Business

92. According to the rational model, the decision-making process includes everything except:
    (Functional Aspects of Management)

    A. Assess options

    B. Determine the point of acceptable satisficing

    C. Make decision

    D. Define the problem

    E. Evaluate results

93. Which is a potential disadvantage of group decision-making:
    (Functional Aspects of Management)

    A. Greater error recognition

    B. Improved morale through participation

    C. Greater acceptance of decision by staff

    D. Diffusion of responsibility

    E. Expanded knowledge pool

PRINCIPLES OF MANAGEMENT

94. **Techniques teams can use to stimulate creative problem solving include everything except ___, which is typically used by individuals:**
    (Functional Aspects of Management)

    A. Brainstorming

    B. Delphi technique

    C. Cross-fertilization

    D. Nominal group technique

    E. Devil's advocacy

95. **Fast, repetitive production environments are facilitated by a ____, and creative environments of dynamic challenges by a _____:**
    (Functional Aspects of Management)

    A. Industrial system, organic system

    B. Mechanistic system, organic system

    C. Natural system, Mechanistic system

    D. Industrial system, natural system

    E. Mechanistic system, mechanistic system

96. **Horizontal organizations are unique because:**
    (Functional Aspects of Management)

    A. They formed as a result of horizontal integration with other organizations

    B. They have a small number of employees per manager

    C. They emphasize functional integration and personal empowerment over hierarchy

    D. They give greater authority to employees than management

    E. They are the inverse of vertical organizations

97. **Perceptual errors in leadership do not include:**
    (Functional Aspects of Management)

    A. Halo effect

    B. Strictness or leniency

    C. Expectancy effect

    D. Projection effect

    E. Selective perception

98. **Which type of team is best when highly specialized operations are involved:**
    (Functional Aspects of Management)

    A. Dysfunctional team

    B. Cross-functional team

    C. Functional team

    D. Vertical team

    E. Project

99. **What type of team is best for executive operations:**
    (Basic Economic Concepts)

    A. Dysfunctional team

    B. Cross-functional team

    C. Functional team

    D. Vertical team

    E. Project team

100. **Groupthink is:**
    (Functional Aspects of Management)

    A. A form of group brainstorming

    B. The collective culture of an organization

    C. The aggregate knowledge set of a team

    D. The innovation created in large groups of highly specialized people

    E. A state in which conformity takes priority over critical thought

PRINCIPLES OF MANAGEMENT

Answer Key

Question Number	Correct Answer	Your Answer	Question Number	Correct Answer	Your Answer	Question Number	Correct Answer	Your Answer
1	B		36	C		71	B	
2	C		37	A		72	C	
3	C		38	A		73	D	
4	B		39	B		74	C	
5	C		40	B		75	B	
6	C		41	E		76	D	
7	D		42	A		77	C	
8	B		43	C		78	C	
9	B		44	D		79	B	
10	A		45	D		80	D	
11	B		46	A		81	A	
12	C		47	B		82	B	
13	E		48	A		83	C	
14	B		49	A		84	B	
15	A		50	A		85	A	
16	A		51	A		86	C	
17	B		52	D		87	A	
18	E		53	A		88	D	
19	A		54	C		89	A	
20	B		55	C		90	C	
21	A		56	A		91	A	
22	A		57	E		92	B	
23	A		58	C		93	D	
24	E		59	B		94	C	
25	A		60	C		95	B	
26	A		61	E		96	C	
27	A		62	C		97	B	
28	B		63	B		98	C	
29	E		64	E		99	B	
30	B		65	B		100	E	
31	B		66	D				
32	C		67	C				
33	A		68	B				
34	A		69	A				
35	E		70	A				

PRINCIPLES OF MANAGEMENT

RATIONALES

1. **According to equity theory:**
   (Operational Aspects of Management)

   A. (Employee B's rewards/Employee A's input) = (Employee A's rewards/Employee B's input)

   B. (Employee A's rewards/Employee A's input) = (Employee B's rewards/Employee B's input)

   C. (Employee A's rewards/Employee B's input) = (Employee B's rewards/Employee A's input)

   D. (Employee A's rewards/Employee A's input) > (Employee B's rewards/Employee B's input)

   E. (Employee A's rewards/Employee A's input) < (Employee B's rewards/Employee B's input)

The answer is B
Equity theory states that an employee compares the amount of work they do and the amount of reward they get to that of others.

2. **Productivity is:**
   (Operational Aspects of Management)

   A. Input*Output

   B. Input/Output

   C. Output/Input

   D. (Output-Input)/Output

   E. (Input-Output)/Input

The answer is C
The amount of output produced per unit of input is simple measure of productivity

PRINCIPLES OF MANAGEMENT

3. **The use of a neutral third party tasked with resolving a dispute but who doesn't have the authority to enforce the outcome is known as:**
   (Organization and Human Resources)

   A. Mediation

   B. Conciliation

   C. Arbitration

   D. Bargaining

   E. Litigation

The answer is C
Arbitration involves the use of an impartial "judge" who attempts to help people find a solution, and makes a determination, but it is not legally binding.

4. **___ is not one of Porter's five forces of environmental scanning:**
   (International Management and Contemporary Issues)

   A. Bargaining power of suppliers

   B. Regulation of governments

   C. Bargaining power of customers

   D. Threat of new entrants

   E. Threat of substitutes

The answer is B
Suppliers, Customers, Competitors, new entrants, substitutes

PRINCIPLES OF MANAGEMENT

5. ___ is an example of ethnocentrism:
   (International Management and Contemporary Issues)

   A. Opening a wholly-foreign owned enterprise before attempting licensing

   B. Mistranslations of promotional materials

   C. Managing team dynamics in foreign offices as in home offices

   D. Using the same asset management analytics in each global office

   E. Structuring a business by functional division rather than geography

The answer is C
Ethnocentrism occurs when you apply domestic standards of behavior to foreign workers.

6. ___ is an example of the maintenance group role:
   (Functional Aspects of Management)

   A. Making acquisition decisions for upcoming projects

   B. Collecting feedback on an internal policy change

   C. Alleviating office friction during end of fiscal year

   D. Playing "Devil's Advocate"

   E. Scheduling project milestones in line with final deadline

The answer is C
Maintenance means doing what's necessary to maximize cohesion within a group.

PRINCIPLES OF MANAGEMENT

7. **The highest degree of group autonomy is found in _____ groups:**
   (Functional Aspects of Management)

   A. Traditional

   B. Semi-autonomous

   C. Cross-functional

   D. Self-managed

   E. Virtual

The answer is D
Self-managed groups make most or all operational decisions themselves.

8. **A management method training employees on the operations of the company and the role of their primary function within it:**
   (Organization and Human Resources)

   A. Job enlargement

   B. Job rotation

   C. Job enrichment

   D. Job reengineering

   E. Job intensification

The answer is B
By briefly performing other jobs within the organization, you can learn the details of the inputs, outputs, and processes of others, improving coordination between job roles.

PRINCIPLES OF MANAGEMENT

9. **Equity theory requires the use of objective measurements of input because:**
   (Operational Aspects of Management)

   A. So that employees know what to expect in their rewards

   B. The endowment effect means each person values their own contributions more than equivalent contributions by others

   C. So that inputs and outputs can be readily calculated

   D. To set a prediction reference point relative to actual outcomes

   E. To set a reference point for negotiations in future exchanges

The answer is B
Each person places more value of their own contributions than on the contributions of others, making relative reward seem persistently inequitable, but this can be alleviated by tying rewards to clear and constant performance metrics.

10. **What type of plan is this**
    "Over the next 5 years we will expand the total market by targeting previously untouched demographics":
    (Functional Aspects of Management)

    A. Strategic

    B. Tactical

    C. Operational

    D. Project

    E. Contingency

The answer is A
Strategic plans deal with the broad direction a company takes, rather than the detailed functions which allow it to pursue its strategy. That's also the difference between a CEO and a COO – CEO makes a plan, COO makes it happen.

PRINCIPLES OF MANAGEMENT

11. **Who is in charge of establishing operational plans:**
    (Functional Aspects of Management)

    A. Middle managers

    B. First-line managers

    C. Executive managers

    D. Financial managers

    E. Shift managers

The answer is B
First-line managers are the people who direct the day-to-day activities of production staff.

12. **The best contingency plans:**
    (Functional Aspects of Management)

    A. Deviate from the optimal plan at the point of change, preserving the value of the previous steps

    B. Are fully established plans wholly separate from the optimal plan

    C. Set alternatives for each step which feed back into the optimal plan

    D. Should be pursued simultaneously to the optimal plan

    E. Should only be developed if the optimal plan fails

The answer is C
To avoid sunk costs from aimless floundering, each step in a plan has its own contingency plan to get back on track.

PRINCIPLES OF MANAGEMENT

13. **In change management, all the following are part of the unfreezing process except:**
    (Functional Aspects of Management)

    A. Surveying employees about their jobs and how they can be improved

    B. Quantify the operational, competitive, and financial impact of elements to be changed

    C. Reinforcing the negative aspects of current methods in the minds of the staff

    D. Communicating controlled isolation of the problem with plans for improvement that doesn't extend into the rest of the organization

    E. Implementing new policies

The answer is E
Unfreezing involves preparing the organization to change by sowing discontent with those things which are going to be changed.

14. **At 6σ, the ideal goal of Six Sigma quality management, there are ____ DPMO with a ____ percentage yield:**
    (Operational Aspects of Management)

    A. 0.019, 99.9999981

    B. 3.4, 99.99966

    C. 233, 99.977

    D. 6,210, 99.38

    E. 66,807, 93.3

The answer is B
3.4 defective parts per million opportunities lies at 6 standard deviations from the mean, according to 6σ.

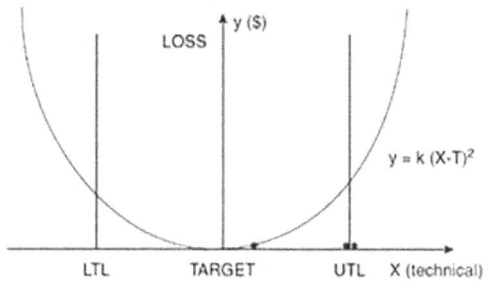

15. The Taguchi Loss Function states:
(Operational Aspects of Management)

A. Deviations from target specifications create a loss which increases exponentially and must not exceed upper and lower limits

B. Quality management operations must be effective enough to be financially viable, but not to the point that its costs exceed its benefits

C. The defective parts per million opportunities will increase the costs of fixing/reconstructing defective output more than the costs of preventing them

D. Increasing losses create deviations from planned growth rates which become unsustainable at upper and lower limits

E. Losses are a function of parabolic curves

The answer is A
As a quality management tool, the TLF is used to estimate the amount of loss associated with missed specification targets.

16. $100,000 earned at complete project
    Planned 10 week deadline, linear PV
    $60,000 EV at 5 weeks
    What is the SPI:
    (Operational Aspects of Management)

    A. 120%

    B. 83%

    C. 10%

    D. -10%

    E. 100%

The answer is A
If a project is exactly on budget and deadline then the schedule performance index will be 100%. If it's ahead of schedule and/or under budget, it'll be over 100%.

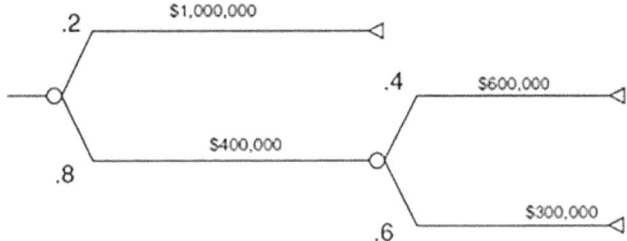

17. The adjusted values at the 2nd node of this decision tree are:
    (Functional Aspects of Management)

    A. -$200,000, $100,000

    B. $240,000, $180,000

    C. $300,000, -$300,000

    D. $200,000, $320,000

    E. $240,000, $300,000

The answer is B
Each potential choice is valued using a combination of the earned value of success, adjusted for the probability of success.

Severity \ Probability		Frequent A	Likely B	Occasional C	Seldom D	Unlikely E
Catastrophic	I	E	E	H	H	M
Critical	II	E	H	H	M	L
Moderate	III	H	M	M	L	L
Negligible	IV	M	L	L	L	L

18. In the management of a fire department, the risk to individual staff members is: *(Functional Aspects of Management)*

    A. None

    B. Low (L)

    C. Moderate (M)

    D. High (H)

    E. Extreme (E)

The answer is E
Fire fighters are at least likely to encounter a fire as it is the nature of their jobs, and the threat fire poses is quite high. Such an extreme risk warrants a large degree of mitigation.

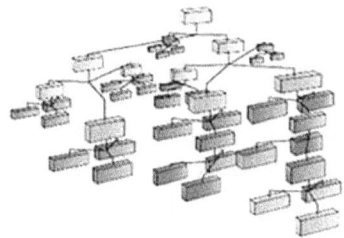

19. Models such as this are most commonly used to depict: *(Functional Aspects of Management)*

    A. Organizational hierarchy

    B. Product portfolio

    C. Subsidiary structure

    D. Capital assets

    E. Team motivation drivers

The answer is A
Positional authority structure determines the shape, and each box is a different job, with its own functions, required skills, etc.

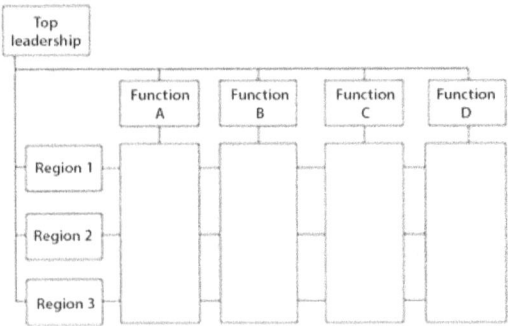

20. **This represents:**
    (Functional Aspects of Management)

    A. Divisional management

    B. Matrix management

    C. Micromanagement

    D. Tight matrix

    E. Organizational spreadsheet

The answer is B:
Matrix structures are difficult to execute due to the high potential for conflicting requests, orders, and loyalties.

PRINCIPLES OF MANAGEMENT

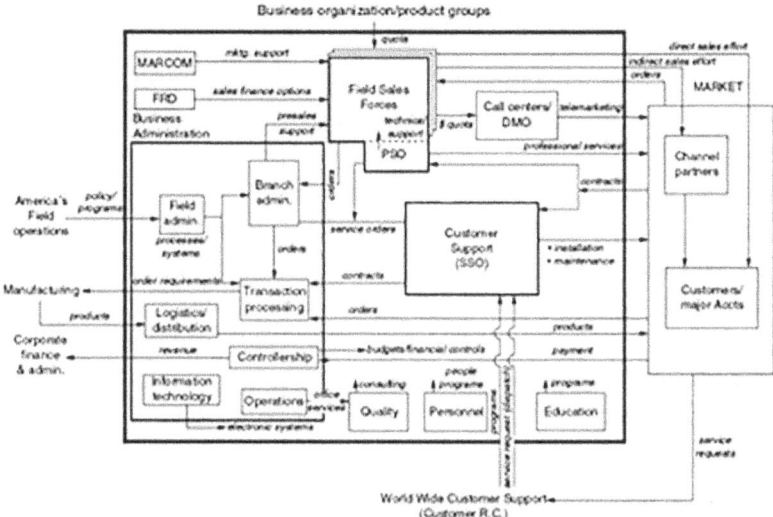

21. This is called ____ which represents ____:
    (Functional Aspects of Management)

    A. Process flowchart, dynamic operations of an organization

    B. Organizational structure, management hierarchy

    C. Schematic diagram, an electrical circuit

    D. Organizational structure, dynamic operations of an organization

    E. Process flowchart, management hierarchy

The answer is A
Every function of an organization can be modeled using a process flowchart.

22. **In Maslow's Hierarchy of Needs, self-actualization is found at:**
    (Organization and Human Resources)

    A. 1

    B. 2

    C. 3

    D. 4

    E. 5

The answer is A
Typically, before a person can pursue self-actualization, they must first meet their baser needs, such as getting paid enough for shelter, and having confidence in their abilities. This is what makes pursuing the life of an artist or writer often so challenging – the pursuit starts with self-actualization.

PRINCIPLES OF MANAGEMENT

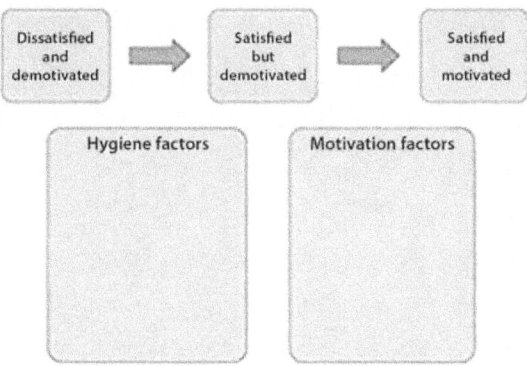

23. In Herzberg's Two-Factor Theory of Motivation, ____ is a hygiene factor and ___ is a motivator:
    (Organization and Human Resources)

    A. Wages, prestige

    B. Responsibility, working conditions

    C. Promotions, job security

    D. Sense of purpose, clear expectations

    E. Recognition, professional relationships

The answer is A
Hygiene factors will keep their jobs over hygiene factors, reducing the costs of employment turnover, but for them to strive for excellence they must be motivated.

PRINCIPLES OF MANAGEMENT

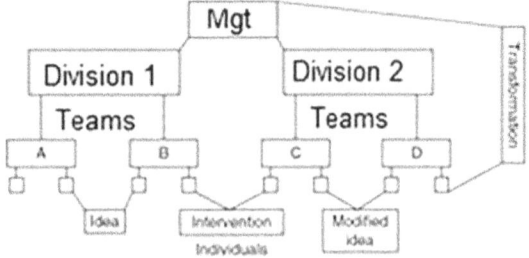

24. This graph illustrates:
(Functional Aspects of Management)

A. Structure of authority

B. Team-based project management

C. Organizational decision making process

D. Bottom-up communication

E. The flow of information in managing continuous improvement

The answer is E:
A productive company culture starts with management, but is customized by individuals, shaping the way management makes future decisions about the people and structures of which culture is composed.

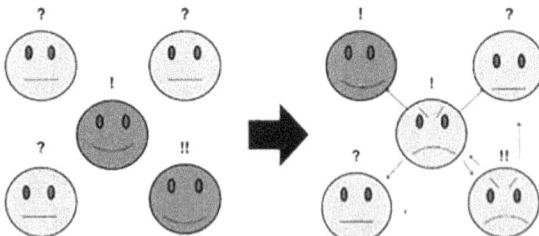

25. This diagram on conflict creation illustrates the need for:
(Functional Aspects of Management)

A. Clear direction and dissemination of information from management

B. The need for arbitration during the decision making process

C. Multiple styles of negotiations

D. Constructive forms of persuasion

E. Team development programs

The answer is A
Conflict comes from differences in ideas about the way things should be. Confusion or lack of clear direction breeds a lot of conflict.

PRINCIPLES OF MANAGEMENT

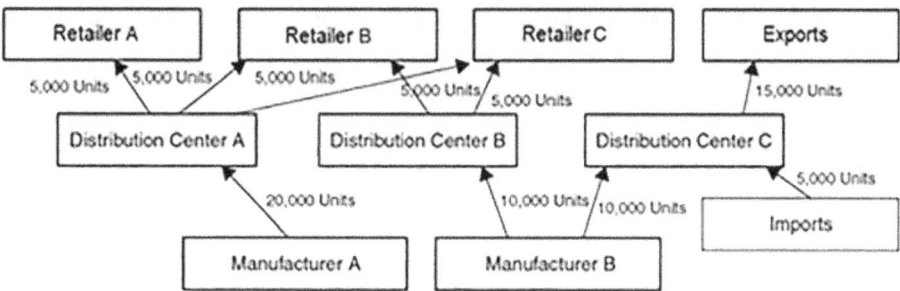

26. **Which manufacturer has the lowest-risk supply chain:**
    (Operational Aspects of Management)

    A. Manufacturer B because 100% of their production has multiple channels to the end consumer

    B. Manufacturer A because their primary distribution center sells to 50% more retailers than 2nd highest

    C. Manufacturer A because they are not competing with foreign imports

    D. Manufacturer B because they have domestic and foreign sales

    E. Both manufacturers A and B have equal risk of disrupted supply chains

The answer is A
Ensuring you have multiple options – plans and contingency plans – is the key to mitigating risk.

27. **___ is a form of ____ given to first-line managers, though ____ is often reserved for middle management:**
    (Functional Aspects of Management)

    A. Reward authority, legitimate power, coercive authority

    B. Personal power, legitimate power, positional authority

    C. Referent authority, personal power, coercive authority

    D. Reward authority, personal power, coercive authority

    E. Coercive authority, legitimate power, positional authority

The answer is A
The authority to give bonuses, hold contests, and so forth improves the dynamic between managers and employees, but those things which can harm morale is frequently reserved for managers which the employees don't usually interact with regularly.

PRINCIPLES OF MANAGEMENT

28. ___ is acquired by being charismatic or motivational, rather than having any formal power:
    (Functional Aspects of Management)

    A. Expert authority

    B. Referent authority

    C. Positional authority

    D. Reward authority

    E. Coercive authority

The answer is B
Much of the power people hold over us is freely given just by nature of the social dynamic; expert authority is given because someone knows more about a topic than you, and referent authority is given just because that person can talk us into acting.

29. Compartmentalization of operations to prevent interaction and communication is typically used to:
    (Functional Aspects of Management)

    A. This is never done in a healthy organization

    B. To create an immersive environment during job rotation training

    C. To prevent interaction between men and women in some highly orthodox cultures

    D. To prevent conflict with competing individuals or teams

    E. Prevent any person from having access to the whole of proprietary information

The answer is E
For secret, proprietary information related to your strategic advantage or core operations, it can be useful to split the function into multiple parts and separate those parts so that "the right hand doesn't know what the left is doing", so to speak.

30. **The point in the team development process in which members conflict with each other as they establish roles and culture is called:**
    (Functional Aspects of Management)

    A. Forming

    B. Storming

    C. Norming

    D. Performing

    E. Adjourning

The answer is B
Until the members of a team all hold the same ideas of how operations and interpersonal interactions should be, minor conflicts will persist.

31. **The point in which a manager will most likely need to validate the credentials of a member is:**
    (Functional Aspects of Management)

    A. Adjourning

    B. Forming

    C. Storming

    D. Norming

    E. Performing

The answer is B
If someone is introduced to a team and the rest of the team isn't familiar with them, it's up to management to validate competence in order to expedite the building of trust and incorporation into a group.

32. **According to Kohlberg's Stages of Moral Development, how should a manager address an individual at Stage 4:**
    (Functional Aspects of Management)

    A. Emphasize conditioning systems of reward and punishment

    B. Emphasize personal gain to be earned in negotiated terms

    C. Emphasize the importance of policies and organizational authority

    D. Emphasize the mutual benefits of constructed operations and dynamics

    E. Emphasize conforming to organizational roles and cultures as a means of acceptance

The answer is C
People at Stage 4 look to authority and structure to make decisions of morality

33. **According to Kohlberg's Moral Development, how should a manager address an individual at Stage 3:**
    (Functional Aspects of Management)

    A. Emphasize conforming to organizational roles and cultures as a means of acceptance

    B. Emphasize the importance of policies and organizational authority

    C. Emphasize the mutual benefits of constructed operations and dynamics

    D. Emphasize conditioning systems of reward and punishment

    E. Emphasize personal gain to be earned in negotiated terms

The answer is A
People at Stage 3 rely on assessments of what other people want, and what will maximize social inclusion, for moral decisions.

PRINCIPLES OF MANAGEMENT

34. Motivation is mathematically represented as:
(Organization and Human Resources)

    A. (Expectancy*Value)/(1+Impulsiveness*Delay)

    B. Expectancy*Value

    C. (Expectancy*Value)/(1+Impulsiveness)

    D. Expected Value – Expected Costs

    E. Expected Value/(Impulsiveness*Delay)

The answer is A
Motivation is driven by future expectations, but mitigated by a person's inability to maintain a given level of activity over longer periods of time.

35. The negotiating style which incluldes offering either fake or inconsequential concessions in order to gain on those things which matter to you is called:
(Functional Aspects of Management)

    A. Accommodating

    B. Avoiding

    C. Collaborating

    D. Competing

    E. Compromising

The answer is E
False compromise that is clear to others can create distrust, actually making the true issues at hand more difficult to negotiate. Best to be as genuine as possible.

PRINCIPLES OF MANAGEMENT

36. The negotiating style which involves intentionally keeping negotiations on aspects which are not issues of conflict in order to draw the other person in is called:
    (Functional Aspects of Management)

    A. Collaborating

    B. Competing

    C. Avoiding

    D. Accommodating

    E. Compromising

The answer is C
Avoiding the true topics of contention can make secondary matters easier to resolve if you don't intend to use them as negotiation pieces, and it creates a unique dynamic wherein the other person is pursuing you, thus putting them at a disadvantage so long as you can maintain avoidance longer than their ability to be patient about it.

37. Employees each produce 10 units per day, units sell for $100 each with a total cost of $90 per unit entirely composed of labor. If it takes 5 days to train a new employee, what is the turnover cost:
    (Organization and Human Resources)

    A. $5,000

    B. $4,500

    C. $500

    D. $450

    E. $0

The answer is A
Even assuming management can instantly replace a lost employee, the training period results in $1,000 per day of lost revenues, which is the amount of differential between maintaining an employee and training a new one.

PRINCIPLES OF MANAGEMENT

38. Per day, experienced staff produce 500 units and earn $100.
    Per day, new staff produce 300 units and earn $50.
    Training takes 5 days and each unit produced is worth $1
    The calculation to analyze the wage productivity differential is:
    (Organization and Human Resources)

    A. (500/100)n – ((300/50)n-250)

    B. ((300/50)n-250)-(500/100)n

    C. (100/500)n-(300/50)n

    D. (500/100)n-(300/50)n

    E. (500-300)n/100-250

The answer is A
In changing labor markets, new employees often don't have the same amount of bargaining power, allowing for lower relative costs, but the cost savings must be more than the amount of lost productivity and the cost of training.

39. Setup costs = $10
    Demand = 100
    Production cost = $20
    Interest rate = 100%
    EOQ is:
    (Operational Aspects of Management)

    A. 5

    B. 10

    C. 50

    D. 100

    E. 500

The answer is B
$\sqrt{(2SD)/(PI)}$

PRINCIPLES OF MANAGEMENT

COSTS	IN-HOUSE	OUTSOURCED
Billing department costs	$118,000	$4,000
Software and hardware costs	$7,500	$500
Direct claim processing costs	$3,600	$122,500
Software and hardware costs	$5,500	$2,000
% of billings collected	60%	70%
Collections	$1,370,900	$1,623,000
Collections costs	$129,100	$127,000
Collections, net of costs		

40. **Decide whether to outsource:**
    (Organization and Human Resources)

    A. Do not outsource to prevent losing $254,200

    B. Outsource to gain $254,200

    C. Do both to gain $254,200

    D. End function completely to prevent losing $254,200

    E. Panic

The answer is B
Using transfer pricing, the amount of cost and revenue created from each production function can be calculated, and then if an outside company can perform that function more effectively then outsourcing it the best option.

41. **It is best to use an authoratarian leadership style when:**
    (Functional Aspects of Management)

    A. During skill development programs

    B. When interpersonal conflict begins to hinder basic work functions

    C. When seeking input for revision of internal policies

    D. When managing skilled experts working in creative conditions

    E. During times of crisis when change must be rapid

The answer is E
Authoritarian leadership is the fastest and most decisive, but is likely to be rejected by others unless it is acknowledged that such emergency actions are warranted.

PRINCIPLES OF MANAGEMENT

42. **A pacesetting leadership style intended to facilitate the staff's activities is best used when:**
    (Functional Aspects of Management)

    A. When managing skilled experts working in creative conditions

    B. When seeking input for revision of internal policies

    C. When interpersonal conflict begins to hinder basic work functions

    D. During times of crisis when change must be rapid

    E. During skill development programs

The answer is A
If employees already have the expertise and motivation to accomplish their goals, then it is up to management to create an environment where they can best apply their skills.

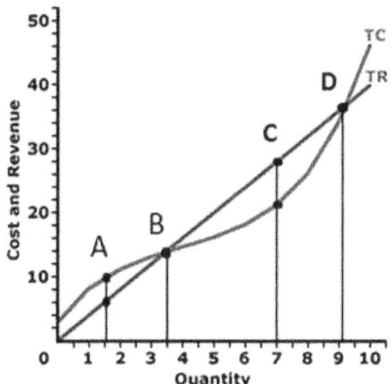

43. **For profit-maximizing firms efficiency is optimized at __ and for revenue-maximizing firms at ___:**
    (Operational Aspects of Management)

    A. B, C

    B. D, C

    C. C, D

    D. C, B

    E. B, D

The answer is C
Profit maximization is best when using a differentiation/quality strategy, while revenue maximization is best for price leadership strategies.

PRINCIPLES OF MANAGEMENT

44. Under generic competitive conditions, productive efficiency is achieved at:
(Operational Aspects of Management)

    A. MC=FC

    B. FC=AC

    C. VC=FC

    D. MC=AC

    E. MC=TC

The answer is D
Marginal cost will start under average cost due to the role of fixed cost, bringing average cost down, but after marginal cost surpasses average cost, then the average will increase again.

45. Which is not a type of team dysfunction:
(Functional Aspects of Management)

    A. Groupthink

    B. Interpersonal conflict

    C. Freeriding

    D. Comprehensive input

    E. Lack of individualization

The answer is D
Teams have a lot of problems that need to be controlled, but having more people contribute their ideas and feedback is a good thing.

PRINCIPLES OF MANAGEMENT

46. Analysis paralysis typically results from:
(Functional Aspects of Management)

A. Lack of decisive confidence

B. Too much information

C. Too little information

D. Too much or too little information

E. Rapidly changing business environment

The answer is A
All decisions are made without perfect information, and if faced with too much information it's up to management to quickly decide what information to use and how quickly the decision must be made.

47. The shareholder wealth maximization model is concerned with:
(International Management and Contemporary Issues)

A. Increasing current profitability

B. Increasing the value of company equity

C. Maximizing the value that the company creates for those which it influences

D. Increasing company revenue growth

E. Increasing NPV of company investments

The answer is B
It is up to management to do whatever is best for the owners of a company, and in a corporation the owners are the shareholders.

PRINCIPLES OF MANAGEMENT

48. **Which of the following is not a stakeholder:**
    (International Management and Contemporary Issues)

    A. Competitors

    B. Shareholders

    C. Employees

    D. Customers

    E. Partners

The answer is A
The formal definition of a stakeholder is "those groups without whose support the organization would cease to exist."

49. **Agency problems result from:**
    (International Management and Contemporary Issues)

    A. Executives who manage a company in a manner contrary to that which benefits the shareholders

    B. Executives who manage a company in a manner contrary to that which benefits the stakeholders

    C. Contradictions between the benefits of the shareholders and stakeholders

    D. Managers who embezzle money from the company

    E. Inefficient functions such as bid rigging and nepotism

The answer is A
The separation of ownership and management creates conflicts of interest and other problems of agency.

PRINCIPLES OF MANAGEMENT

50. A short organization is one which has:
(Functional Aspects of Management)

    A. Few degrees of management with a larger volume of staff per manager

    B. More degrees of management with a lower volume of staff per manager

    C. Few degrees of management with a lower volume of staff per manager

    D. More degrees of management with a with a larger volume of staff per manager

    E. Few degrees of management with higher staff empowerment

The answer is A
"Tall" and "short" refer to the height of the organizational structure – the number of levels of authority in a chain of command.

51. SIPOC analysis includes each except:
(Organization and Human Resources)

    A. Competitors

    B. Supplier

    C. Inputs

    D. Processes

    E. Outputs

The answer is A
The "C" stands for customers – SIPOC is all about value creation.

PRINCIPLES OF MANAGEMENT

52. **According to Lean-Six Sigma, the 8 sources of waste include everything except:**
    (Operational Aspects of Management)

    A. Defects

    B. Overproduction

    C. Non-utilized talent

    D. Overtime

    E. Inventory-in-process

The answer is D
The sources of waste can be remembered using "DOWNTIME", but overtime contributes to production, not waste.

53. **The most integrated way to create a direct presence within a foreign market is through:**
    (International Management and Contemporary Issues)

    A. WFOE

    B. Licensing

    C. Joint venture

    D. Exporting

    E. Outsourcing

The answer is A
Subsidiary ownership is most immersive option of foreign expansion

PRINCIPLES OF MANAGEMENT

54. **In SWOT, ___ is an example of "W" and ___ is an example of "O":**
    (Operational Aspects of Management)

    A. Small HR pool in area, small population leading to insufficient revenues

    B. Efficient inventory management, cost-leader strategy from low costs

    C. Low brand recognition, cult following with potential for niche market strategy

    D. High materials costs, price competition

    E. Unique product, lack of sustainable advantage due to no IP registration

The answer is C
Sometimes companies with low brand recognition garner the attention of niche markets specifically because they are aren't well-known yet.

55. **Something must be ___ and ___ to maintain a sustainable competitive advantage:**
    (Operational Aspects of Management)

    A. Valuable, exchangeable

    B. Unsubstitutable, irreplaceable

    C. Rare, inimitable

    D. Rare, exchangeable

    E. Valuable, irreplaceable

The answer is C
Rare, valuable, inimitable, unsubstitutable

PRINCIPLES OF MANAGEMENT

56. ___ is the person who influences decisions by using indirect information to guide other to come to the desired conclusion:
    (Functional Aspects of Management)

    A. Idea planters

    B. Predictors

    C. Trend setters

    D. Persuaders

    E. Negotiators

The answer is A
Idea planters stimulate inception within others

57. According to JIT ____:
    (Functional Aspects of Management)

    A. Reserve inventory should always be held to account for variations from predicted sales volume

    B. The only reserve inventory to be held is that which will be used in the next month

    C. The only reserve inventory to be held is that which will be used biweekly

    D. The only reserve inventory to be held is that which will be used in the next week

    E. No reserve inventory should be held

The answer is E
It's the goal of just-in-time inventory management to strive to make products available just as customers need them in order to limit storage costs.

PRINCIPLES OF MANAGEMENT

58. **How is PESTEL different in a global environment than a domestic one:**
    (International Management and Contemporary Issues)

    A. Economical factors must include a corrective index to account for different economic structures

    B. Sociocultural factors become impossible to predict in foreign nations

    C. The interaction between nations creates dynamics more complex than both nations by themselves

    D. You must include political factors

    E. There is no difference

The answer is C
Each nation has its own environment, but the way these environments influence each other adds a complexity that must also be considered.

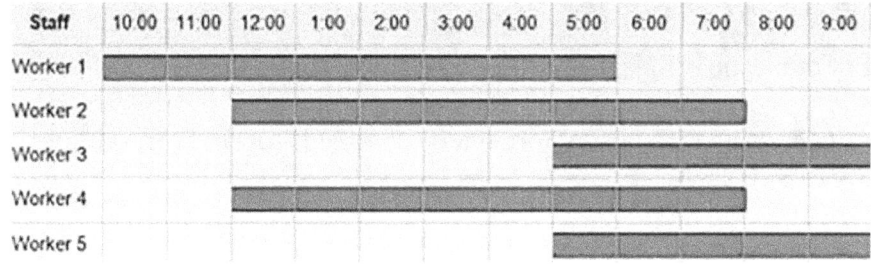

59. **What does this say about operations:**
    (Organization and Human resources)

    A. Open from 10am-9pm with a shift change at 7pm and mornings are busier than evening

    B. Open from 10am-9pm with a shift change at 5pm and mornings are busier than evenings

    C. A one-day project starting at 10am with a deadline of 9pm has up to 5 workers on it at any time

    D. One person opens at 10am, 2 people close at 9pm, and there are 4 employees to the manager

    E. The period of 5pm-7pm is the busiest, requiring the most people

The answer is B
Gantt charts are a great way to visualize staff scheduling

PRINCIPLES OF MANAGEMENT

60. **Decentralization requires ____ in order to ____:**
    (Organization and Human Resources)

    A. Decreased authority in first-line management, empower employees

    B. Increased authority in middle management, maintain control

    C. Increased authority in first-line management, be responsive to customers

    D. Empowerment of middle management, make decisions

    E. Centralization, maintain order

The answer is C
If lower-level staff aren't empowered to make decisions, decentralization will bring operations to a halt.

61. **The Foreign Corrupt Practices Act:**
    (International Management and Contemporary Issues)

    A. Bans the bribing of domestic officials by US or foreign citizens

    B. Bans the bribing of domestic officials by foreigners, and holds foreign corporations listed domestically to SEC laws

    C. Bans US citizens from banning foreign officials or domestic officials

    D. Bans the bribing of foreign officials, bans the bribing of domestic officials by foreigners

    E. Bans the bribing of foreign officials, and holds foreign corporations listed domestically to SEC laws

The answer is E
The FCPA dictates the interaction of Americans with foreign officials, and the manner in which foreign corporations interact with domestic shareholders.

PRINCIPLES OF MANAGEMENT

62. According to _____, management involves using the scientific method to break-down each function into rigid specializations in a mass-production environment:
    (International Management and Contemporary Issues)

    A. Henri Fayol

    B. David Aaker

    C. FW Taylor

    D. Charon Drotter

    E. Max Weber

The answer is C
This has been dubbed Taylorism.

63. Henry Ford, founder of the Ford Motor Company, paid twice the standard salary because:
    (Organization and Human Resources)

    A. It allowed employees to purchase the products they were making

    B. Paying standard wages gave people little incentive to stay, creating huge turnover costs

    C. To attract highly-skilled workers

    D. To increase aggregate demand using the income effect

    E. To motivate employees to be more productive

The answer is B
The turnover costs associated

PRINCIPLES OF MANAGEMENT

64. According to ____, management must include participative setting of objectives:
    (International Management and Contemporary Issues)

    A. Frederick Herzberg

    B. Geert Hoftsede

    C. Abraham Maslow

    D. FW Taylor

    E. Peter Drucker

The answer is E
When employees are included in setting objectives, they take greater ownership and have greater acceptance of them.

65. Lower wages do not lead to higher employment because:
    (Organization and Human Resources)

    A. Fewer people are willing to work at a given price level despite their need to survive

    B. Companies will never hire more people than they need to meet production demand, regardless of wage level

    C. Lower wages cause greater per-person output

    D. Higher employment requires higher price levels to increase supply

    E. Unions prevent labor negotiations

The answer is B
At the same time, companies will continue to hire as many people as they need to meet production demands regardless of gradual increases in minimum wages.

PRINCIPLES OF MANAGEMENT

66. According to Blanchard and Hersey, the ___ management style is used when employees are most developed, and ___ when they are least developed:
    (Functional Aspects of Management)

    A. Coaching, directing

    B. Delegating, supporting

    C. Coaching, supporting

    D. Delegating, directing

    E. Directing, delegating

The answer is D
Managers can continuously give autonomy to individual employees, changing the management style from directing, to coaching, to supporting, to delegating.

67. **The 20-70-10 rule states:**
    (Organization and Human Resources)

    A. Employees in the bottom 70% of productivity must be replaced, those in the top 10% supported, and the remaining 20% coached

    B. Employees get 10% of their skills from training, 70% from working, and the remaining 20% from work socialization

    C. Employees in the bottom 20% of productivity must be replaced, those in the top 10% supported, and the remaining 70% coached

    D. Employees in the bottom 10% of productivity must be replaced, those in the top 20% supported, and the remaining 70% coached

    E. Employees get 70% of their skills from training, 10% from working, and the remaining 20% from work socialization

The answer is C
The 20-70-10 rule has been largely rejected for its tendency to create frictional, low-morale working environment in which 1/5 of the company is constantly at risk.

PRINCIPLES OF MANAGEMENT

68. According to Hofstede, the degree to which a culture values gain and achievement over social cohesion is called:
    (International Management and Contemporary Issues)

    A. Indulgence

    B. Masculinity

    C. Individualism

    D. Time orientation

    E. Power distance

The answer is B
The dimension of masculinity/femininity has been criticized for its application of gender stereotypes to the label.

69. Hofstede and GLOBE share which cultural dimension:
    (International Management and Contemporary Issues)

    A. Uncertainty avoidance

    B. Gender egalitarianism

    C. Performance orientation

    D. In-group collectivism

    E. Humane orientation

The answer is A
Power distance is also found in both.

PRINCIPLES OF MANAGEMENT

70. According to the original Civil Rights Act of 1964, it was legal to discriminate employment based on:
    (Organization and Human Resources)

    A. Disability

    B. Gender

    C. Race

    D. Religion

    E. Color

The answer is A
The Age Discrimination Act of 1967 makes it illegal to discriminate against those aged 40 and over, but not under the age of 40.

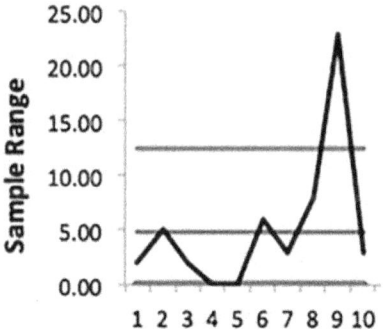

71. In statistical process control, this is typical of:
    (Functional Aspects of Management)

    A. A systematic flaw causing consistent variability

    B. An anomalous or temporary flaw in the production cycle

    C. Volatile production growth

    D. Seasonal production variations

    E. Normal production quality

The answer is B
Short, periodic deviations of quality outside production parameters result from problems which are not systematic, making them more difficult to identify.

301

PRINCIPLES OF MANAGEMENT

72. **A behavior is considered unlawful harassment when:**
    (Organization and Human Resources)

    A. The behavior is not appropriate in the workplace

    B. An individual perceives the behavior as offensive

    C. It is persistent or severe enough to make the workplace intimidating

    D. The behavior breaks other laws

    E. The behavior is socially inappropriate

The answer is C
Even if a behavior is not considered acceptable, to be considered unlawful there must either be a consistent pattern of that behavior, or the behavior must be relatively severe.

73. **A company is held liable for harassment within the workplace when:**
    (Organization and Human Resources)

    A. Companies are never held liable, only people

    B. It fails to act on any harassment brought to its attention

    C. It fails to provide workplace equality training during orientation

    D. It fails to act on harassment brought to its attention, or immediately when supervisors harass

    E. Companies are always immediately liable for what happens

The answer is D
If a behavior is not brought to the attention of management then they can't necessarily be expected to know it's happening, but if the behavior comes from a manager then they inherently know about it

PRINCIPLES OF MANAGEMENT

74. __ is not a type of compensation:
    (Organization and Human Resources)

    A. Wages

    B. Insurance benefits

    C. Flex time

    D. 401(k) matching

    E. Pensions

The answer is C
Flex time is a benefit, but it is not a form of remuneration.

75. **Each limits the bargaining power of individual employees except:**
    (Organization and Human Resources)

    A. The high cost of developing new skills relative to low income

    B. Government regulation

    C. The majority of labor does not have the savings to survive for extended negotiations or job search

    D. Low skill requirements for those jobs most vulnerable

    E. Lack of equivalent access to legal and PR resources

The answer is B
With the rise of unions in the early-20th century, government regulation actually facilitated the right to collective bargaining.

PRINCIPLES OF MANAGEMENT

76. **Performance appraisals must be all except:**
    (Organization and Human Resources)

    A. Performed regularly

    B. Clear and specific

    C. Objectively measured

    D. Strict

    E. Individualized

The answer is D
Rather than strict or lenient, it's important to be fair.

77. **Which is not a tool used to create a cohesive virtual environment:**
    (Functional Aspects of Management)

    A. Instant messaging

    B. Cloud computing

    C. Database management systems

    D. Collaborative workspace

    E. Video conferencing

The answer is C
Databases do not increase connectivity between individuals in a virtual organization, but they can be shared using methods which do.

78. _____ is not one of the reasons workplace diversity is important:
(Organization and Human Resources)

   A. Different perspectives increases innovation and improves idea pool

   B. Larger labor pools increase total labor potential

   C. Affirmative action requires special consideration for underrepresented groups

   D. Demographic equivalence improves responsiveness to changing markets

   E. Workplace diversity expands market size and/or market share

The answer is C
Data has shown that increased diversity improves the growth of both the organization, and the economy as a whole.

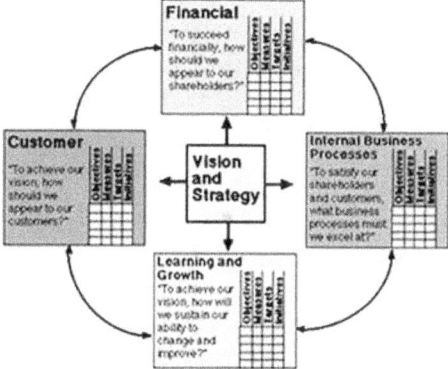

79. This is _____, which _____:
(Functional Aspects of Management)

   A. Balanced scorecard, evaluates the degree to which different functions are prepared to pursue a strategy initiative before execution

   B. Balanced scorecard, assesses the degree to which operations support the overall strategy

   C. Balanced scorecard, calculates the resource utilization of different functions dedicated to a strategic initiative

   D. Strategic operations chart, defines the way in which organizational operations must function to achieve strategic goals

   E. Strategy control graph, assesses the degree to which operations support the overall strategy

The answer is B:
It's used to visualize the degree to which the functions of an organization are all working toward a single goal.

PRINCIPLES OF MANAGEMENT

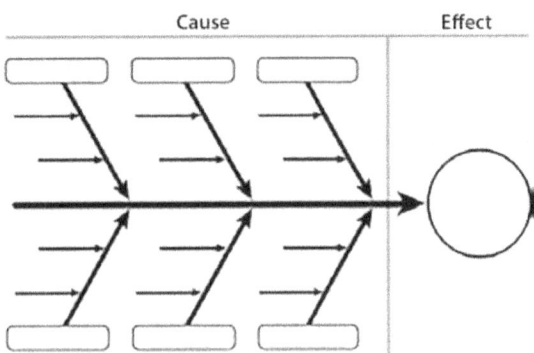

80. This is ____ :
(Functional Aspects of Management)

   A. Causal loop diagram

   B. Cause-effect graph

   C. Why-because analysis

   D. Ishikawa diagram

   E. Causal diagram

The answer is D
Developed by Kaoru Ishikawa, this is colloquially known as a fishbone diagram.

81. In a corporation, top management is hired by:
(Organization and Human Resources)

   A. Board of directors

   B. Shareholders

   C. Stakeholders

   D. Executives

   E. Front-line management

The answer is A
The board of directors is in charge of hiring executive management, among other things. This often leads to conflicts of interest and agency problems as the boards of directors often place themselves into those management roles.

PRINCIPLES OF MANAGEMENT

82. **In a corporation, board of directors is hired by:**
    (Organization and Human Resources)

    A. Board of directors

    B. Shareholders

    C. Stakeholders

    D. Executives

    E. Front-line management

The answer is B
Though it's difficult to coordinate the shareholders of a large corporation with broadly distributed shares, this is what's required to fire someone from the board of directors should decisions be made which are clearly contrary to the best interests of the shareholders.

83. **The four functions of management does not include:**
    (Functional Aspects of Management)

    A. Planning

    B. Organizing

    C. Marketing

    D. Leading

    E. Controlling

The answer is C
Planning, organizing, leading, controlling

PRINCIPLES OF MANAGEMENT

84. According to Mintzberg, the role of the manager which involves communicating information to people outside the organization is:
    (Functional Aspects of Management)

    A. Disseminator

    B. Spokesperson

    C. Monitor

    D. Figurehead

    E. Liaison

The answer is B
This is one of the informational roles, and contrasts the role of Disseminator, which involves communicating to people inside the organization.

85. According to Mintzberg, the role of the manager which includes networking within and outside the organization is:
    (Functional Aspects of Management)

    A. Liaison

    B. Spokesperson

    C. Figurehead

    D. Disseminator

    E. Monitor

The answer is A
This is one of the interpersonal roles, requiring a manager to function as a representative of the company.

PRINCIPLES OF MANAGEMENT

86. **According to Mintzberg, the role of the manager which involves defending the interests of the business is:**
    (Functional Aspects of Management)

    A. Disturbance handler

    B. Entrepreneur

    C. Negotiator

    D. Resource allocator

    E. Leader

The answer is C
This is one of the decisional categories, which is the only category with 4 roles rather than 3.

87. **Which are traditionally listed as part of the managerial skill set:**
    (Functional Aspects of Management)

    A. Technical skills, human skills

    B. Human skills, marketing skills

    C. Conceptual skills, accounting skills

    D. Technical skills, marketing skills

    E. Human skills, accounting skills

The answer is A
Technical, human, conceptual

88. ___ refers to those actions and behaviors which people believe to be important:
(Functional Aspects of Management)

    A. Morals

    B. Principles

    C. Beliefs

    D. Values

    E. Ethics

The answer is D
Both individuals and companies have values

89. **Setting goals does not:**
(Functional Aspects of Management)

    A. Function has a comprehensive plan

    B. Provide guidance and direction

    C. Create a foundation for organized planning

    D. Establish challenging milestones to motivate staff

    E. Provide a method for evaluating performance

The answer is A
Goals are only one small part of a plan, intended to guide the actions which lead to the successful fulfillment of the plan.

PRINCIPLES OF MANAGEMENT

90. **The official parameters set by an organization outlining an activity or response is called:**
    (Functional Aspects of Management)

    A. Regulations

    B. Rules

    C. Procedures

    D. Laws

    E. Norms

The answer is C
Procedures vary in how strictly they must be followed, sometimes being more lax such as social norms, or sometimes more strict even to the degree that a violation breaks the law.

91. **Which type of grand strategy can involve selling current business units:**
    (Functional Aspects of Management)

    A. Retrenchment

    B. Global

    C. Growth

    D. Stability

    E. Business

The answer is A
"Retrenchment" is a fancy way of saying that the company needs to get smaller if it wants to survive at all.

PRINCIPLES OF MANAGEMENT

92. According to the rational model, the decision-making process includes everything except:
    (Functional Aspects of Management)

    A. Assess options

    B. Determine the point of acceptable satisficing

    C. Make decision

    D. Define the problem

    E. Evaluate results

The answer is B
Satisficing is not a part of the rational model, although an assessment of the cost of one's own time relative to the benefits of additional decision-making is a rational consideration.

93. Which is a potential disadvantage of group decision-making:
    (Functional Aspects of Management)

    A. Greater error recognition

    B. Improved morale through participation

    C. Greater acceptance of decision by staff

    D. Diffusion of responsibility

    E. Expanded knowledge pool

The answer is D
If no one can be held fully responsible, or they don't feel they can be, then decisions will often be more risky.

PRINCIPLES OF MANAGEMENT

94. **Techniques teams can use to stimulate creative problem solving include everything except ___, which is typically used by individuals:**
    (Functional Aspects of Management)

    A. Brainstorming

    B. Delphi technique

    C. Cross-fertilization

    D. Nominal group technique

    E. Devil's advocacy

The answer is C
Cross-fertilization occurs when an individual contacts a professional from another field for information.

95. **Fast, repetitive production environments are facilitated by a ____, and creative environments of dynamic challenges by a _____:**
    (Functional Aspects of Management)

    A. Industrial system, organic system

    B. Mechanistic system, organic system

    C. Natural system, Mechanistic system

    D. Industrial system, natural system

    E. Mechanistic system, mechanistic system

The answer is B
The operating environment must be conducive to the type of operations being performed.

PRINCIPLES OF MANAGEMENT

96. **Horizontal organizations are unique because:**
    (Functional Aspects of Management)

    A. They formed as a result of horizontal integration with other organizations

    B. They have a small number of employees per manager

    C. They emphasize functional integration and personal empowerment over hierarchy

    D. They give greater authority to employees than management

    E. They are the inverse of vertical organizations

The answer is C
Horizontal organizations have greater cross-functionality than traditional models.

97. **Perceptual errors in leadership do not include:**
    (Functional Aspects of Management)

    A. Halo effect

    B. Strictness or leniency

    C. Expectancy effect

    D. Projection effect

    E. Selective perception

The answer is B
Strictness and leniency is erroneous, but not perceptual

PRINCIPLES OF MANAGEMENT

98. **Which type of team is best when highly specialized operations are involved:**
    (Functional Aspects of Management)

    A. Dysfunctional team

    B. Cross-functional team

    C. Functional team

    D. Vertical team

    E. Project

The answer is C
A group of experts in a single field can accomplish highly specialized tasks

99. **What type of team is best for executive operations:**
    (Basic Economic Concepts)

    A. Dysfunctional team

    B. Cross-functional team

    C. Functional team

    D. Vertical team

    E. Project team

The answer is B
Teams of people from different organizational functions are effective in determining things like product development.

100. Groupthink is:
(Functional Aspects of Management)

A. A form of group brainstorming

B. The collective culture of an organization

C. The aggregate knowledge set of a team

D. The innovation created in large groups of highly specialized people

E. A state in which conformity takes priority over critical thought

The answer is E
Groupthink generally involves one person becoming the authority figure who is surrounded by "yes men", although blind agreement with the first person to have an idea also occurs, as people try to trade thought and responsibility for social inclusion.

PRINCIPLES OF MARKETING

Description of the Examination

The Principles of Marketing examination covers the material that is usually taught in a one-semester introductory course in marketing. Such a course is usually known as Basic Marketing, Introduction to Marketing, Fundamentals of Marketing, Marketing, or Marketing Principles. The exam is concerned with the role of marketing in society and within a firm, understanding consumer and organizational markets, marketing strategy planning, the marketing mix, marketing institutions, and other selected topics, such as international marketing, ethics, marketing research, services and not-for-profit marketing. The candidate is also expected to have a basic knowledge of the economic/demographic, social/cultural, political/legal, and technological trends that are important to marketing.

The examination contains approximately 100 questions to be answered in 90 minutes. Some of these are pretest questions that will not be scored. Any time candidates spend on tutorials and providing personal information is in addition to the actual testing time.

Knowledge and Skills Required

The subject matter of the Principles of Marketing examination is drawn from the following topics in the approximate proportions indicated. The percentages next to the main topics indicate the approximate percentage of exam questions on that topic.

8-13% **Role of Marketing in Society**
- Ethics
- Nonprofit Marketing
- International Marketing

17-24% **Role of Marketing in a Firm**
- Marketing Concept
- Marketing Strategy
- Marketing Environment
- Marketing Decision System
  - Marketing research
  - Marketing Information System

22-27% **Target Marketing**
- Consumer Behavior
- Segmentation
- Positioning
- B2B Markets

40-50% **Marketing Mix**
- Produce and Service Management
- Branding
- Pricing Policies
- Distribution Channels and Logistics
- Integrated Marketing Communications and Promotion
- Marketing Application in e-Commerce

PRINCIPLES OF MARKETING

SAMPLE TEST

DIRECTIONS: Read each item and select the best response.

1. **In marketing, commercialization is:**
   (Role of Marketing in a Firm)

   A. The development of commercial ads

   B. The point at which a new product is launched onto the market

   C. The point at which a new product is tested in a small market before wider launch

   D. The point at which research is performed for the production of a new product

   E. A shift of social values toward material goods

2. **When performing market research, primary research is ____ but _____ then secondary research:**
   (Role of Marketing in a Firm)

   A. Easier to find, subject to interpretation

   B. Less detailed, cheaper

   C. More detailed, more expensive

   D. More detailed, cheaper

   E. Less detailed, more expensive

3. **The least integrated way to create a direct presence within a foreign market is through:**
   (Role of Marketing in Society)

   A. Wholly-owned subsidiaries

   B. Joint ventures

   C. Franchising

   D. Licensing

   E. Exporting

4. **____ is a restriction which prevents the importing of particular goods:**
   (Role of Marketing in Society)

   A. Tariff

   B. Quota

   C. Credit restriction

   D. Exchange control

   E. Embargo

5. **Success in marketing relies on:**
   (Role of Marketing in a Firm)

   A. Executive partnerships

   B. Production efficiency

   C. Customer satisfaction

   D. Assertive staff

   E. Constant innovation

PRINCIPLES OF MARKETING

6. **During what stage of the product lifecycle should a marketer build product awareness:**
   (Marketing Mix)

   A. Decline

   B. Maturity

   C. Introduction

   D. Growth

   E. Replacement

7. **When demand is highly elastic:**
   (Marketing Mix)

   A. Seasonal fluctuations are very strong

   B. Price will change very slowly in response to a change in demand

   C. Price will change quickly in response to a change in demand

   D. It will change quickly in response to a change in price

   E. It will change very slowly in response to a change in price

8. **The 4 P's of the marketing mix are:**
   (Marketing Mix)

   A. Product, price, promotion, placement

   B. Product, price, place, promotion

   C. Produce properly priced products

   D. Product, promotion, placement, profit

   E. Product, price, place, profit

9. **A company operating at low PED will benefit most from a ___ strategy:**
   (Marketing Mix)

   A. Price leader

   B. Penetration

   C. Niche

   D. 2nd mover

   E. Premium pricing

10. **A company operating at high PED will benefit most from a ___ strategy:**
    (Marketing Mix)

    A. Price leader

    B. Premium pricing

    C. Niche

    D. 2nd mover

    E. Penetration

PRINCIPLES OF MARKETING

11. **The two most common pricing schemes for online advertising are:**
    (Marketing Mix)

    A. PPC and monthly rates

    B. PPC & PPI

    C. Daily and monthly rates

    D. PPV and monthly rates

    E. PPC and daily rates

12. **The use of hard sales methods and high pressure tactics is typical of:**
    (Role of Marketing in a Firm)

    A. Market orientation

    B. Production orientation

    C. Sales orientation

    D. Social orientation

    E. Push orientation

13. **The use of opportunities to develop and better humanity by integrating products and services into current trends is typical of:**
    (Role of Marketing in a Firm)

    A. Social orientation

    B. Market orientation

    C. Push orientation

    D. Production orientation

    E. Sales orientation

14. **Which of the following is unique to online marketing:**
    (Marketing Mix)

    A. The amount of electronic transactions

    B. The use of banner ads

    C. The use of catalogue-design ordering

    D. The lack of security in payment information

    E. Integration into customers' lives and activities beyond the product offered

15. **Which is not an example of a free strategy:**
    (Role of Marketing in a Firm)

    A. Coupons

    B. Offering free services by selling ad space

    C. Giving away free samples to attract customers

    D. Loyalty rewards programs

    E. Casino comps

16. **Which is not a factor of the external environment:**
    (Role of Marketing in a Firm)

    A. Procedural

    B. Sociocultural

    C. Legal

    D. Environmental

    E. Technological

17. **Which is not a factor of the internal environment:**
    (Role of Marketing in a Firm)

    A. Procedural

    B. Competitive

    C. Distributional

    D. Resources

    E. Partners

18. **SWOT is:**
    (Role of Marketing in a Firm)

    A. An outdated term for an advertising firm

    B. Analysis of strengths, weaknesses, opportunities and trust

    C. A global strategy of subsidiaries, web, outsourcing, and trade

    D. Analysis of strategy, wording, orientation, and tactics

    E. Analysis of strengths, weaknesses, opportunities, and threats

19. **Which is not an example of a tie-in:**
    (Marketing Mix)

    A. Development of a downloadable expansion pack for a video game

    B. Development of a video game based on an upcoming movie

    C. Creation of an online community discussion board for players of the same video game

    D. Publishing of a book series set in the same setting as a popular video game

    E. Sales of t-shirts portraying video game characters

PRINCIPLES OF MARKETING

20. **Seasonal closing of operations is not common in:**
    (Marketing Mix)

    A. Tourism-based industries

    B. Retail-based industries

    C. Agricultural-based industries

    D. Education-based industries

    E. Event planning-based industries

21. **A strategy to increase sales of existing products by identifying new markets is known as:**
    (Role of Marketing in a Firm)

    A. Market development

    B. Product development

    C. Diversification

    D. Market penetration

    E. Target marketing

22. **What trait is not required to maintain a sustainable competitive advantage:**
    (Role of Marketing in a Firm)

    A. Discretionary

    B. Inimitable

    C. Valuable

    D. Unsubstitutable

    E. Rare

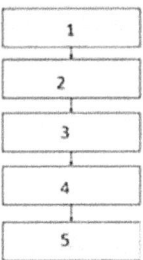

23. **What comes first in the consumer decision process:**
    (Target Marketing)

    A. Purchase decision

    B. Evaluation of alternatives

    C. Post-purchase evaluation

    D. Information search

    E. Problem recognition

24. **What comes 3rd in the consumer decision process:**
    (Target Markets)

    A. Problem recognition

    B. Post-purchase evaluation

    C. Information search

    D. Purchase decision

    E. Evaluation of alternatives

25. ___ is the person who decides which information to be made available in the decision-buying process:
    (Target Marketing)

    A. Gatekeeper

    B. Decider

    C. Purchaser

    D. Influencer

    E. Key bearer

26. Which of the following is not an activity associated with white-hat SEO:
    (Marketing Mix)

    A. Spamdexing

    B. Backlinking

    C. Blogging

    D. Press releases

    E. Use of metatags

27. The primary difference between MLM and an illegal pyramid scheme is:
    (Marketing Mix)

    A. Emphasis on sales or recruiting

    B. Organizational structure

    C. Sales orientation

    D. Management style

    E. Organizational culture

28. Sam's Club is an example of a(n):
    (Marketing Mix)

    A. Department store

    B. Big box retailer

    C. Wholesaler

    D. Warehouse

    E. Discount store

29. Prospect theory states that:
    (Target Marketing)

    A. People will use rules of thumb in making decisions

    B. The search for information costs time and resources

    C. Consumers consider the extreme possibilities of gain/loss rather than the likely outcomes

    D. People value their own possessions more than equivalents owned by others

    E. Consumers will accept "good enough" rather than maximize value

30. Which is not direct marketing:
    (Marketing Mix)

    A. Email advertising

    B. Website advertising

    C. Telemarketing

    D. Relationship selling

    E. Catalogues

PRINCIPLES OF MARKETING

31. Unit sales = 30,000
    Market unit sales = 120,000
    Calculate market share:
    (Target Marketing)

    A. 400%

    B. 90,000

    C. 30%

    D. 40%

    E. 400

32. Coca Cola uses ____ distribution and Maserati uses ____ distribution:
    (Marketing Mix)

    A. Selective, intensive

    B. Exclusive, intensive

    C. Intensive, exclusive

    D. Intensive, selective

    E. Exclusive, selective

33. ____ is not part of the promotion mix:
    (Marketing Mix)

    A. Advertising

    B. Pricing strategy

    C. Public relations

    D. Personal selling

    E. Sales promotion

34. ____ integration occurs between competitors at equivalent points in the supply chain:
    (Role of Marketing in a Firm)

    A. Horizontal

    B. Vertical

    C. Diagonal

    D. Orthogonal

    E. Direct

35. ____ integration occurs between organizations of different supply chains and at different points in the supply chain:
    (Role of Marketing in a Firm)

    A. Direct

    B. Vertical

    C. Orthogonal

    D. Horizontal

    E. Diagonal

36. ____ is not an example of demographic segmentation:
    (Target Marketing)

    A. Study guides for college students

    B. Group insurance for retired people

    C. Kayaks for outdoors enthusiasts

    D. Neon cereal for children

    E. Modelling for financial firms

37. ____ is not an example of psychographic segmentation:
    (Target Marketing)

    A. Shoes for distance runners

    B. Body jewelry for pierced people

    C. Tutoring for the metro area

    D. Interchangeable needles for knitters

    E. Decanters for scotch drinkers

38. **Increased demand as a result of changes in consumer preferences after repeated exposure through advertising is an example of:**
    (Target Marketing)

    A. Marketing effect

    B. Substitution effect

    C. Income effect

    D. Marginal utility optimization

    E. Mere-exposure effect

39. **The implications of the income effect on an individual company can be calculated by:**
    (Target Markets)

    A. $\Delta D/\Delta P$

    B. $\Delta D/\Delta Y$

    C. $\Delta S/\Delta P$

    D. $\Delta I/\Delta D$

    E. $\Delta D/\Delta I$

40. **A claim about a product such as "the best in town" is known as:**
    (Role of Marketing in Society)

    A. False advertising

    B. Puffery

    C. Exaggeration

    D. Subjective claims

    E. Hype

41. **Lying to consumers violates:**
    (Role of Marketing in Society)

    A. Lying to Consumers Act

    B. Federal Trade Commission Act

    C. Sherman Act

    D. The Truth in Advertising Act

    E. Consumer Product Safety Act

42. **__ is an engaging or interactive form of promotion relying on consumer distribution of media or news:**
    (Marketing Mix)

    A. Social marketing

    B. Viral marketing

    C. Meme marketing

    D. Internet marketing

    E. Publicity stunt

43. A wholesaler selling to retailers is ___ while retailers selling to end users is ___:
    (Marketing Mix)

    A. C2B, B2B

    B. B2C, B2B

    C. B2B, B2C

    D. B2B, C2B

    E. B2B, C2B

44. Value =:
    (Target Marketing)

    A. P-U

    B. Y/P

    C. U-P

    D. U/P

    E. P/U

45. ___ is not an example of a grey market:
    (Marketing Mix)

    A. Buying goods in low-price markets and reselling them at a profit in high-price markets

    B. Buying goods in a nation where they are available and then reselling them in a nation where they are not

    C. Buying limited-supply goods and then reselling them at a profit at auction

    D. Selling used goods on Craigslist

    E. Supply chain intermediaries of exclusive goods selling to non-exclusive retailers

46. A logical positioning strategy is:
    (Target Marketing)

    A. 55 High PES, low production cost, quality strategy

    B. High PES, high R&D cost, second-mover strategy

    C. Low PED, high production cost, price-leader strategy

    D. High PED, low sales cost, niche strategy

    E. 55 High PED, low production cost, price-leader strategy

47. ___ is an example of a Veblen Good:
    (Marketing Mix)

    A. Limited edition releases gaining collector's value

    B. Low-quality wine increasing in demand because of its high price

    C. Paying a high price for a hand-crafted crystal chandelier

    D. Demand increasing for low-quality goods due to prices increasing relative to income

    E. Demand decreasing for high quality goods which belong to others

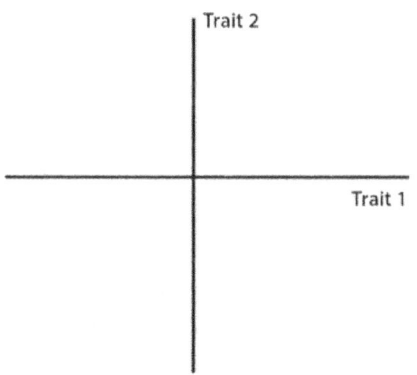

48. What is this:
    (Marketing Mix)

    A. Perceptual map

    B. Supply and demand grid

    C. Sales trend chart

    D. SWOT grid

    E. Competitive map

49. The point at which product availability has been optimized relative to market demand is called:
    (Target Marketing)

    A. Market saturation

    B. Market liquidation

    C. Demand fulfillment

    D. Supply and demand equilibrium

    E. Cannibalization

50. Cannibalization occurs when:
    (Marketing Mix)

    A. Increasing supply outlets decreases sales per outlet as a result of exceeding market saturation

    B. There is a reduction in market share in a competitive market

    C. There is a reduction in market share resulting from new product innovations in the market

    D. New product offerings shrink the sales of old product offerings within a single product portfolio

    E. Integration through hostile takeover results in the full acquisition of a competitor

PRINCIPLES OF MARKETING

51. ___ is an example of a Giffen Good:
    (Target Marketing)

    A. 66 Increase in demand as a result of a shift in consumer preferences

    B. Demand for high-end consumer goods increasing as a result of higher income

    C. Low-quality wine increasing in demand due to its high price

    D. Limited edition releases gaining collector's value

    E. 66 Increase in demand at thrift stores as a result of new-clothing prices increasing relative to income

52. What type of supply chain intermediary does not take title or ownership of inventory:
    (Marketing Mix)

    A. Retailers

    B. Branch offices

    C. Full-service wholesalers

    D. Brokers

    E. General wholesalers

53. Which benefits most from smaller, local distribution points than large points with lower per unit cost:
    (Marketing Mix)

    A. Agricultural goods

    B. Consumer electronics

    C. Mineral Ore

    D. Textiles

    E. Industrial equipment

54. ___ is not a retailer:
    (Marketing Mix)

    A. Vending machines

    B. Door to door sales

    C. Home shopping channel

    D. Catalogues

    E. Pharmaceutical sales reps

55. A business operating at very high PED should attempt to:
    (Role of Marketing in a Firm)

    A. Build brand equity

    B. Maximize profits

    C. Maximize revenues

    D. Maximize innovation

    E. Maintain the status quo

56. ____ is an example of predatory pricing:
(Role of Marketing in Society)

   A. Selling below cost to prevent threat from new market entrants

   B. Selling below cost to initially penetrate the market and draw attention

   C. Competition between competitors for the lowest price

   D. Selling to different customers at different prices with difference in cost

   E. Manufacturer suggested retail prices

57. You might use competitor indexing to:
(Marketing Mix)

   A. Track the relative market positions of competitors

   B. Identify substitutes in addition to direct competitors

   C. Measure the relative market share of competitors

   D. Price your product to establish a brand relative to existing competition

   E. Compare the benefits being offered by competing products

58. Price = $100
Units Shipped = 500
Shipping cost = $1,000 FOB
Calculate immediate revenues:
(Marketing Mix)

   A. $4,500

   B. $4,000

   C. $5,000

   D. $0

   E. $500

59. So many product prices end in 9 (e.g.: $5.99) because:
(Marketing Mix)

   A. Consideration for sales taxes

   B. Prices never actually end in 9

   C. Price competition leads to margins as low as possible

   D. People have a natural attraction to the number 9 resulting from millennia of cultural significance

   E. Buyers anchor price to rounding-down, rather than the nearest price, giving the perception of better value

60. Which has the highest global Q-score:
    (Role of Marketing in Society)

    A. Hyundai

    B. University of Michigan

    C. Disney

    D. Nintendo

    E. Northwood

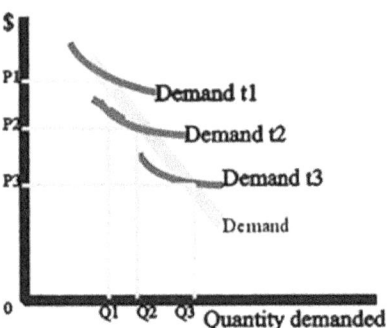

61. What is happening here:
    (Target Marketing)

    A. Price premiums

    B. Discount pricing

    C. Value pricing

    D. Price skimming

    E. Cost-plus pricing

62. Brand Name Price = $14.99
    Brand Name Coupon = 11% off
    Off-Brand Price = $12
    Which is the better deal
    (Marketing Mix)

    A. Both are the same price

    B. Brand name

    C. Off-brand

    D. Typically-off brand, but with coupon brand name is better

    E. Not enough information

63. According to CLV methodology, Expected PV in Year 2 is ____ and Cumulative NPV in Year 3 is ____:
    (Role of Marketing in a Firm)

    A. $209, $210

    B. $210, $209

    C. $200, $200

    D. $210, $215

    E. $215, $209

PRINCIPLES OF MARKETING

64. Sales = 500,000 units monthly
    Inventory storage = $550,000 units
    Storage cost = $5/unit per month
    According to JIT ____
    (Role of Marketing on a Firm)

    A. 500,000 new units per day with 50,000 in storage

    B. 500,000 new units per month with nothing in storage

    C. 16,438 new units per day with 50,000 in storage

    D. 500,000 new units per month with 50,000 in storage

    E. 16,438 new units per day with nothing in storage

65. A lock-in is a risky strategy because:
    (Role of Marketing in Society)

    A. It may violate consumer protection laws

    B. It may violate antitrust laws

    C. It may open opportunities for disruptive technologies

    D. It may alienate vendors

    E. It may alienate customers

High Growth	1	2
Low Growth	3	4
	Low Share	High share

66. Businesses in section 4 are called:
    (Role of Marketing in a Firm)

    A. Stars

    B. Dogs

    C. Zebras

    D. Cash cows

    E. Question marks

High Growth	1	2
Low Growth	3	4
	Low Share	High share

67. Businesses in section 1 are called:
    (Role of Marketing in a Firm)

    A. Cash cows

    B. Stars

    C. Question marks

    D. Dogs

    E. Zebras

	1	2
Broad Scope		
Narrow Scope	3	4
	Low Cost	Unique Benefits

68. According to Porter's Generic Strategies, businesses in section 1 should use a ____ strategy: *(Target Marketing)*

    A. Differentiation

    B. Cost leadership

    C. Focused cost leadership

    D. Focused differentiation

    E. Unfocused cost leadership

	1	2
Broad Scope		
Narrow Scope	3	4
	Low Cost	Unique Benefits

69. According to Porter's Generic Strategies, businesses in section 2 include examples like: *(Target Marketing)*

    A. High-end department stores

    B. Discount mattress stores

    C. Chain mega stores

    D. Artisan specialty stores

    E. Independent breweries

70. Porter's Five Forces model includes threat of new entrants, bargaining power of supplier, bargaining power of buyers, ____ and ____: *(Marketing Mix)*

    A. Threat of substitutes, rivalry among existing competitors

    B. Technological change, rivalry among existing competitors

    C. Threat of substitutes, technological change

    D. Government regulation, technological change

    E. Government regulation, rivalry among existing competitors

71. ___ is not considered in PESTEL environmental scanning: *(Target Marketing)*

    A. Political

    B. Suppliers

    C. Environmental

    D. Legal

    E. Economical

72. **Which is not an example of disruptive technology:**
    (Target Marketing)

    A. Digital cameras putting traditional film manufacturing out of business

    B. Napster forcing the record industry to switch to digital media

    C. Sales of the SUV taking market share from van and truck sales

    D. Solar and wind energy replacing fossil fuels

    E. Refrigerators replacing the ice box and ice delivery service

73. **___ is not a type of spam:**
    (Role of Marketing in Society)

    A. Instant messenger connection requests from business accounts

    B. Ads in social media comments

    C. Unsolicited email advertisements

    D. Telemarketer fundraising

    E. Repeated posting of a message in an online newsgroup

74. **Black markets are born when:**
    (Role of Marketing in Society)

    A. Criminals can make money

    B. People want to break the law

    C. Counterfeit goods are easy to make

    D. Governments overregulate markets

    E. Market demand is not being met through accepted means

75. **Which of the following has not been used to successfully fight counterfeiting:**
    (Role of Marketing in Society)

    A. Offering additional features not easily copied

    B. Ending distribution to markets with prevalent counterfeiting operations

    C. Maintaining searchable database of ID numbers on each unit

    D. Increasing market presence through carefully controlled distribution channels

    E. Brand and price positioning so that target market is careful to buy the real thing, leaving counterfeit sales to markets who can't afford the real thing anyway

76. During competitive analysis, ___ is an important activity when one competitor is clearly the best as some function:
    (Role of Marketing in a Firm)

    A. Aversion strategy

    B. Reengineering

    C. Modelling

    D. Benchmarking

    E. Copying

77. When communicating with a target audience, the ___ must ___ the message in a manner so that the ___ will ___ it the same way:
    (Target Marketing)

    A. Talker, say, listener, hear

    B. Sender, decode, receiver, encode

    C. Sender, encode, receiver, decode

    D. Receiver, encode, sender, decode

    E. Receiver decode, sender, encode

78. Anything causing the receiver to understand something different than the intention of the receiver is called:
    (Target Marketing)

    A. Mistranslation

    B. Misunderstanding

    C. Noise

    D. Disruption

    E. Static

79. A company whose competitive advantage is in managing supply chain will benefit most from a ___ strategy:
    (Marketing Mix)

    A. First mover

    B. Price leader

    C. Niche

    D. Differentiation

    E. Second mover

80. A toy with "batteries sold separately" and requiring two AA batteries has a cost of $20. A 3-pack of batteries is $6. The derived demand is:
    (Marketing Mix)

    A. $20 for the toy minus batteries

    B. $26 for toy and batteries

    C. $6 in batteries

    D. $14 for the toy less battery cost

    E. $4 in batteries

81. A global company with standardized products will set divisions by:
    (Target Marketing)

    A. Function

    B. Geography

    C. Product line

    D. Target market

    E. No divisions will be set

82. A global company which is highly responsive to local tastes will set divisions by:
    (Target Marketing)

    A. Function

    B. Geography

    C. Product line

    D. Target market

    E. No divisions will be set

83. In market research, a survey must do everything except:
    (Target Marketing)

    A. Provide a scale of potential answers for closed-ended questions

    B. Provide a method for measuring the responses given

    C. Guide the respondents answers

    D. Ask questions clearly and thoroughly

    E. Protect the privacy and safety of the respondents

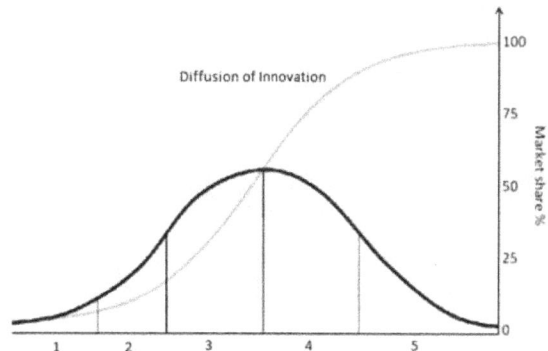

84. Which customers are at point 2:
    (Target Marketing)

    A. Early majority

    B. 9 Laggards

    C. Late majority

    D. Innovators

    E. 9 Early adopters

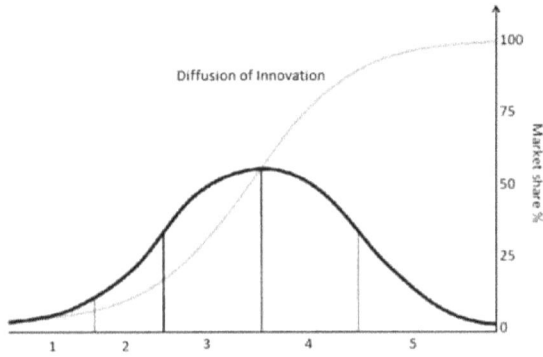

85. Which customers are at 1: *(Target Marketing)*

    A. Innovators

    B. Early majority

    C. Laggards

    D. Late majority

    E. Early adopters

86. The customer experience begins when ____ and ends when ____: *(Marketing Mix)*

    A. They purchase something, that thing reaches the end of its useful life

    B. They begin searching for possible purchases within your market, they make the purchase decision

    C. They become aware of your company, they forget your company exists

    D. They enter your store, they leave your store

    E. They begin any interaction with your company, they end that interaction

87. The internet has facilitated research into CEM by all except: *(Marketing Mix)*

    A. Making satisfaction surveys available

    B. Collecting consistent data on product usage

    C. Providing opportunities to allow customers to interact with other customers while engaging with their products

    D. Increasing ease of follow-up sales such as add-ons and replacement parts

    E. Providing a convenient avenue to offer tips and information of product usage

88. When will brand equity have a negative value: *(Marketing Mix)*

    A. Brand equity can never be negative

    B. After a PR gaffe by an executive which gave the impression of judgmental elitism

    C. After long-standing perceptions of low quality left unmitigated

    D. After an ethical/legal scandal which harms broad perceptions about the nature of core operations

    E. After a major recall which makes people question the quality of the product

89. Chris buys a car for $1,000 but it needs someone to do $4,000 of repairs. What is the derived factor demand:
(Marketing Mix)

   A. $4,000

   B. $5,000

   C. $10,000

   D. $2,000

   E. $3,000

Market Attractive	1	2
Not Market Attractive	3	4
	Weak Position	Strong Position

90. When assessing a market portfolio, how do you respond to a product in section 2:
(Marketing Mix)

   A. Divest or withdrawal

   B. Develop improvements

   C. Diversify

   D. Maintain position

   E. Invest in greater expansion

Market Attractive	1	2
Not Market Attractive	3	4
	Weak Position	Strong Position

91. When assessing a market portfolio, how do you respond to a product in section 3:
(Marking Mix)

   A. Divest of withdrawal

   B. Develop improvements

   C. Invest in greater expansion

   D. Maintain position

   E. Diversify

92. Common metrics of customer engagement on websites include all except:
(Marketing Mix)

   A. Click through rate

   B. Visitor ISP

   C. Number of pages viewed

   D. Duration of visit

   E. Number of unique visitors

Course Topic	Market Segmentation	Price Research	Brand Tracking Studies
Class Session Length	45 minutes	30 minutes	60 minutes
Number of classes per course	4	4	6
Format	Pre-recorded	Live Instructor	Pre-recoded
Availability	24/7 for 15 days	24/7 for 7 days	24/7 for 30 days
Q&A session	By email to instructor	At the end of each class with live instructor	Not available
Interactivity	None, static slides showing content and voice over	Tutorial with interactive exercises	Tutorial with interactive exercises
Price	$$	$$$$	$$

93. This is a _____:
    (Marketing Mix)

    A. Option comparison

    B. Side-by-side analysis

    C. Sales sheet

    D. Conjoint analysis

    E. Opportunity cost

94. Innovation games are a part of which step of product development:
    (Marketing Mix)

    A. Screening

    B. Idea generation

    C. Concept testing

    D. Test marketing

    E. Product development

95. Omaha NE makes a good test market for national brands because:
    (Marketing mix)

    A. It's in the middle of the country

    B. Its demographics match that of the nation very closely

    C. It stays secret because no one knows what's happening there

    D. It's densely populated

    E. The population is small

96. "Place" in the marketing mix means everything except:
    (Marketing Mix)

    A. Where customers will be when they need the product

    B. Where customers live and go

    C. Who lives in a target region

    D. The shipping channels necessary

    E. The distribution nodes required

97. "Promotion" in the marketing mix means everything except:
    (Marketing Mix)

    A. Methods of sales

    B. Company role in society

    C. The location of store fronts

    D. Brand management

    E. Resource-based view of the firm

98. **"Price" is influenced by everything except:**
(Marketing Mix)

   A. Competitor pricing

   B. Production costs

   C. Profit margin

   D. Perceived value

   E. Customer income

99. **Objectives should be everything except:**
(Marketing Mix)

   A. Specific

   B. Competitive

   C. Measurable

   D. Actionable

   E. Time oriented

100. **Views on the difference between products and services include everything except:**
(Marketing Mix)

   A. Services are exclusively rent-based

   B. Services to not offer ownership

   C. The production of services perishes at the time of production

   D. Services are not tangible

   E. Services add value through expertise

PRINCIPLES OF MARKETING

Answer Key

Question Number	Correct Answer	Your Answer	Question Number	Correct Answer	Your Answer	Question Number	Correct Answer	Your Answer
1	B		34	A		67	C	
2	C		35	D		68	B	
3	C		36	C		69	A	
4	E		37	C		70	A	
5	C		38	E		71	B	
6	C		39	B		72	C	
7	D		40	B		73	D	
8	B		41	D		74	E	
9	E		42	B		75	B	
10	A		43	C		76	D	
11	B		44	D		77	C	
12	C		45	D		78	C	
13	A		46	E		79	B	
14	E		47	B		80	E	
15	A		48	A		81	A	
16	A		49	A		82	B	
17	B		50	A		83	C	
18	E		51	E		84	E	
19	A		52	D		85	A	
20	B		53	A		86	C	
21	A		54	E		87	A	
22	A		55	C		88	D	
23	E		56	A		89	A	
24	D		57	D		90	E	
25	A		58	C		91	A	
26	A		59	E		92	B	
27	A		60	C		93	D	
28	B		61	D		94	C	
29	E		62	C		95	B	
30	B		63	B		96	C	
31	D		64	E		97	E	
32	C		65	B		98	C	
33	B		66	D		99	B	
						100	D	

RATIONALES

1. **In marketing, commercialization is:**
   (Role of Marketing in a Firm)

   A. The development of commercial ads

   B. The point at which a new product is launched onto the market

   C. The point at which a new product is tested in a small market before wider launch

   D. The point at which research is performed for the production of a new product

   E. A shift of social values toward material goods

The answer is B
In the product development process, commercialization is the step at which a product first reaches the broader market after success in the test market

2. **When performing market research, primary research is ____ but ____ than secondary research:**
   (Role of Marketing in a Firm)

   A. Easier to find, subject to interpretation

   B. Less detailed, cheaper

   C. More detailed, more expensive

   D. More detailed, cheaper

   E. Less detailed, more expensive

The answer is C
Secondary research was performed for other reasons, so it's cheaper but leaves a greater degree of uncertainty

3. **The least integrated way to create a direct presence within a foreign market is through:**
   (Role of Marketing in Society)

   A. Wholly-owned subsidiaries

   B. Joint ventures

   C. Franchising

   D. Licensing

   E. Exporting

The answer is C
When first entering foreign markets, even a franchise will have a strong impact on brand value in that nation, but still poses less financial risk than direct ownership.

4. **____ is a restriction which prevents the importing of particular goods:**
   (Role of Marketing in Society)

   A. Tariff

   B. Quota

   C. Credit restriction

   D. Exchange control

   E. Embargo

The answer is E
An embargo is a government policy which bans trade with a particular nation and/or trade on a particular type of good

5. **Success in marketing relies on:**
   (Role of Marketing in a Firm)

   A. Executive partnerships

   B. Production efficiency

   C. Customer satisfaction

   D. Assertive staff

   E. Constant innovation

The answer is C
The underlying philosophy behind marketing is to offer a product that satisfy customer desires, and make it available in a place they need it, at a time when they need it.

6. **During what stage of the product lifecycle should a marketer build product awareness:**
   (Marketing Mix)

   A. Decline

   B. Maturity

   C. Introduction

   D. Growth

   E. Replacement

The answer is C
During the introduction stage of the produce lifecycle, it's critical that the market be made aware of the benefits a product offers by using information marketing, as opposed to trying to maintain awareness.

PRINCIPLES OF MARKETING

7. When demand is highly elastic:
(Marketing Mix)

A. Seasonal fluctuations are very strong

B. Price will change very slowly in response to a change in demand

C. Price will change quickly in response to a change in demand

D. It will change quickly in response to a change in price

E. It will change very slowly in response to a change in price

The answer is D
$\Delta D/\Delta P$

8. The 4 P's of the marketing mix are:
(Marketing Mix)

A. Product, price, promotion, placement

B. Product, price, place, promotion

C. Produce properly priced products

D. Product, promotion, placement, profit

E. Product, price, place, profit

The answer is B
Marketing focuses on offering valuable products, at a time and place that the customers will need it, at a price they can afford, communicating the benefits to them in a manner they'll understand. "Place" is often called "distribution", but "3 P's and a D" just isn't as nifty.

9. **A company operating at low PED will benefit most from a ___ strategy:** *(Marketing Mix)*

    A. Price leader

    B. Penetration

    C. Niche

    D. 2nd mover

    E. Premium pricing

The answer is E
With low price elasticity of demand, price increases will raise profitability faster than it drop revenues, thus maximizing growth potential through a strategy of quality that maximizes profits rather than revenues.

10. **A company operating at high PED will benefit most from a ___ strategy:** *(Marketing Mix)*

    A. Price leader

    B. Premium pricing

    C. Niche

    D. 2nd mover

    E. Penetration

The answer is A
With high price elasticity of demand, customer demand increases faster than profits drop, thus maximizing growth potential through a strategy of price competition that maximizes revenues rather than profits.

11. **The two most common pricing schemes for online advertising are:**
    (Marketing Mix)

    A. PPC and monthly rates

    B. PPC & PPI

    C. Daily and monthly rates

    D. PPV and monthly rates

    E. PPC and daily rates

The answer is B

Online advertising is generally priced per click or per impression, often using an auction method wherein an advertiser offers a maximum bid price and is charged only slightly over the next highest bid.

12. **The use of hard sales methods and high pressure tactics is typical of:**
    (Role of Marketing in a Firm)

    A. Market orientation

    B. Production orientation

    C. Sales orientation

    D. Social orientation

    E. Push orientation

The answer is C

Sales orientation includes sales methods like door-to-door sales, relationship sales, and the use of methods intended to obligate a person to buy.

PRINCIPLES OF MARKETING

13. **The use of opportunities to develop and better humanity by integrating products and services into current trends is typical of:**
    (Role of Marketing in a Firm)

    A. Social orientation

    B. Market orientation

    C. Push orientation

    D. Production orientation

    E. Sales orientation

The answer is A
The social orientation involves associating your brand with humanitarian efforts to attract customers who want to feel like they're helping, as well as making programs such as that your customers.

14. **Which of the following is unique to online marketing:**
    (Marketing Mix)

    A. The amount of electronic transactions

    B. The use of banner ads

    C. The use of catalogue-design ordering

    D. The lack of security in payment information

    E. Integration into customers' lives and activities beyond the product offered

The answer is E
Many of the things seen online are common of other media, but as internet technology is integrated more into our lives there are increasing opportunities for companies to play a role in activities outside of product scope.

PRINCIPLES OF MARKETING

15. Which is not an example of a free strategy:
    (Role of Marketing in a Firm)

    A. Coupons

    B. Offering free services by selling ad space

    C. Giving away free samples to attract customers

    D. Loyalty rewards programs

    E. Casino comps

The answer is A
Coupons rely on discounts rather than offers of free stuff

16. Which is not a factor of the external environment:
    (Role of Marketing in a Firm)

    A. Procedural

    B. Sociocultural

    C. Legal

    D. Environmental

    E. Technological

The answer is A
Company procedures are within the control of the company, making it part of the internal environment.

PRINCIPLES OF MARKETING

17. Which is not a factor of the internal environment:
    (Role of Marketing in a Firm)

    A. Procedural

    B. Competitive

    C. Distributional

    D. Resources

    E. Partners

The answer is B
Competition exists outside the control of a company, so it is internal

18. SWOT is:
    (Role of Marketing in a Firm)

    A. An outdated term for an advertising firm

    B. Analysis of strengths, weaknesses, opportunities and trust

    C. A global strategy of subsidiaries, web, outsourcing, and trade

    D. Analysis of strategy, wording, orientation, and tactics

    E. Analysis of strengths, weaknesses, opportunities, and strengths

The answer is E
A SWOT analysis is created to discover a company's internal strengths and weaknesses, and then align them with external opportunities and threats

PRINCIPLES OF MARKETING

19. **Which is not an example of a tie-in:**
    (Marketing Mix)

    A. Development of a downloadable expansion pack for a video game

    B. Development of a video game based on an upcoming movie

    C. Creation of an online community discussion board for players of the same video game

    D. Publishing of a book series set in the same setting as a popular video game

    E. Sales of t-shirts portraying video game characters

The answer is A
A tie-in is a product intended to benefit from the success of an otherwise unrelated product, while an expansion pack is simply an additional feature of the original product.

20. **Seasonal closing of operations is not common in:**
    (Marketing Mix)

    A. Tourism-based industries

    B. Retail-based industries

    C. Agricultural-based industries

    D. Education-based industries

    E. Event planning-based industries

The answer is B
The majority of retail operates year-round

PRINCIPLES OF MARKETING

21. **A strategy to increase sales of existing products by identifying new markets is known as:**
    (Role of Marketing in a Firm)

    A. Market development

    B. Product development

    C. Diversification

    D. Market penetration

    E. Target marketing

The answer is A

Market development seeks to expand target market, while product development seeks to expand the product portfolio

22. **What trait is not required to maintain a sustainable competitive advantage:**
    (Role of Marketing in a Firm)

    A. Discretionary

    B. Inimitable

    C. Valuable

    D. Unsubstitutable

    E. Rare

The answer is A

A sustainable competitive advantage is one that is rare, valuable, unsubstitutable, and inimitable. Discretion does not play a role, except perhaps to keep trade secrets.

23. **What comes first in the consumer decision process:** *(Target Marketing)*

   A. Purchase decision

   B. Evaluation of alternatives

   C. Post-purchase evaluation

   D. Information search

   E. Problem recognition

The answer is E
Before a consumer will try to buy something, they must first recognize that a problem exists which a product can resolve.

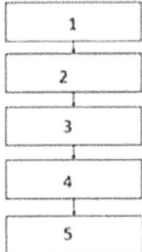

24. **What comes 3rd in the consumer decision process:** *(Target Markets)*

   A. Problem recognition

   B. Post-purchase evaluation

   C. Information search

   D. Purchase decision

   E. Evaluation of alternatives

The answer is D
After a consumer collects information on the products which may resolve their problems, they'll compare the options available before making a decision.

PRINCIPLES OF MARKETING

25. ___ is the person who decides which information to be made available in the decision-buying process:
    (Target Marketing)

    A. Gatekeeper

    B. Decider

    C. Purchaser

    D. Influencer

    E. Key bearer

The answer is A
Making it through the gatekeeper is a common challenge in B2B marketing, since the person who makes purchasing decisions often has an assistant or secretary which manages what information makes it through.

26. **Which of the following is not an activity associated with white-hat SEO:**
    (Marketing Mix)

    A. Spamdexing

    B. Backlinking

    C. Blogging

    D. Press releases

    E. Use of metatags

The answer is A
White-hat SEO is intended to increase brand awareness on the internet, while black-hat SEO exploits search engine algorithms, which major search engines recognize this pattern and can punish such activities.

PRINCIPLES OF MARKETING

27. **The primary difference between MLM and an illegal pyriamid scheme is:**
    (Marketing Mix)

    A. Emphasis on sales or recruiting

    B. Organizational structure

    C. Sales orientation

    D. Management style

    E. Organizational culture

The answer is A
US law recognized an illegal pyramid scheme as one whose primary activities are focused on recruiting more salespeople to exploit, rather than actually selling a product. Multi-level marketing is very similar, but focuses almost entirely on selling a legitimate product.

28. **Sam's Club is an example of a(n):**
    (Marketing Mix)

    A. Department store

    B. Big box retailer

    C. Wholesaler

    D. Warehouse

    E. Discount store

The answer is B
Big box retailers sell large volumes of common goods to small businesses and end consumers.

PRINCIPLES OF MARKETING

29. **Prospect theory states that:**
    (Target Marketing)

    A. People will use rules of thumb in making decisions

    B. The search for information costs time and resources

    C. Consumers consider the extreme possibilities of gain/loss rather than the likely outcomes

    D. People value their own possessions more than equivalents owned by others

    E. Consumers will accept "good enough" rather than maximize value

The answer is E
Casinos and insurance are examples of industries which exist exclusively because of prospect theory

30. **Which is not direct marketing:**
    (Marketing Mix)

    A. Email advertising

    B. Website advertising

    C. Telemarketing

    D. Relationship selling

    E. Catalogues

The answer is B
Direct marketing directs materials to directly to specific customers through personal channels, rather than through broad broadcasts

PRINCIPLES OF MARKETING

31. Unit sales = 30,000
    Market unit sales = 120,000
    Calculate market share:
    (Target Marketing)

    A. 400%

    B. 90,000

    C. 30%

    D. 40%

    E. 400

The answer is D
The most basic calculation of market share is unit sales/market sales as a percentage

32. Coca Cola uses ____ distribution and Maserati uses ____ distribution:
    (Marketing Mix)

    A. Selective, intensive

    B. Exclusive, intensive

    C. Intensive, exclusive

    D. Intensive, selective

    E. Exclusive, selective

The answer is C
Intensive distribution focuses on being in as many places as possible, selective distribution focuses on being in areas only in particular markets, and exclusive distribution highly limits availability except to people who seek specifically that brand.

PRINCIPLES OF MARKETING

33. ___ is not part of the promotion mix:
(Marketing Mix)

    A. Advertising

    B. Pricing strategy

    C. Public relations

    D. Personal selling

    E. Sales promotion

The answer is B
Though price is part of the marketing mix, the promotion mix exclusively describes the promotion part of the marketing mix.

34. ____ integration occurs between competitors at equivalent points in the supply chain:
(Role of Marketing in a Firm)

    A. Horizontal

    B. Vertical

    C. Diagonal

    D. Orthogonal

    E. Direct

The answer is A
Horizontal integration connects two companies at the same point in two different supply chains – competitors or complements.

PRINCIPLES OF MARKETING

35. ____ integration occurs between organizations of different supply chains and at different points in the supply chain:
(Role of Marketing in a Firm)

   A. Direct

   B. Vertical

   C. Orthogonal

   D. Diagonal

   E. Horizontal

The answer is D
Diagonal integration creates a conglomerate

36. ___ is not an example of demographic segmentation:
(Target Marketing)

   A. Study guides for college students

   B. Group insurance for retired people

   C. Kayaks for outdoors enthusiasts

   D. Neon cereal for children

   E. Modelling for financial firms

The answer is C
Demographic segmentation targets people with the same demographic trait, such as age, stage of life cycle, or religion.

37. ____ is not an example of psychographic segmentation:
    (Target Marketing)

    A. Shoes for distance runners

    B. Body jewelry for pierced people

    C. Tutoring for the metro area

    D. Interchangeable needles for knitters

    E. Decanters for scotch drinkers

The answer is C
Psychographic segmentation targets people with the same interests or subculture.

38. Increased demand as a result of changes in consumer preferences after repeated exposure through advertising is an example of:
    (Target Marketing)

    A. Marketing effect

    B. Substitution effect

    C. Income effect

    D. Marginal utility optimization

    E. Mere-exposure effect

The answer is E
The mere-exposure effect is what causes people to appreciate an acquired taste, or start to enjoy a song after hearing it a bunch of times.

39. **The implications of the income effect on an individual company can be calculated by:**
    (Target Markets)

    A. $\Delta D/\Delta P$

    B. $\Delta D/\Delta Y$

    C. $\Delta S/\Delta P$

    D. $\Delta I/\Delta D$

    E. $\Delta D/\Delta I$

The answer is B
The income effect measures the amount that demand changes in response to a change in consumer income.

40. **A claim about a product such as "the best in town" is known as:**
    (Role of Marketing in Society)

    A. False advertising

    B. Puffery

    C. Exaggeration

    D. Subjective claims

    E. Hype

The answer is B
Puffery is a claim which says great things about a company or product, but uses subjective assessments rather than objective facts.

PRINCIPLES OF MARKETING

41. **Lying to consumers violates:**
    (Role of Marketing in Society)

    A. Lying to Consumers Act

    B. Federal Trade Commission Act

    C. Sherman Act

    D. The Truth in Advertising Act

    E. Consumer Product Safety Act

The answer is D
The Truth in Advertising Act was created to enforce specific aspects of the Federal Trade Commission Act to ensure that companies cannot lie to customers.

42. **__ is an engaging or interactive form of promotion relying on consumer distribution of media or news**
    (Marketing Mix)

    A. Social marketing

    B. Viral marketing

    C. Meme marketing

    D. Internet marketing

    E. Publicity stunt

The answer is B
Viral marketing is called "viral" because it spreads from person to person

PRINCIPLES OF MARKETING

43. A wholesaler selling to retailers is ___ while retailers selling to end users is ____:
    (Marketing Mix)

    A. C2B, B2B

    B. B2C, B2B

    C. B2B, B2C

    D. B2B, C2B

    E. B2B, C2B

The answer is C
Although businesses can be customers if they're the ones which eventually consume the product, B2B refers to selling to businesses because of the unique purchasing behavior exhibited by businesses as compared to consumers.

44. Value =:
    (Target Marketing)

    A. P-U

    B. Y/P

    C. U-P

    D. U/P

    E. P/U

The answer is D
The amount of utility derived from a product divided by the price of the product is the formal calculation of value – greater utility or lower price increases the value.

PRINCIPLES OF MARKETING

45. ___ is not an example of a grey market:
(Marketing Mix)

    A. Buying goods in low-price markets and reselling them at a profit in high-price markets

    B. Buying goods in a nation where they are available and then reselling them in a nation where they are not

    C. Buying limited-supply goods and then reselling them at a profit at auction

    D. Selling used goods on Craigslist

    E. Supply chain intermediaries of exclusive goods selling to non-exclusive retailers

The answer is D
The grey market is not illegal, but includes distribution channels not formally intended by the supplier. Selling used goods means that the initial purchase was made through formal distribution channels.

46. A logical positioning strategy is:
(Target Marketing)

    A. High PES, low production cost, quality strategy

    B. High PES, high R&D cost, second-mover strategy

    C. Low PED, high production cost, price-leader strategy

    D. High PED, low sales cost, niche strategy

    E. High PED, low production cost, price-leader strategy

The answer is E
A business strategy is a natural extension of the internal and external environments.

PRINCIPLES OF MARKETING

47. ___ is an example of a Veblen Good:
    (Marketing Mix)

    A. Limited edition releases gaining collector's value

    B. Low-quality wine increasing in demand because of its high price

    C. Paying a high price for a hand-crafted crystal chandelier

    D. Demand increasing for low-quality goods due to prices increasing relative to income

    E. Demand decreasing for high quality goods which belong to others

The answer is B
Veblen goods increase in demand simply as a result of the higher price, typically because of their role as a status symbol

48. What is this:
    (Marketing Mix)

    A. Perceptual map

    B. Supply and demand grid

    C. Sales trend chart

    D. SWOT grid

    E. Competitive map

The answer is A
A perceptual map is a 2-dimensional plane which compares products or brands by two traits such as "price" and "quality"

PRINCIPLES OF MARKETING

49. The point at which product availability has been optimized relative to market demand is called:
(Target Marketing)

A. Market saturation

B. Market liquidation

C. Demand fulfillment

D. Supply and demand equilibrium

E. Cannibalization

The answer is A
At market saturation, demand for the product has been fully supplied, and any additional supply will result in cannibalization or lack of success

50. Cannibalization occurs when:
(Marketing Mix)

A. Increasing supply outlets decreases sales per outlet as a result of exceeding market saturation

B. There is a reduction in market share in a competitive market

C. There is a reduction in market share resulting from new product innovations in the market

D. New product offerings shrink the sales of old product offerings within a single product portfolio

E. Integration through hostile takeover results in the full acquisition of a competitor

The answer is A
Cannibalization occurs when a single company makes 2+ distribution channels available to the same market, reducing sales per channel.

PRINCIPLES OF MARKETING

51. ___ is an example of a Giffen Good:
(Target Marketing)

   A. Increase in demand as a result of a shift in consumer preferences

   B. Demand for high-end consumer goods increasing as a result of higher income

   C. Low-quality wine increasing in demand due to its high price

   D. Limited edition releases gaining collector's value

   E. Increase in demand at thrift stores as a result of new-clothing prices increasing relative to income

The answer is E
A Giffen good is also called an inferior good

52. What type of supply chain intermediary does not take title or ownership of inventory:
(Marketing Mix)

   A. Retailers

   B. Branch offices

   C. Full-service wholesalers

   D. Brokers

   E. General wholesalers

The answer is D
Brokers facilitate an exchange between buyer and seller, but never take ownership themselves.

PRINCIPLES OF MARKETING

53. Which benefits most from smaller, local distribution points than large points with lower per unit cost:
(Marketing Mix)

- A. Agricultural goods
- B. Consumer electronics
- C. Mineral Ore
- D. Textiles
- E. Industrial equipment

The answer is A
Perishable goods benefit from short distribution channels that maintain carefully-managed environmental conditions

54. ____ is not a retailer:
(Marketing Mix)

- A. Vending machines
- B. Door to door sales
- C. Pharmaceutical sales reps
- D. Catalogues
- E. Home shopping channel

The answer is E
Retailers sell directly to end-users rather than intermediaries

PRINCIPLES OF MARKETING

55. **A business operating at very high PED should attempt to:**
    (Role of Marketing in a Firm)

    A. Build brand equity

    B. Maximize profits

    C. Maximize revenues

    D. Maximize innovation

    E. Maintain the status quo

The answer is C
High PED means that a decrease in price will create disproportionately high increase in sales, making revenue maximization the best growth strategy

56. **____ is an example of predatory pricing:**
    (Role of Marketing in Society)

    A. Selling below cost to prevent threat from new market entrants

    B. Selling below cost to initially penetrate the market and draw attention

    C. Price competition between competitors for the lowest price

    D. Selling to different customers at different prices with difference in cost

    E. Manufacturer suggested retail prices

The answer is A
Predatory pricing includes pricing strategies intended to hinder competition

PRINCIPLES OF MARKETING

57. You might use competitor indexing to:
    (Marketing Mix)

    A. Track the relative market positions of competitors

    B. Identify substitutes in addition to direct competitors

    C. Measure the relative market share of competitors

    D. Price your product to establish a brand relative to existing competition

    E. Compare the benefits being offered by competing products

The answer is D
Competitor indexing begins by assessing the price positions used by competitors, and then sets your own price position relative to them

58. Price = $100
    Units Shipped = 500
    Shipping cost = $1,000 FOB
    Calculate immediate revenues:
    (Marketing Mix)

    A. $4,500

    B. $4,000

    C. $5,000

    D. $0

    E. $500

The answer is C
FOB – free on board – means the buyer is paying for distribution costs

PRINCIPLES OF MARKETING

59. **So many product prices end in 9 (e.g.: $5.99) because:**
    (Marketing Mix)

    A. Consideration for sales taxes

    B. Prices never actually end in 9

    C. Price competition leads to margins as low as possible

    D. People have a natural attraction to the number 9 resulting from millennia of cultural significance

    E. Buyers anchor price to rounding-down, rather than the nearest price, giving the perception of better value

The answer is E
Psychological pricing takes advantages of natural consumer behaviors, such as pricing products just barely below the next highest dollar so that they perceive the lower whole number instead.

60. **Which has the highest global Q-score:**
    (Role of Marketing in Society)

    A. Hyundai

    B. University of Michigan

    C. Disney

    D. Nintendo

    E. Northwood

The answer is C
Q-score is a measurement of consumer awareness of brand. Disney and Coca Cola are two of the most recognized brands in the world, more than religious symbols.

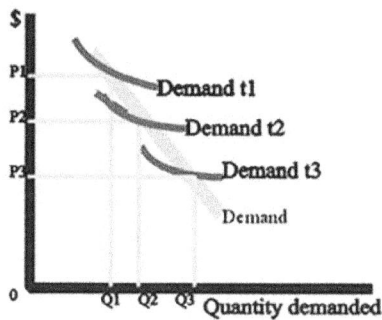

61. What is happening here: *(Target Marketing)*

A. Price premiums

B. Discount pricing

C. Value pricing

D. Price skimming

E. Cost-plus pricing

The answer is D
Price skimming occurs when a business starts with a very high price, and gradually brings the price down over time. This is common especially among tech, wherein price skimming strategies correlate with very short product lifecycles.

**62. Brand Name Price = $14.99
Brand Name Coupon = 11% off
Off-Brand Price = $12
Which is the better deal**
(Marketing Mix)

A. Both are the same price

B. Brand name

C. Off-brand

D. Typically-off brand, but with coupon brand name is better

E. Not enough information

The answer is C
Even with a coupon, the off-brand price is better, which is very common, leading many experts to advise consumers against relying on coupons.

	Year 0	Year 1	Year 2	Year 3	Year 4	Year 5
Revenue per Customer		$400	$400	$400	$400	$400
One-time Acquisition Cost	-$480					
Mailing Cost		-$9.60	-$9.60	-$9.60	-$9.60	-$9.60
Profit per Customer in Year	-$480	$390	$390	$390	$390	$390
Expected Present Value in Year	-$480	$355		$124	$73	$43
Cumulative Net Present Value	-$480	-$125	$85		$282	$325

63. **According to CLV methodology, Expected PV in Year 2 is ____ and Cumulative NPV in Year 3 is _____:**
    (Role of Marketing in a Firm)

    A. $209, $210

    B. $210, $209

    C. $200, $200

    D. $210, $215

    E. $215, $209

The answer is B
$PV = FV/(1+r)^t$

64. Sales = 500,000 units monthly
    Inventory storage = $550,000 units
    Storage cost = $5/unit per month
    According to JIT ____
    (Role of Marketing on a Firm)

    A. 500,000 new units per day with 50,000 in storage

    B. 500,000 new units per month with nothing in storage

    C. 16,438 new units per day with 50,000 in storage

    D. 500,000 new units per month with 50,000 in storage

    E. 16,438 new units per day with nothing in storage

The answer is E
Just-in-time manufacturing/inventory management seeks to cut storage costs by carefully managing supply so that it matches demand at nearly the same time, often utilizing analytical computer programs and inventory management software to instantly reorder products as they are bought.

65. A lock-in is a risky strategy because:
    (Role of Marketing in Society)

    A. It may violate consumer protection laws

    B. It may violate antitrust laws

    C. It may open opportunities for disruptive technologies

    D. It may alienate vendors

    E. It may alienate customers

The answer is B
Antitrust laws were established to increase market competition by ending monopolies

PRINCIPLES OF MARKETING

High Growth	1	2
Low Growth	3	4
	Low Share	High share

66. Businesses in section 4 are called:
(Role of Marketing in a Firm)

   A. Stars

   B. Dogs

   C. Zebras

   D. Cash cows

   E. Question marks

The answer is D
Cash cows have very low growth rates, but have a large market share, making them dominant players in a stable market

High Growth	1	2
Low Growth	3	4
	Low Share	High share

67. Businesses in section 1 are called:
(Role of Marketing in a Firm)

   A. Cash cows

   B. Stars

   C. Question marks

   D. Dogs

   E. Zebras

The answer is C
Start-ups are typically considered question marks – their small size makes fast growth easier, but it's yet to be seen whether it can be sustained.

Broad Scope	1	2
Narrow Scope	3	4
	Low Cost	Unique Benefits

68. According to Porter's Generic Strategies, businesses in section 1 should use a _____ strategy:
    (Target Marketing)

    A. Differentiation

    B. Cost leadership

    C. Focused cost leadership

    D. Focused differentiation

    E. Unfocused cost leadership

The answer is B
Wal-Mart is an example of a broad cost leadership strategy

PRINCIPLES OF MARKETING

Broad Scope	1	2
Narrow Scope	3	4
	Low Cost	Unique Benefits

69. According to Porter's Generic Strategies, businesses in section 2 include examples like:
    (Target Marketing)

    A. High-end department stores

    B. Discount mattress stores

    C. Chain mega stores

    D. Artisan specialty stores

    E. Independent breweries

The answer is A
Le Bon Marche sells a broad variety of very expensive goods

70. Porter's Five Forces model includes threat of new entrants, bargaining power of supplier, bargaining power of buyers, ____ and ____:
    (Marketing Mix)

    A. Threat of substitutes, rivalry among existing competitors

    B. Technological change, rivalry among existing competitors

    C. Threat of substitutes, technological change

    D. Government regulation, technological change

    E. Government regulation, rivalry among existing competitors

The answer is A
Porter's Five Forces attempt to describe the forces which define competition within a market

PRINCIPLES OF MARKETING

71. ___ is not considered in PESTEL environmental scanning:
    (Target Marketing)

    A. Political

    B. Suppliers

    C. Environmental

    D. Legal

    E. Economical

The answer is B
Political, Economical, Social, Technological, Environmental, Legal

72. **Which is not an example of disruptive technology:**
    (Target Marketing)

    A. Digital cameras putting traditional film manufacturing out of business

    B. Napster forcing the record industry to switch to digital media

    C. Sales of the SUV taking market share from van and truck sales

    D. Solar and wind energy replacing fossil fuels

    E. Refrigerators replacing the ice box and ice delivery service

The answer is C
Disruptive technology fundamentally changes how customers solve a problem, eliminating obsolete technologies

PRINCIPLES OF MARKETING

73. ___ is not a type of spam:
    (Role of Marketing in Society)

    A. Instant messenger connection requests from business accounts

    B. Ads in social media comments

    C. Unsolicited email advertisements

    D. Telemarketer fundraising

    E. Repeated posting of a message in an online newsgroup

The answer is D
"Spam" refers to mass, unsolicited advertising by computer-based means

74. **Black markets are born when:**
    (Role of Marketing in Society)

    A. Criminals can make money

    B. People want to break the law

    C. 55 Counterfeit goods are easy to make

    D. Governments overregulate markets

    E. 55 Market demand is not being met through accepted means

The answer is E
So long as people will pay money, supply will always be made

PRINCIPLES OF MARKETING

75. **Which of the following has not been used to successfully fight counterfeiting:**
    (Role of Marketing in Society)

    A. Offering additional features not easily copied

    B. Ending distribution to markets with prevalent counterfeiting operations

    C. Maintaining searchable database of ID numbers on each unit

    D. Increasing market presence through carefully controlled distribution channels

    E. Brand and price positioning so that target market is careful to buy the real thing, leaving counterfeit sales to markets who can't afford the real thing anyway

The answer is B
Pulling out of a market completely actually makes counterfeiting worse

76. **During competitive analysis, ___ is an important activity when one competitor is clearly the best as some function:**
    (Role of Marketing in a Firm)

    A. Aversion strategy

    B. Reengineering

    C. Modelling

    D. Benchmarking

    E. Copying

The answer is D
Benchmarking seeks to identify who is best at what, and emulating it

PRINCIPLES OF MARKETING

77. When communicating with a target audience, the ___ must ___ the message in a manner so that the ___ will ___ it the same way:
    (Target Marketing)

    A. Talker, say, listener, hear

    B. Sender, decode, receiver, encode

    C. Sender, encode, receiver, decode

    D. Receiver, encode, sender, decode

    E. Receiver decode, sender, encode

The answer is C
Communication requires the sender to turn an idea into a code of language which the receiver will then decode into their own idea of what the code means

78. Anything causing the receiver to understand something different than the intention of the receiver is called:
    (Target Marketing)

    A. Mistranslation

    B. Misunderstanding

    C. Noise

    D. Disruption

    E. Static

The answer is C
Noise can include misunderstandings of meaning, different written languages, and differences in perceptions of body language, different ideas about the meaning of colors, and even differences in the direction of reading, among other things. Noise often results in humorous translations in product promotion.

PRINCIPLES OF MARKETING

79. A company whose competitive advantage is in managing supply chain will benefit most from a ___ strategy:
    (Marketing Mix)

    A. First mover

    B. Price leader

    C. Niche

    D. Differentiation

    E. Second mover

The answer is B
A well-managed supply chain will result in low costs with efficient production availability, such as Wal-Mart.

80. A toy with "batteries sold separately" and requiring two AA batteries has a cost of $20. A 3-pack of batteries is $6. The derived demand is:
    (Marketing Mix)

    A. $20 for the toy minus batteries

    B. $26 for toy and batteries

    C. $6 in batteries

    D. $14 for the toy less battery cost

    E. $4 in batteries

The answer is E
Derived demand refers to the demand which is inherently created for some good in response to the purchase of a different good.

PRINCIPLES OF MARKETING

81. A global company with standardized products will set divisions by:
(Target Marketing)

A. Function

B. Geography

C. Product line

D. Target market

E. No divisions will be set

The answer is A

Companies seeking global standardization will not be as concerned with differences in local operations, as its likely the customers in each nation are seeking the same benefits. Examples include Rolex watches.

82. A global company which is highly responsive to local tastes will set divisions by:
(Target Marketing)

A. Function

B. Geography

C. Product line

D. Target market

E. No divisions will be set

The answer is B

It's particularly common for food products to carefully customize their products to local tastes, such as the difference between Nestle's chocolate in the US compared to in Europe.

83. **In market research, a survey must do everything except:**
    (Target Marketing)

    A. Provide a scale of potential answers for closed-ended questions

    B. Provide a method for measuring the responses given

    C. Guide the respondents answers

    D. Ask questions clearly and thoroughly

    E. Protect the privacy and safety of the respondents

The answer is C
Survey research must be developed in a manner which is careful to explain the question without influencing the answer that will be given.

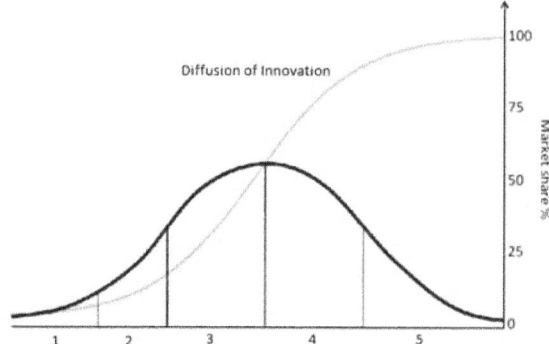

84. **Which customers are at point 2:**
    (Target Marketing)

    A. Early majority

    B. Laggards

    C. Late majority

    D. Innovators

    E. Early adopters

The answer is E
Early adopters are among the first to use new innovations, but typically do not actively track current research in anticipation of its release.

PRINCIPLES OF MARKETING

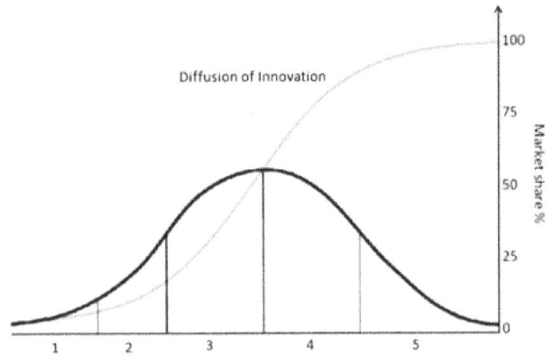

85. **Which customers are at 1:**
    (Target Marketing)

    A. Innovators

    B. Early majority

    C. Laggards

    D. Late majority

    E. Early adopters

The answer is A
Innovators follow current trends in R&D and are among the first to begin using new innovations, including participation as beta testers.

86. **The customer experience begins when ____ and ends when ____:**
    (Marketing Mix)

    A. They purchase something, that thing reaches the end of its useful life

    B. They begin searching for possible purchases within your market, they make the purchase decision

    C. They become aware of your company, they forget your company exists

    D. They enter your store, they leave your store

    E. They begin any interaction with your company, they end that interaction

The answer is C
Customer experience includes the perceptions customers have of your products and brands during their entire awareness of your products and brands, including what they're told, and what they've experienced in the past.

PRINCIPLES OF MARKETING

87. The internet has facilitated research into CEM by all except:
(Marketing Mix)

A. Making satisfaction surveys available

B. Collecting consistent data on product usage

C. Providing opportunities to allow customers to interact with other customers while engaging with their products

D. Increasing ease of follow-up sales such as add-ons and replacement parts

E. Providing a convenient avenue to offer tips and information of product usage

The answer is A
Satisfaction surveys have been available since long before the internet existed

88. When will brand equity have a negative value:
(Marketing Mix)

A. Brand equity can never be negative

B. After a PR gaffe by an executive which gave the impression of judgmental elitism

C. After long-standing perceptions of low quality left unmitigated

D. After an ethical/legal scandal which harms broad perceptions about the nature of core operations

E. After a major recall which makes people question the quality of the product

The answer is D
Negative brand equity means that being associated with a company or brand is a liability and will actually make a market less likely to interact with you. Even low-quality brands have equity in their respective markets.

89. Chris buys a car for $1,000, but it needs someone to do $4,000 of repairs. What is the derived factor demand:
(Marketing Mix)

   A. $4,000

   B. $5,000

   C. $10,000

   D. $2,000

   E. $3,000

The answer is A
The derived demand results from the need to pursue a service because of the purchase of a car

Market Attractive	1	2
Not Market Attractive	3	4
	Weak Position	Strong Position

90. When assessing a market portfolio, how do you respond to a product in section 2:
(Marketing Mix)

   A. Divest or withdrawal

   B. Develop improvements

   C. Diversify

   D. Maintain position

   E. Invest in greater expansion

The answer is E
If you have a strong position in an attractive market, then it is likely that expanding that product in your portfolio will increase overall portfolio returns

	1	2
Market Attractive	1	2
Not Market Attractive	3	4
	Weak Position	Strong Position

91. When assessing a market portfolio, how do you respond to a product in section 3: *(Marking Mix)*

  A. Divest of withdrawal

  B. Develop improvements

  C. Invest in greater expansion

  D. Maintain position

  E. Diversify

The answer is A
If you have a weak position in an unattractive market, then it's likely that you're losing money by pursuing that product

92. Common metrics of customer engagement on websites include all except: *(Marketing Mix)*

  A. Click through rate

  B. Visitor ISP

  C. Number of pages viewed

  D. Duration of visit

  E. Number of unique visitors

The answer is B
The ISP is personally-identifying information and says nothing about how successful your website is

Course Topic	Market Segmentation	Price Research	Brand Tracking Studies
Class Session Length	45 minutes	30 minutes	60 minutes
Number of classes per course	4	4	6
Format	Pre-recorded	Live Instructor	Pre-recoded
Availability	24/7 for 15 days	24/7 for 7 days	24/7 for 30 days
Q&A session	By email to instructor	At the end of each class with live instructor	Not available
Interactivity	None, static slides showing content and voice over	Tutorial with interactive exercises	Tutorial with interactive exercises
Price	$$	$$$$	$$

93. **This is a _____:**
    (Marketing Mix)

    A. Option comparison

    B. Side-by-side analysis

    C. Sales sheet

    D. Conjoint analysis

    E. Opportunity cost

The answer is D
A conjoint analysis compares multiple options using a variety of side-by-side variables for customers to evaluate as a whole, rather than individually

94. **Innovation games are a part of which step of product development:**
    (Marketing Mix)

    A. Screening

    B. Idea generation

    C. Concept testing

    D. Test marketing

    E. Product development

The answer is C
Innovation games are generally used to test new concepts so that they can be assessed and improved upon before release into a test market

PRINCIPLES OF MARKETING

95. **Omaha NE makes a good test market for national brands because:**
    (Marketing mix)

    A. It's in the middle of the country

    B. Its demographics match that of the nation very closely

    C. It stays secret because no one knows what's happening there

    D. It's densely populated

    E. The population is small

The answer is B
The best test markets are those which mirror the target market

96. **"Place" in the marketing mix means everything except:**
    (Marketing Mix)

    A. Where customers will be when they need the product

    B. Where customers live and go

    C. Who lives in a target region

    D. The shipping channels necessary

    E. The distribution nodes required

The answer is C
Place refers to everything associated with the distribution

PRINCIPLES OF MARKETING

97. **"Promotion" in the marketing mix means everything except:**
    (Marketing Mix)

    A. Methods of sales

    B. Company role in society

    C. The location of store fronts

    D. Brand management

    E. Resource-based view of the firm

The answer is E
Promotion refers to everything associated with communicating with the target market

98. **"Price" is influenced by everything except:**
    (Marketing Mix)

    A. Competitor pricing

    B. Production costs

    C. Profit margin

    D. Perceived value

    E. Customer income

The answer is C
Profit margins are influenced by price, but price should never be influenced by profit margins

PRINCIPLES OF MARKETING

99. Objectives should be everything except:
(Marketing Mix)

A. Specific

B. Competitive

C. Measurable

D. Actionable

E. Time oriented

The answer is B
An objective is a goal over which people may or may not compete, but the objectives themselves should not be to compete

100. Views on the difference between products and services include everything except:
(Marketing Mix)

A. Services are exclusively rent-based

B. Services to not offer ownership

C. The production of services perishes at the time of production

D. Services are not tangible

E. Services add value through expertise

The answer is D
Products require expertise, too

XAMonline
The CLEP Specialist
Individual Sample Tests in ebook format with full explanations

eBooks

All 33 CLEP sample tests are available as ebook downloads from retail websites such as **Amazon.com** and **Barnesandnoble.com**

American Government	9781607875130
American Literature	9781607875079
Analyzing and Interpreting Literature	9781607875086
Biology	9781607875222
Calculus	9781607875376
Chemistry	9781607875239
College Algebra	9781607875215
College Composition	9781607875109
College Composition Modular	9781607875437
College Mathematics	9781607875246
English Literature	9781607875093
Financial Accounting	9781607875383
French	9781607875123
German	9781607875369
History of the United States I	9781607875178
History of the United States II	9781607875185
Human Growth and Development	9781607875444
Humanities	9781607875147
Information Systems	9781607875390
Introduction to Educational Psychology	9781607875451
Introductory Business Law	9781607875420
Introductory Psychology	9781607875154
Introductory Sociology	9781607875352
Natural Sciences	9781607875253
Precalculus	9781607875345
Principles of Macroeconomics	9781607875406
Principles of Microeconomics	9781607875468
Principles of Marketing	9781607875475
Principles of Management	9781607875468
Social Sciences and History	9781607875161
Spanish	9781607875116
Western Civilization I	9781607875192
Western Civilization II	9781607875208

TO ORDER or amazon or

XAMonline
CLEP
Full Study Guides

CLEP College Algebra
ISBN: 9781607875598
Price: $34.95

CLEP Biology
ISBN: 9781607875314
Price: $34.95

CLEP Analyzing and
Interpreting Literature
ISBN: 9781607875260
Price: $34.95

CLEP College Composition
and Modular
ISBN: 9781607875277
Price: $19.99

CLEP College Mathematics
ISBN: 9781607875321
Price: $34.95

CLEP Psychology
ISBN: 9781607875291
Price: $34.95

CLEP Spanish
ISBN: 9781607875284
Price: $34.95

  or  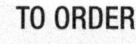 or

XAMonline
CLEP Subject Series
Collection by Topic
Sample Test Approach

CLEP Literature
ISBN: 9781607875833
Price: $34.95

CLEP Foreign Language
ISBN: 9781607875772
Price: $34.95

CLEP History
ISBN: 9781607875789
Price: $34.95

CLEP Sociology
ISBN: 9781607875796
Price: $34.95

CLEP Science
ISBN: 9781607875802
Price: $34.95

CLEP Mathematics
ISBN: 9781607875819
Price: $34.95

CLEP Business
ISBN: 9781607875826
Price: $34.95

  or  or

XAMonline
CLEP Favorites
Collection by Topic
Sample Test Approach

CLEP Five Favorites
ISBN: 9781607875765
Price: $24.95

CLEP Military Favorites
ISBN: 9781607875512
Price: $24.95

      or      or 

www.ingramcontent.com/pod-product-compliance
Lightning Source LLC
Chambersburg PA
CBHW080723230426
43665CB00020B/2600